MW00799570

BMWFILMS.COM PRESENTS
THE HIRE ™

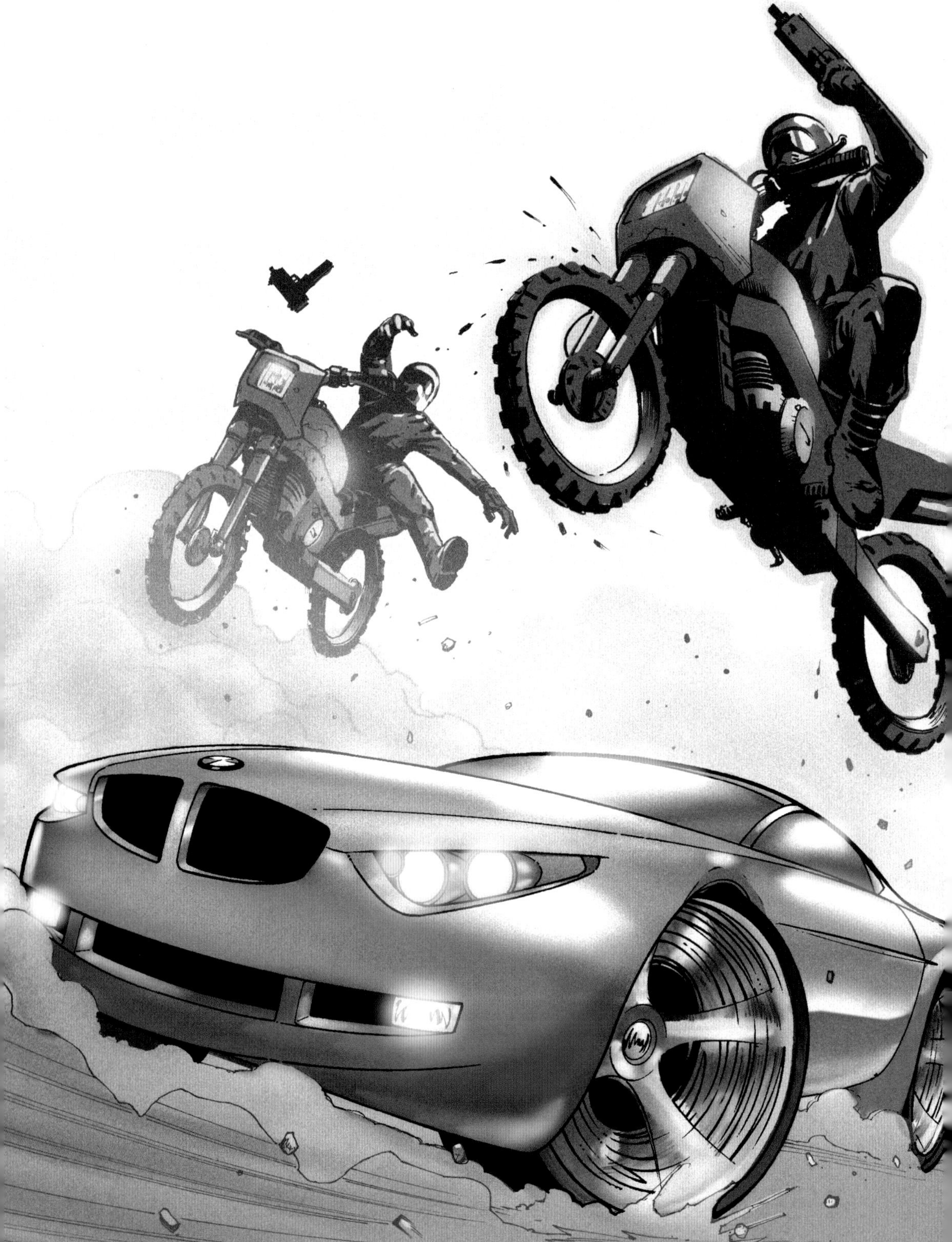

ILLUSTRATION BY FRANCISCO RUIZ VELASCO AND STUDIO F

BMWFILMS.COM PRESENTS

THE HIRE™

ABOUT THE CARS

There's no point in running down to your local BMW dealer to purchase the cars you see in these stories. See, they don't exist . . . yet.

In The Hire films on www.bmwfilms.com, the Driver is always equipped with the latest model from BMW. In comics, since the action need not be bound by the limitations of which car an actor can actually get in and drive, we've availed ourselves of BMW's own design department and given the driver the latest BMW concept cars. All of the BMWs used in these comics are unmistakably BMWs, but a generation beyond anything currently on the road.

DARK HORSE BOOKS™

LETTERER **MICHAEL DAVID THOMAS** COVER ART **MATT WAGNER** AND **WIL GLASS** PUBLISHER **MIKE RICHARDSON**
DESIGNER **TINA ALESSI** ART DIRECTOR **LIA RIBACCHI** ASSISTANT EDITOR **DAVE MARSHALL** EDITOR **RANDY STRADLEY**

BMWFILMS.COM Presents The Hire

Text and illustrations for The Hire are © 2004 BMW of North America, LLC & ™. All rights reserved. Used under authorization.
The BMW name and logo are registered trademarks. Dark Horse Comics® and the Dark Horse logo are trademarks of Dark Horse
Comics, Inc., registered in various categories and countries. All rights reserved. No portion of this publication may be reproduced
or transmitted, in any form or by any means, without the express written permission of Dark Horse Comics, Inc. Names, characters,
places, and incidents featured in this publication either are the product of the author's imagination or are used fictitiously.
Any resemblance to actual persons (living or dead), events, institutions, or locales, without satiric intent, is coincidental.

THIS VOLUME COLLECTS ISSUES #1 THROUGH #4 OF THE **DARK HORSE**
COMIC-BOOK SERIES **BMWFILMS.COM PRESENTS THE HIRE.**

TO FIND A COMICS SHOP IN YOUR AREA, CALL THE **COMIC SHOP LOCATOR SERVICE** TOLL-FREE AT 1-888-266-4226
PUBLISHED BY **DARK HORSE BOOKS** / A DIVISION OF **DARK HORSE COMICS, INC.**
10956 SE MAIN STREET / MILWAUKIE, OR 97222

FIRST EDITION: APRIL 2006
ISBN: 1-59307-183-3

1 3 5 7 9 10 8 6 4 2
Printed in China

darkhorse.com / bmwfilms.com

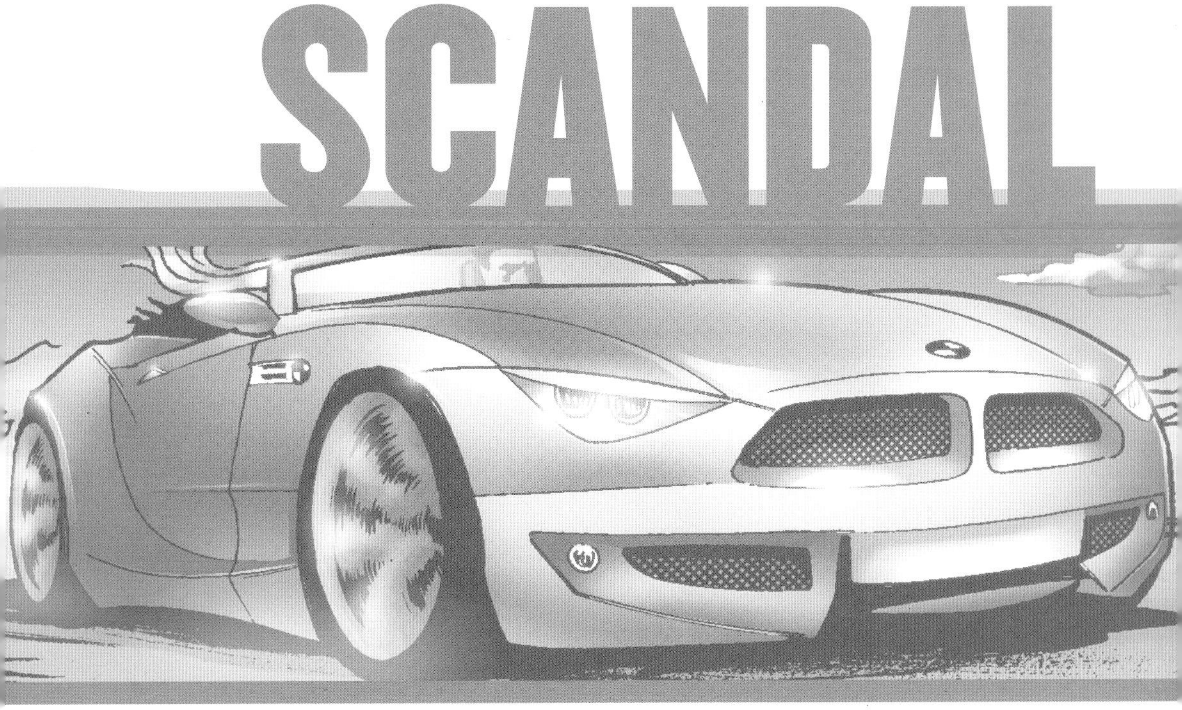
SCANDAL

SCRIPT MATT WAGNER ART MATT WAGNER
AND FRANCISCO RUIZ VELASCO COLORS WIL GLASS

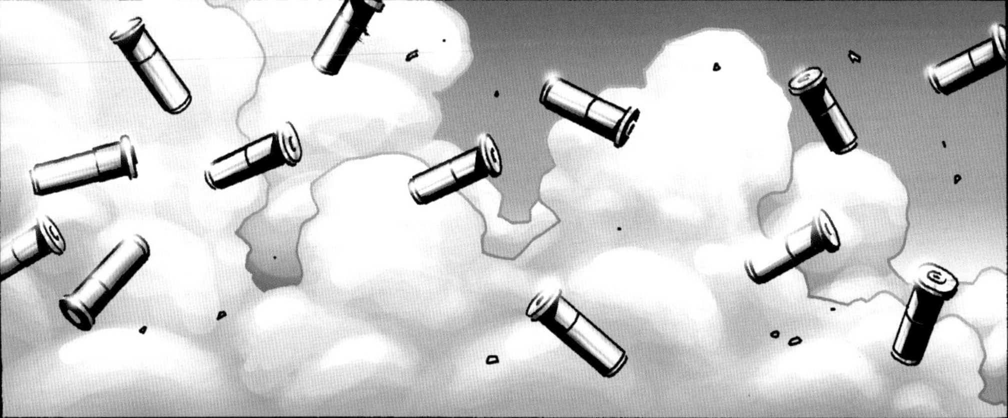

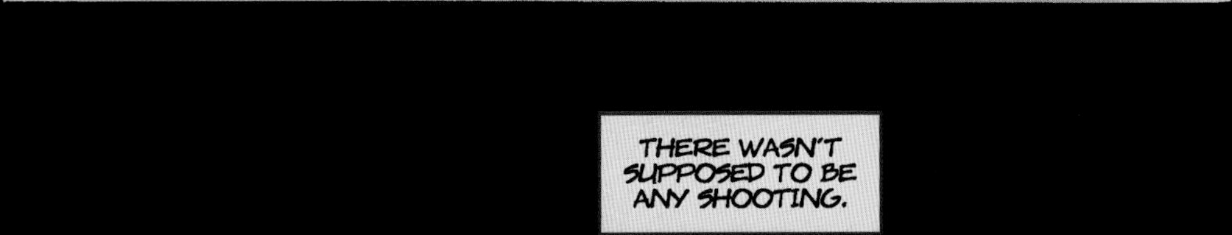
THERE WASN'T SUPPOSED TO BE ANY SHOOTING.

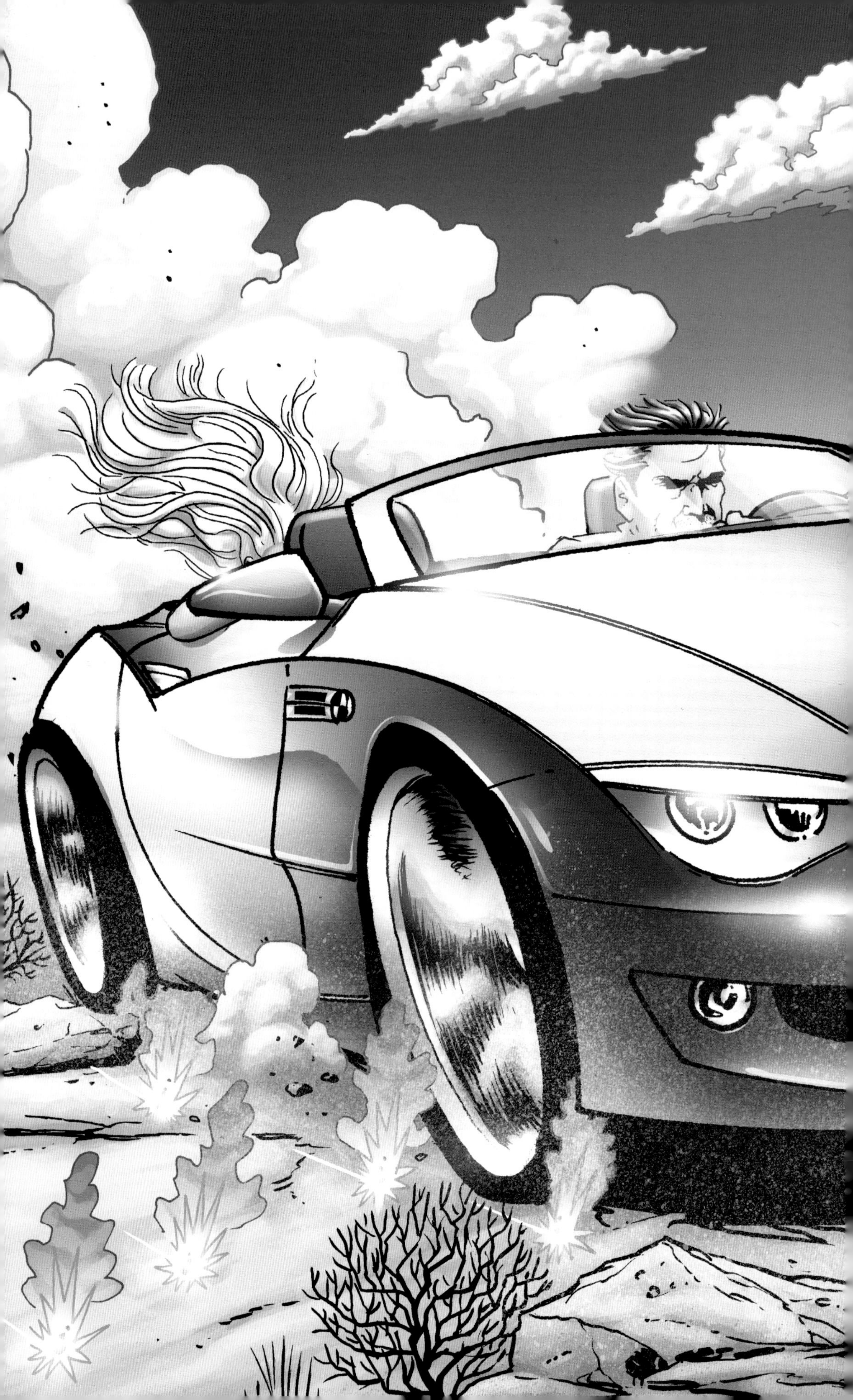

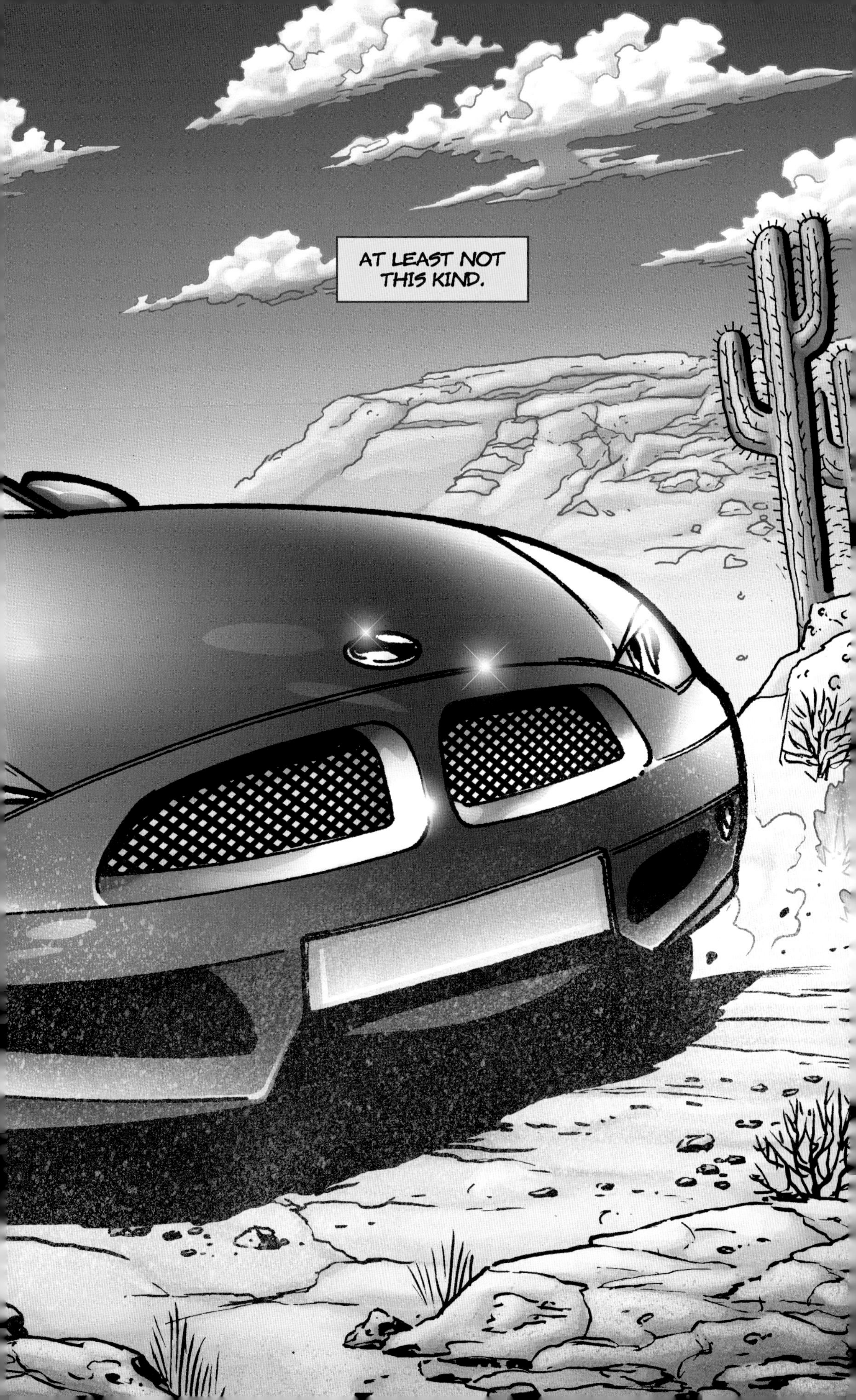
AT LEAST NOT THIS KIND.

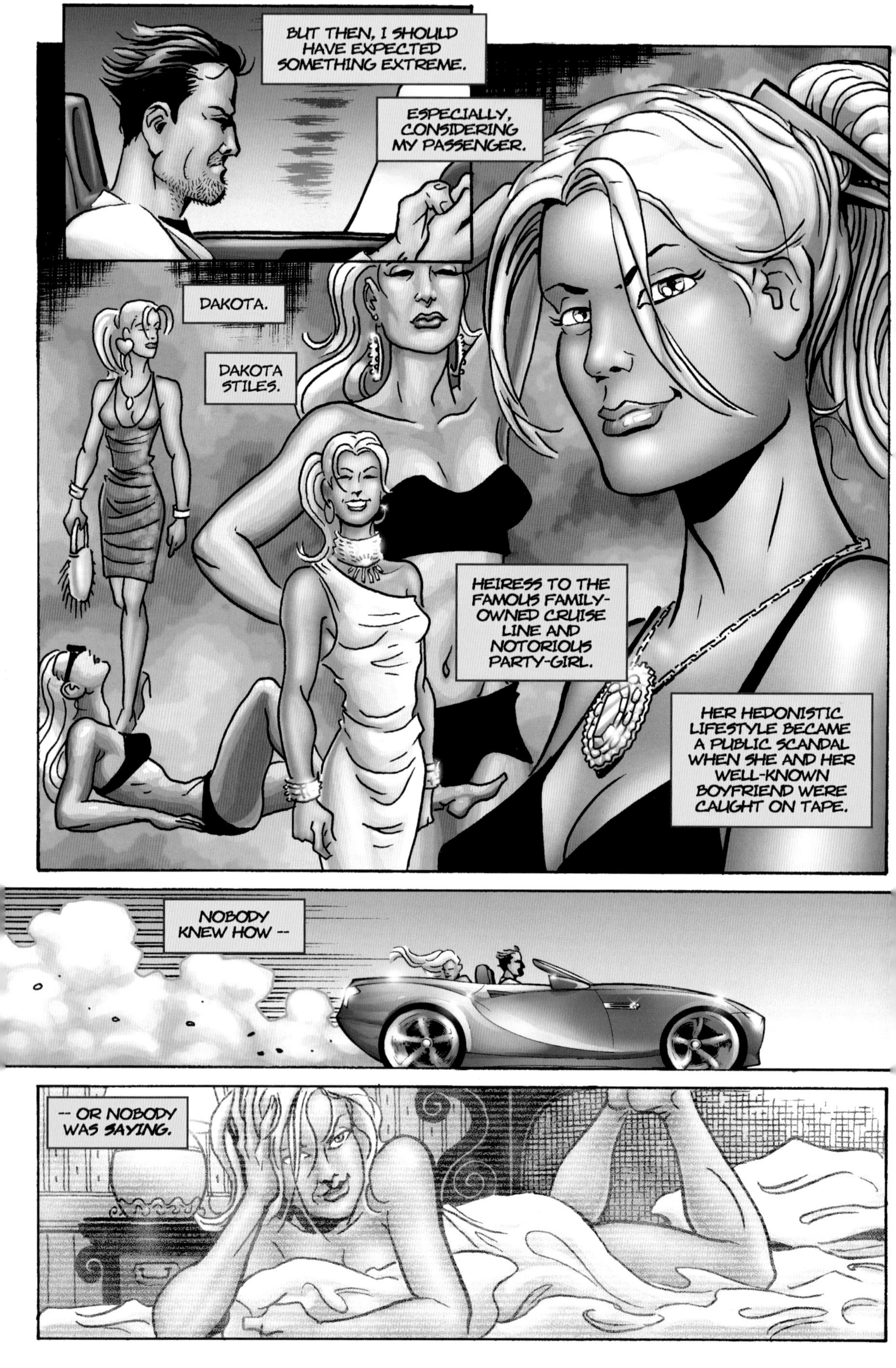
BUT THEN, I SHOULD HAVE EXPECTED SOMETHING EXTREME.
ESPECIALLY, CONSIDERING MY PASSENGER.
DAKOTA.
DAKOTA STILES.
HEIRESS TO THE FAMOUS FAMILY-OWNED CRUISE LINE AND NOTORIOUS PARTY-GIRL.
HER HEDONISTIC LIFESTYLE BECAME A PUBLIC SCANDAL WHEN SHE AND HER WELL-KNOWN BOYFRIEND WERE CAUGHT ON TAPE.
NOBODY KNEW HOW --
-- OR NOBODY WAS SAYING.

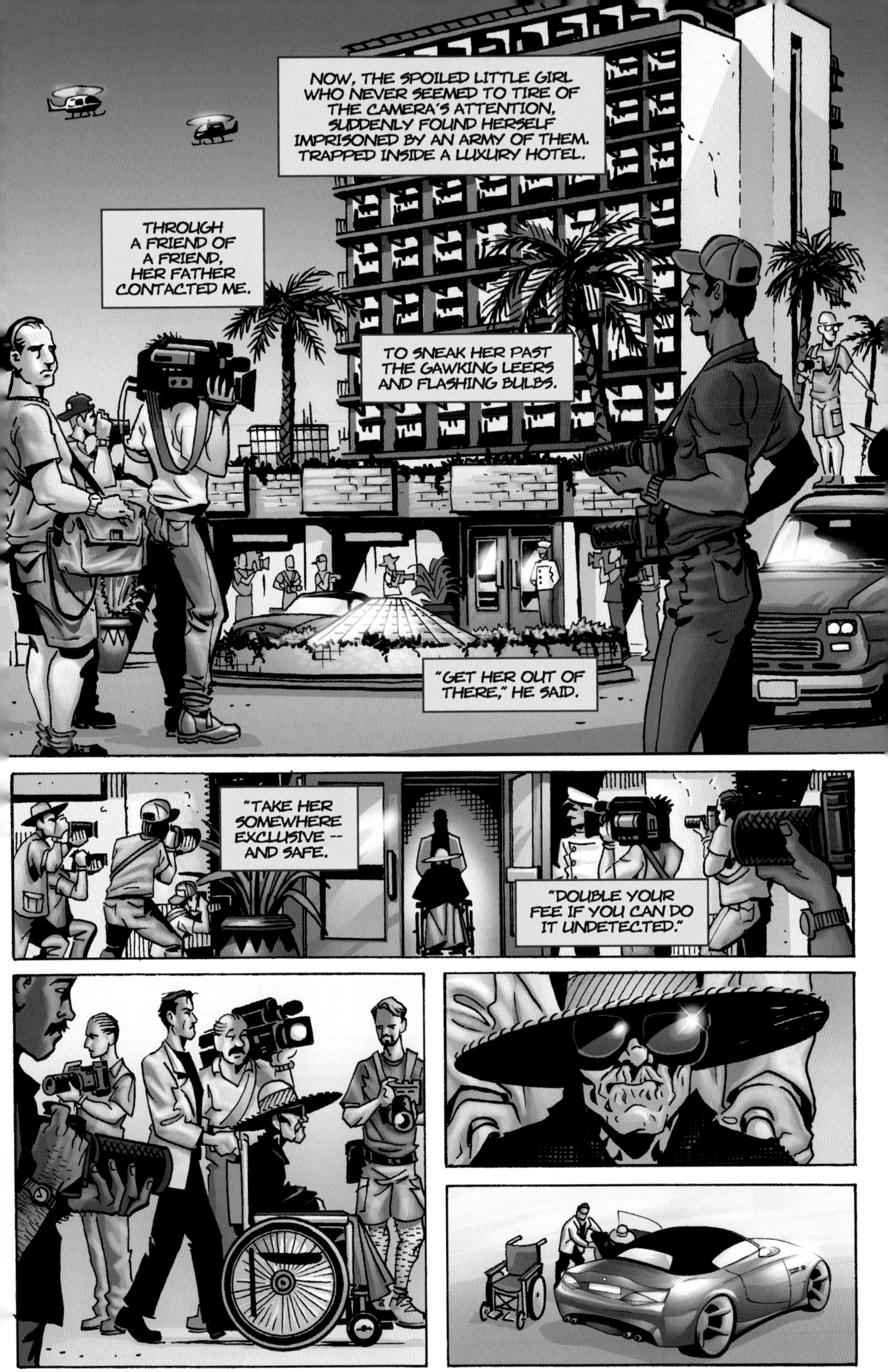
NOW, THE SPOILED LITTLE GIRL WHO NEVER SEEMED TO TIRE OF THE CAMERA'S ATTENTION, SUDDENLY FOUND HERSELF IMPRISONED BY AN ARMY OF THEM. TRAPPED INSIDE A LUXURY HOTEL.
THROUGH A FRIEND OF A FRIEND, HER FATHER CONTACTED ME.
TO SNEAK HER PAST THE GAWKING LEERS AND FLASHING BULBS.
"GET HER OUT OF THERE," HE SAID.
"TAKE HER SOMEWHERE EXCLUSIVE -- AND SAFE.
"DOUBLE YOUR FEE IF YOU CAN DO IT UNDETECTED."

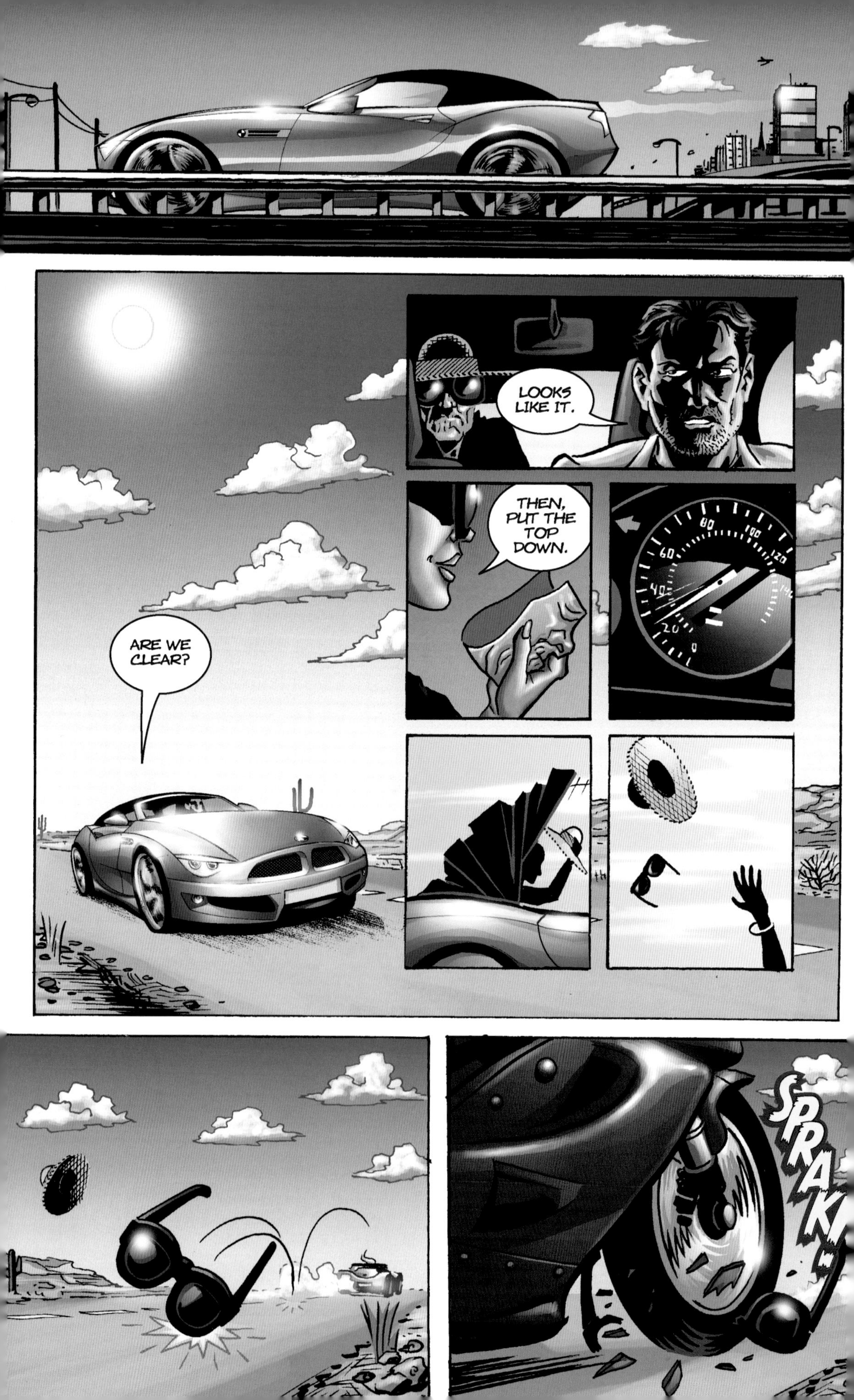
ARE WE CLEAR?
LOOKS LIKE IT.
THEN, PUT THE TOP DOWN.
SPRAK!

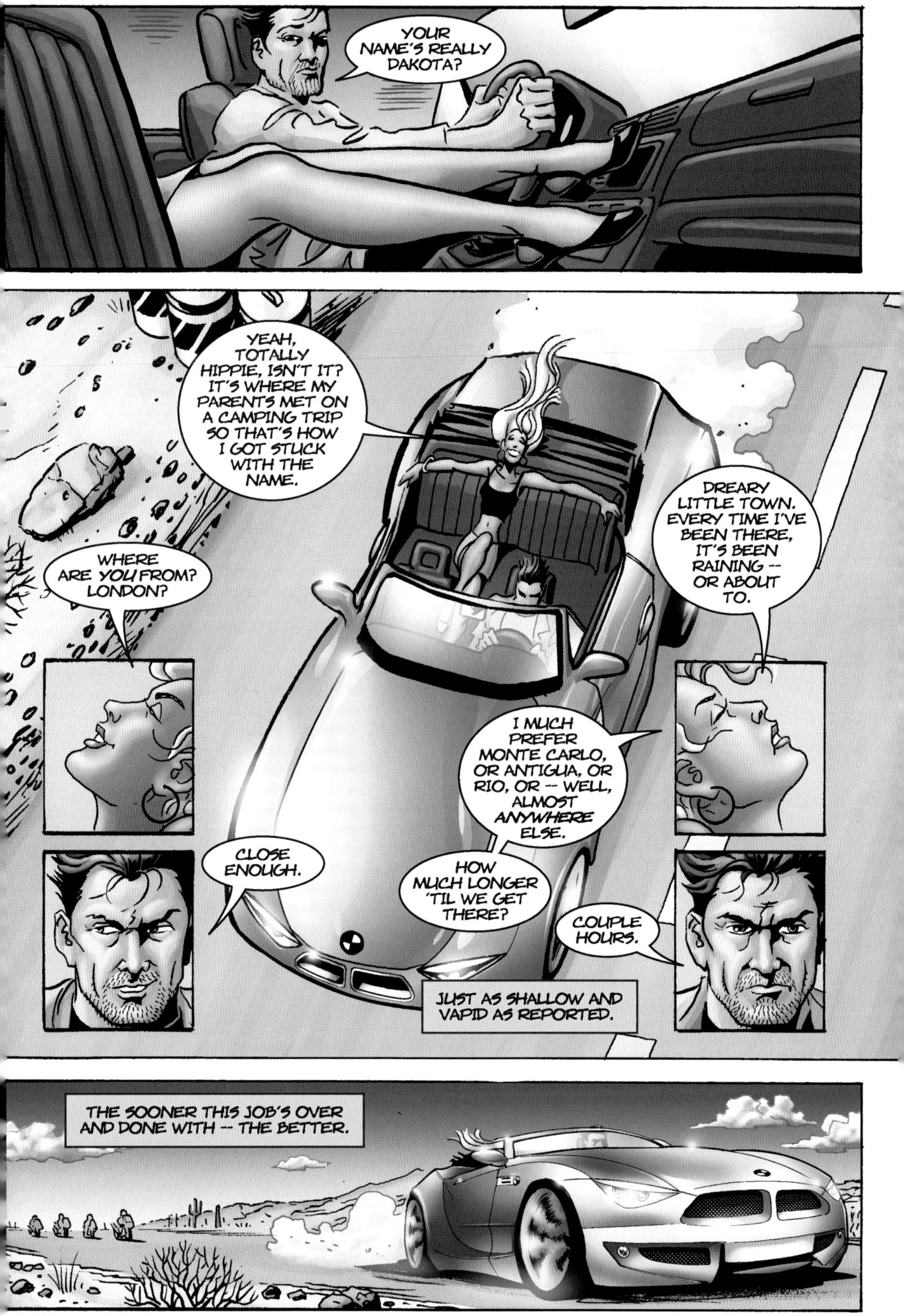
YOUR NAME'S REALLY DAKOTA?
YEAH, TOTALLY HIPPIE, ISN'T IT? IT'S WHERE MY PARENTS MET ON A CAMPING TRIP SO THAT'S HOW I GOT STUCK WITH THE NAME.
WHERE ARE YOU FROM? LONDON?
CLOSE ENOUGH.
DREARY LITTLE TOWN. EVERY TIME I'VE BEEN THERE, IT'S BEEN RAINING -- OR ABOUT TO.
I MUCH PREFER MONTE CARLO, OR ANTIGUA, OR RIO, OR -- WELL, ALMOST ANYWHERE ELSE.
HOW MUCH LONGER 'TIL WE GET THERE?
COUPLE HOURS.
JUST AS SHALLOW AND VAPID AS REPORTED.
THE SOONER THIS JOB'S OVER AND DONE WITH -- THE BETTER.

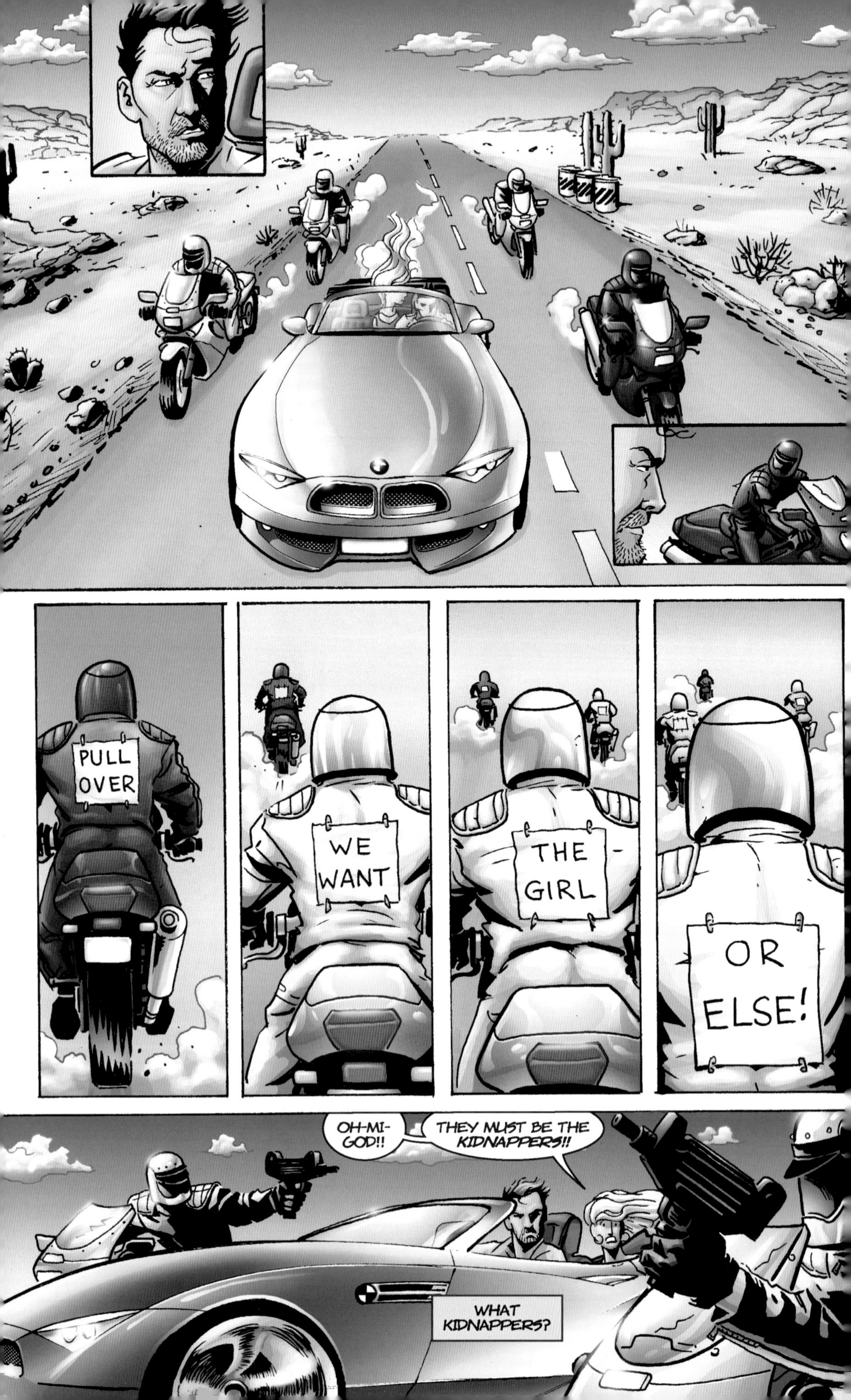
PULL OVER
WE WANT
THE GIRL
OR ELSE!
OH-MI-GOD!!
THEY MUST BE THE KIDNAPPERS!!
WHAT KIDNAPPERS?

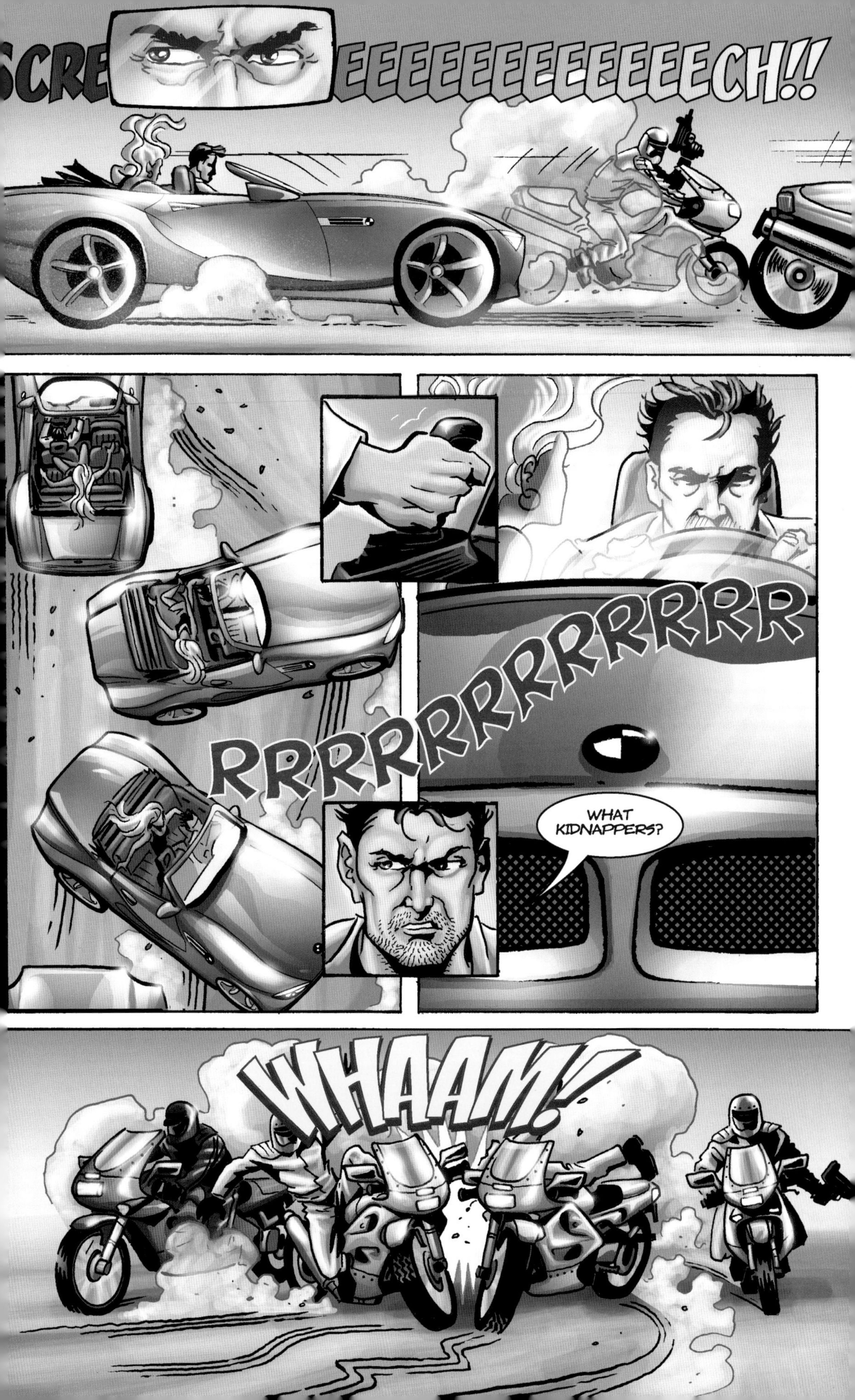
SCREEEEEEEEEEEEEEECH!!
RRRRRRRRRRRRR
WHAT KIDNAPPERS?
WHAAM!

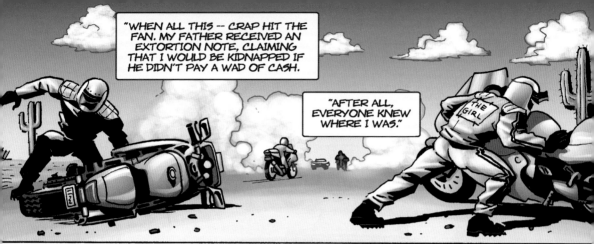

"WHEN ALL THIS -- CRAP HIT THE FAN. MY FATHER RECEIVED AN EXTORTION NOTE, CLAIMING THAT I WOULD BE KIDNAPPED IF HE DIDN'T PAY A WAD OF CASH.

"AFTER ALL, EVERYONE KNEW WHERE I WAS."

HE JUST WROTE IT OFF AS SOME PUBLICITY-HUNGRY NUT-CASE. I MEAN --

-- WHO THE HELL SENDS A RANSOM DEMAND BEFORE THEY HAVE A HOSTAGE?

SOMEONE WHO'S CONFIDENT OF GETTING WHAT THEY WANT.

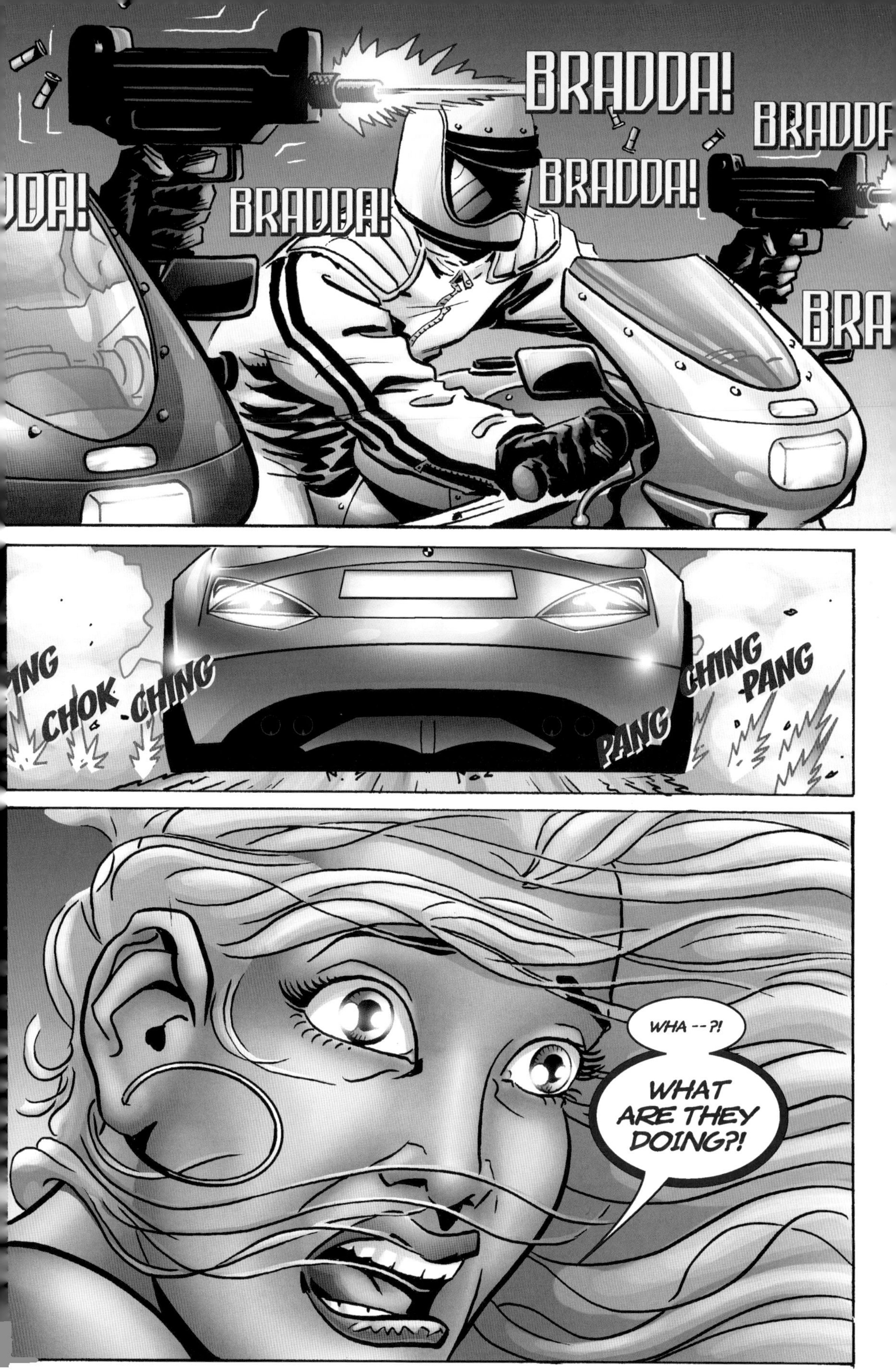

DDA!
BRADDA!
BRADDA!
BRADDA!
BRADDA
BRA
PING
CHOK
CHING
PANG
CHING
PANG
WHA --?!
WHAT ARE THEY DOING?!

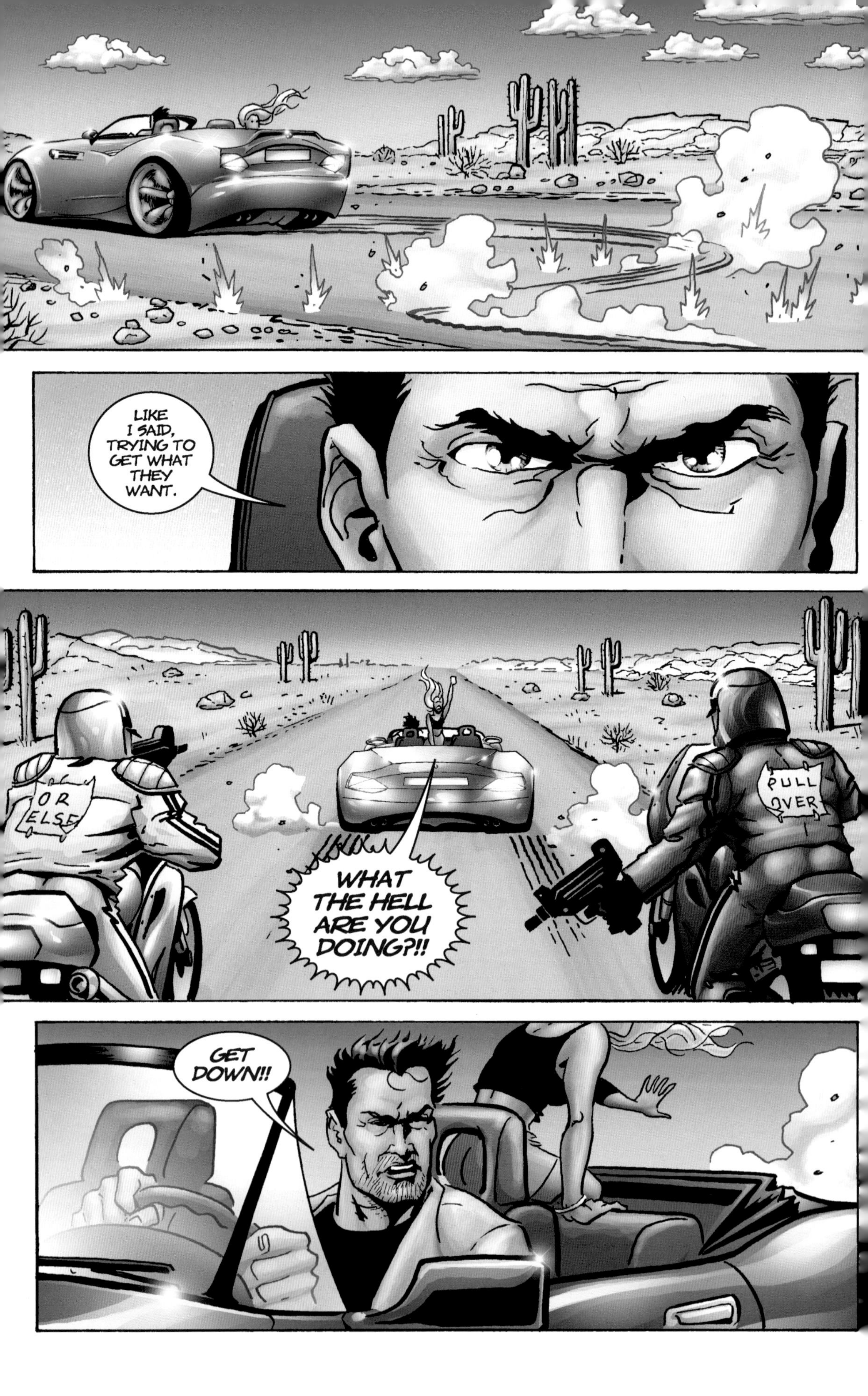
LIKE I SAID, TRYING TO GET WHAT THEY WANT.
OR ELSE
PULL OVER
WHAT THE HELL ARE YOU DOING?!!
GET DOWN!!

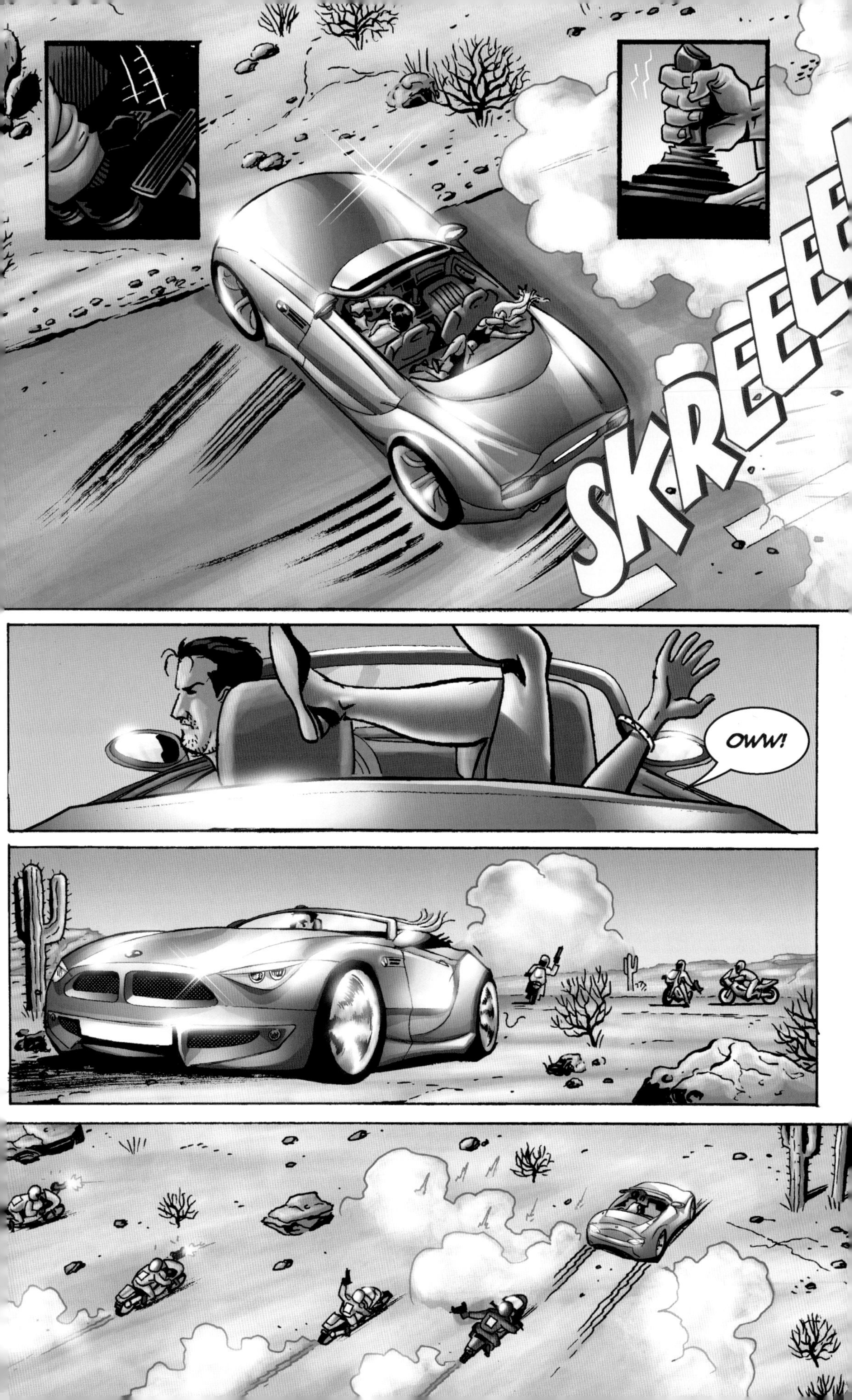
SKREEEEE
OWW!

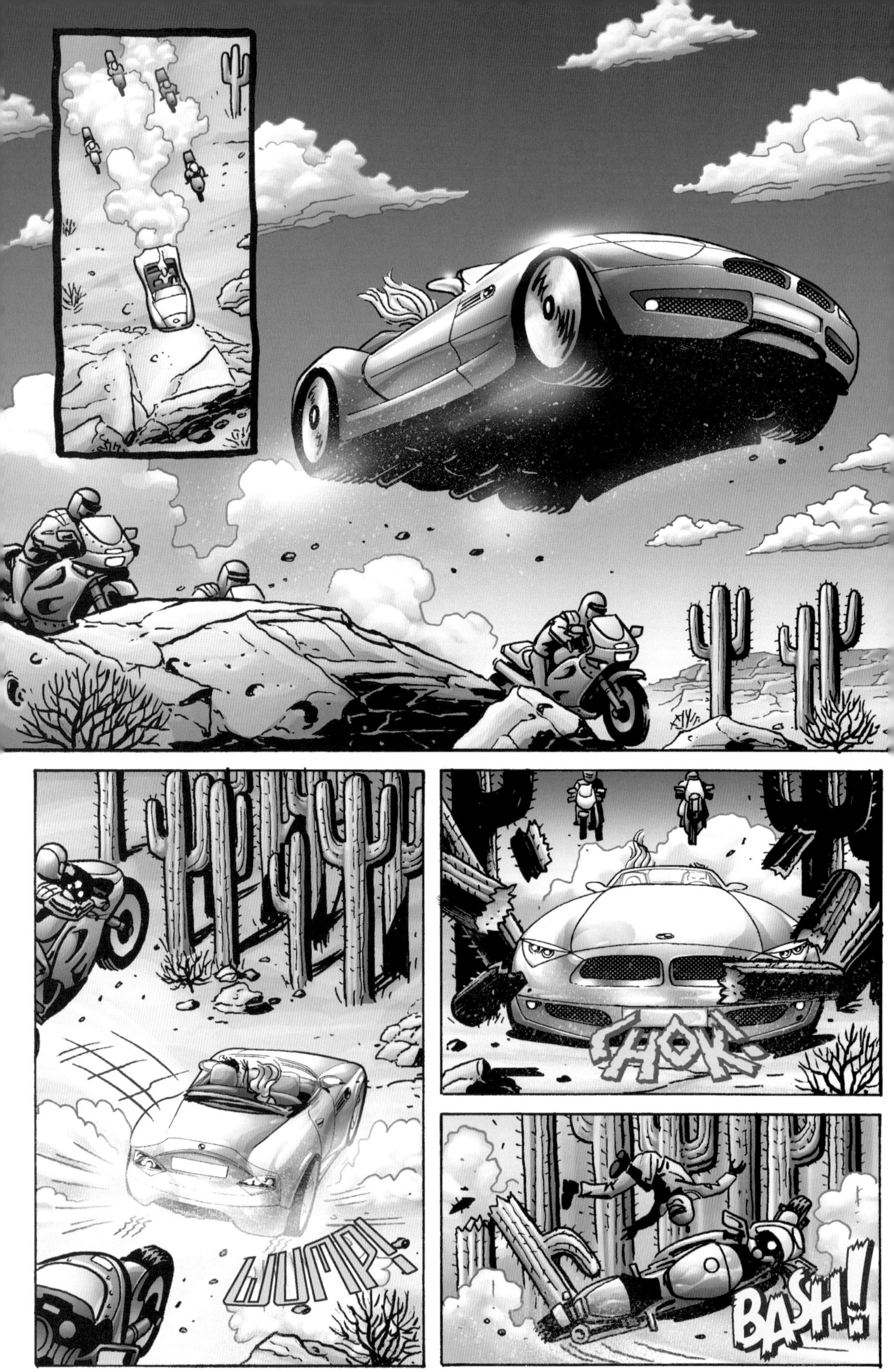
WUMP!
CHOK!
BASH!

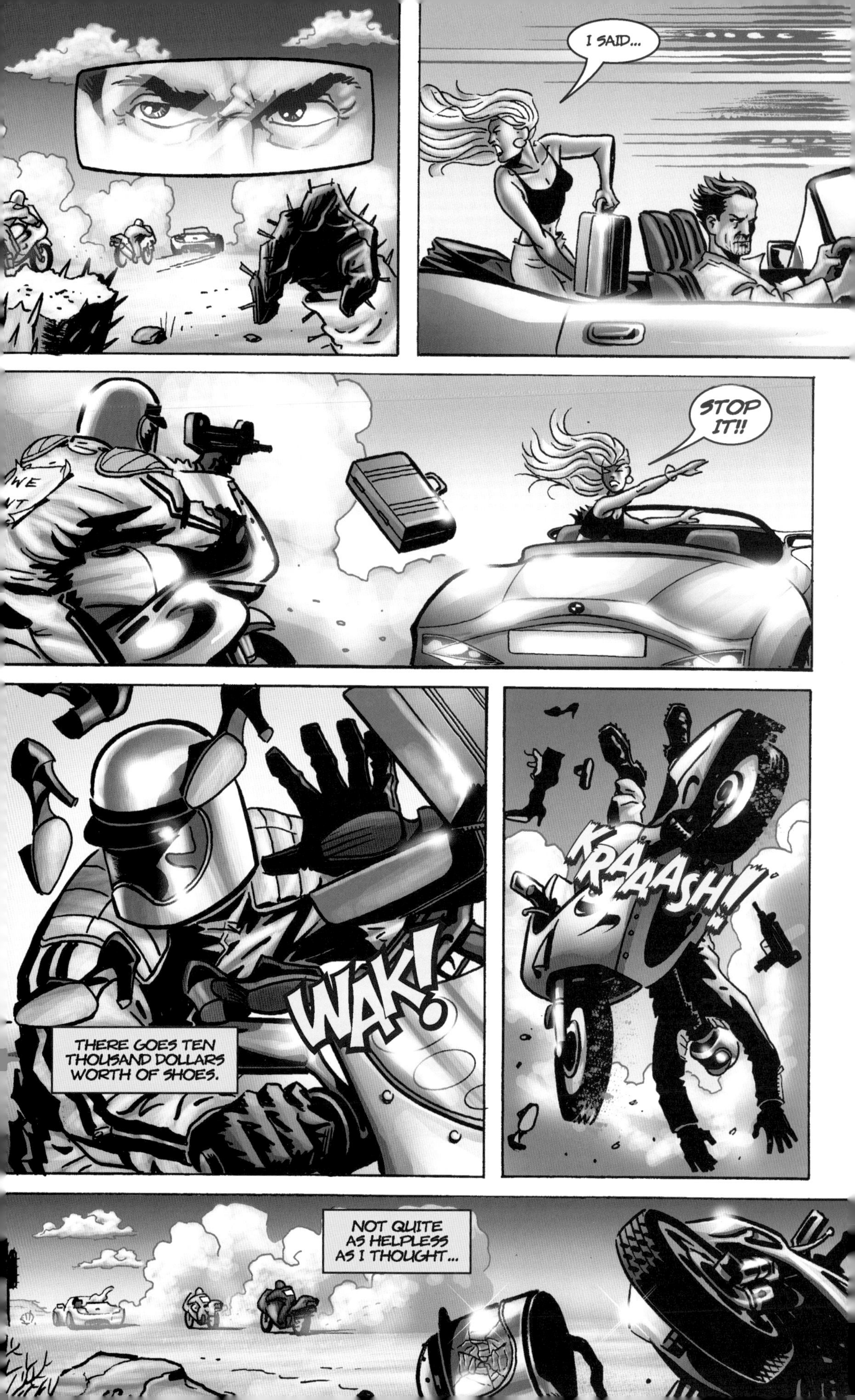
I SAID...
STOP IT!!
THERE GOES TEN THOUSAND DOLLARS WORTH OF SHOES.
WAK!
KRAAASH!
NOT QUITE AS HELPLESS AS I THOUGHT...

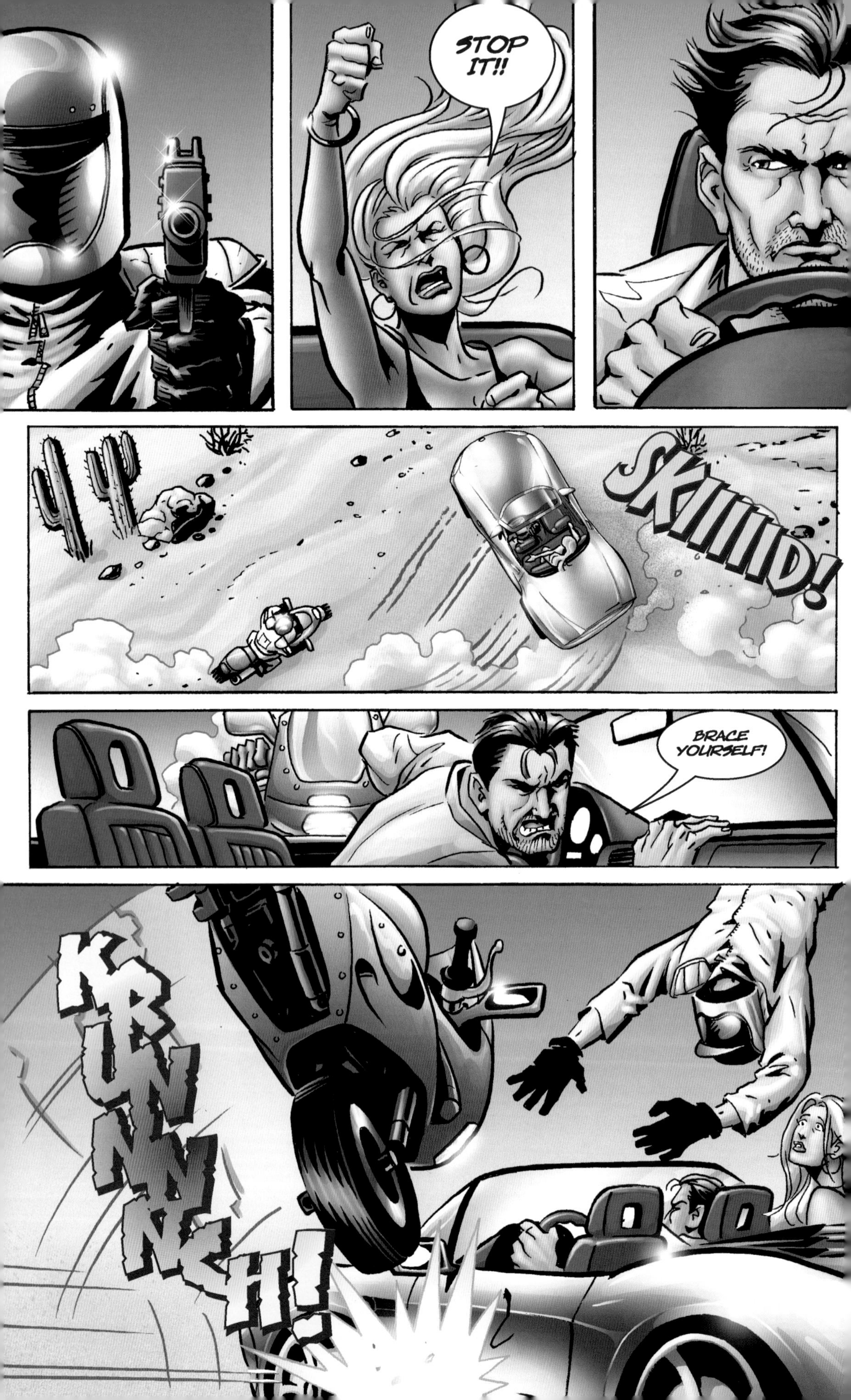
STOP IT!!
SKIIIIID!
BRACE YOURSELF!
KRUNNCH!!

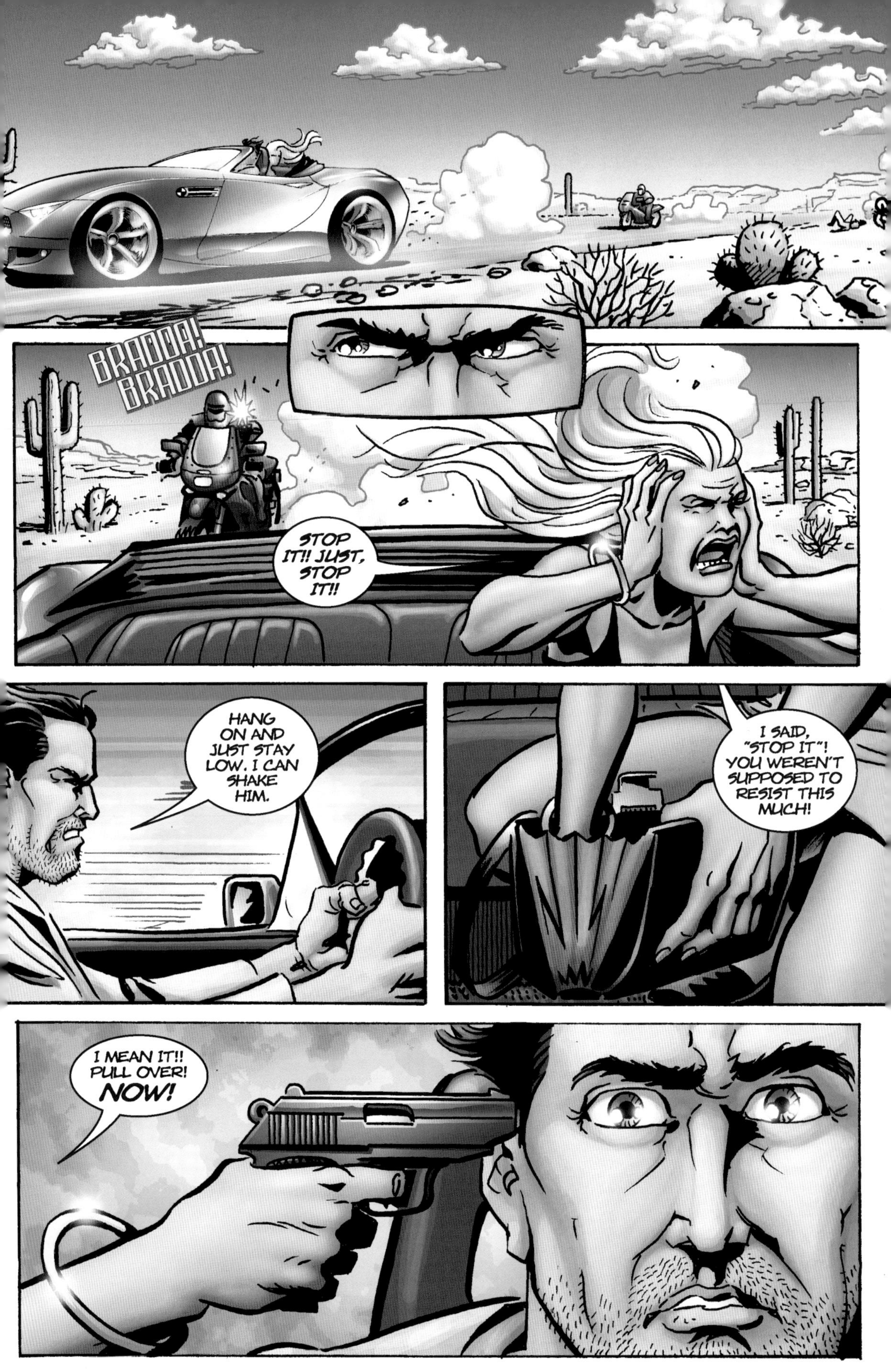
BRADDA! BRADDA!
STOP IT!! JUST, STOP IT!!
HANG ON AND JUST STAY LOW. I CAN SHAKE HIM.
I SAID, "STOP IT"! YOU WEREN'T SUPPOSED TO RESIST THIS MUCH!
I MEAN IT!! PULL OVER! NOW!

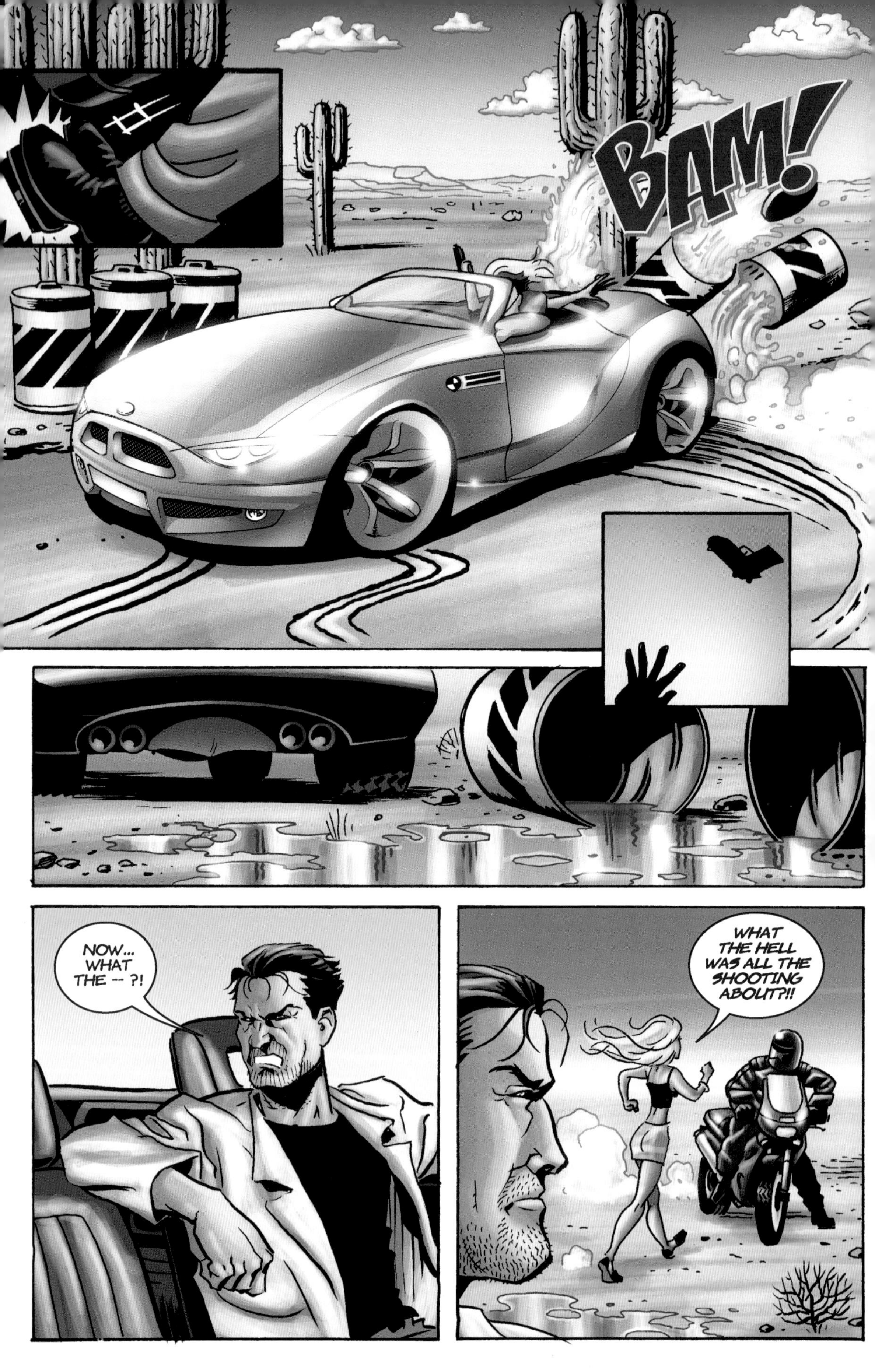
BAM!
NOW... WHAT THE -- ?!
WHAT THE HELL WAS ALL THE SHOOTING ABOUT?!!

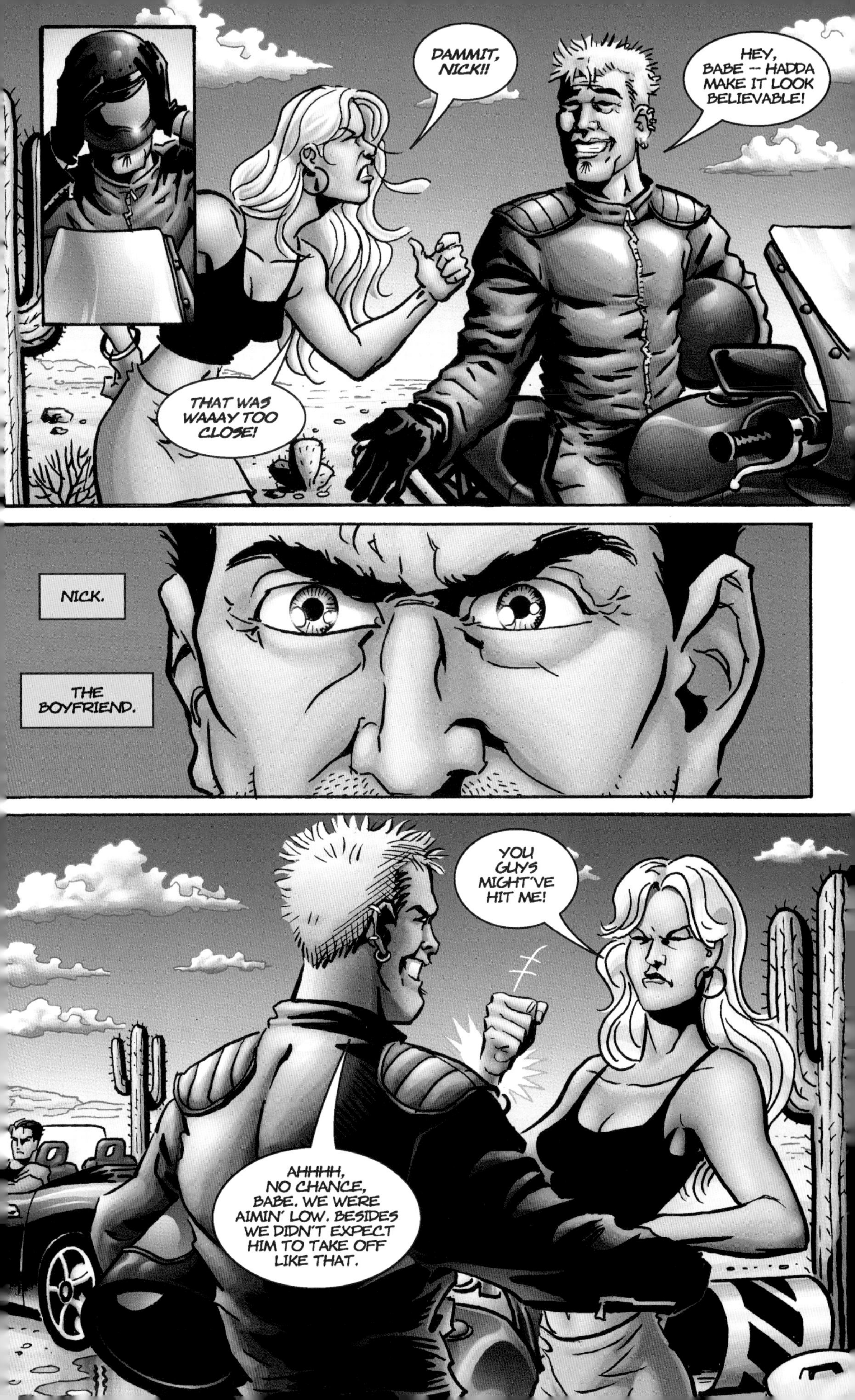
DAMMIT, NICK!!
THAT WAS WAAAY TOO CLOSE!
HEY, BABE -- HADDA MAKE IT LOOK BELIEVABLE!
NICK.
THE BOYFRIEND.
YOU GUYS MIGHT'VE HIT ME!
AHHHH, NO CHANCE, BABE. WE WERE AIMIN' LOW. BESIDES WE DIDN'T EXPECT HIM TO TAKE OFF LIKE THAT.

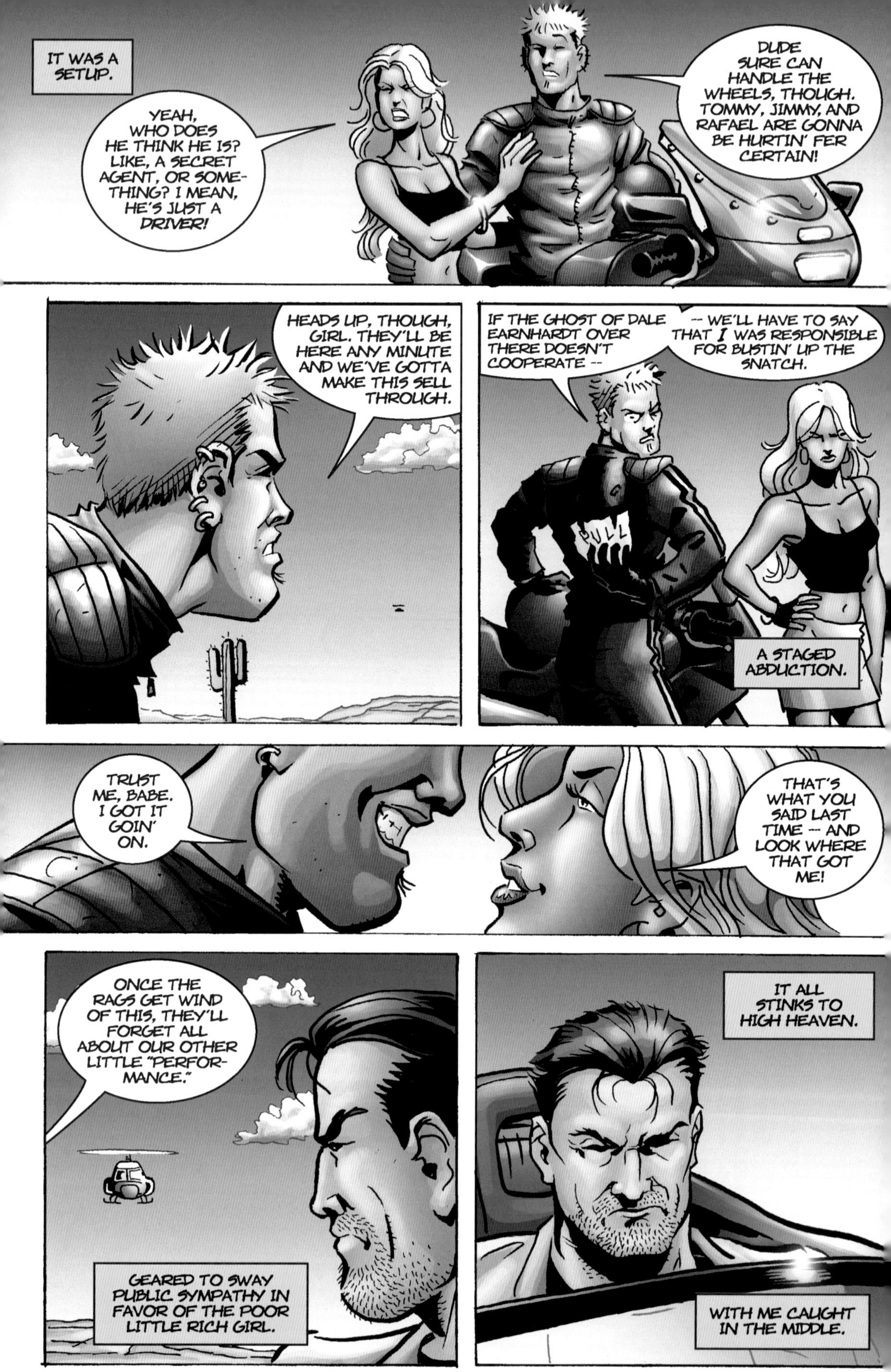
IT WAS A SETUP.
YEAH, WHO DOES HE THINK HE IS? LIKE, A SECRET AGENT, OR SOME-THING? I MEAN, HE'S JUST A DRIVER!
DUDE SURE CAN HANDLE THE WHEELS, THOUGH. TOMMY, JIMMY, AND RAFAEL ARE GONNA BE HURTIN' FER CERTAIN!
HEADS UP, THOUGH, GIRL. THEY'LL BE HERE ANY MINUTE AND WE'VE GOTTA MAKE THIS SELL THROUGH.
IF THE GHOST OF DALE EARNHARDT OVER THERE DOESN'T COOPERATE --
-- WE'LL HAVE TO SAY THAT I WAS RESPONSIBLE FOR BUSTIN' UP THE SNATCH.
A STAGED ABDUCTION.
TRUST ME, BABE. I GOT IT GOIN' ON.
THAT'S WHAT YOU SAID LAST TIME -- AND LOOK WHERE THAT GOT ME!
ONCE THE RAGS GET WIND OF THIS, THEY'LL FORGET ALL ABOUT OUR OTHER LITTLE "PERFOR-MANCE."
GEARED TO SWAY PUBLIC SYMPATHY IN FAVOR OF THE POOR LITTLE RICH GIRL.
IT ALL STINKS TO HIGH HEAVEN.
WITH ME CAUGHT IN THE MIDDLE.

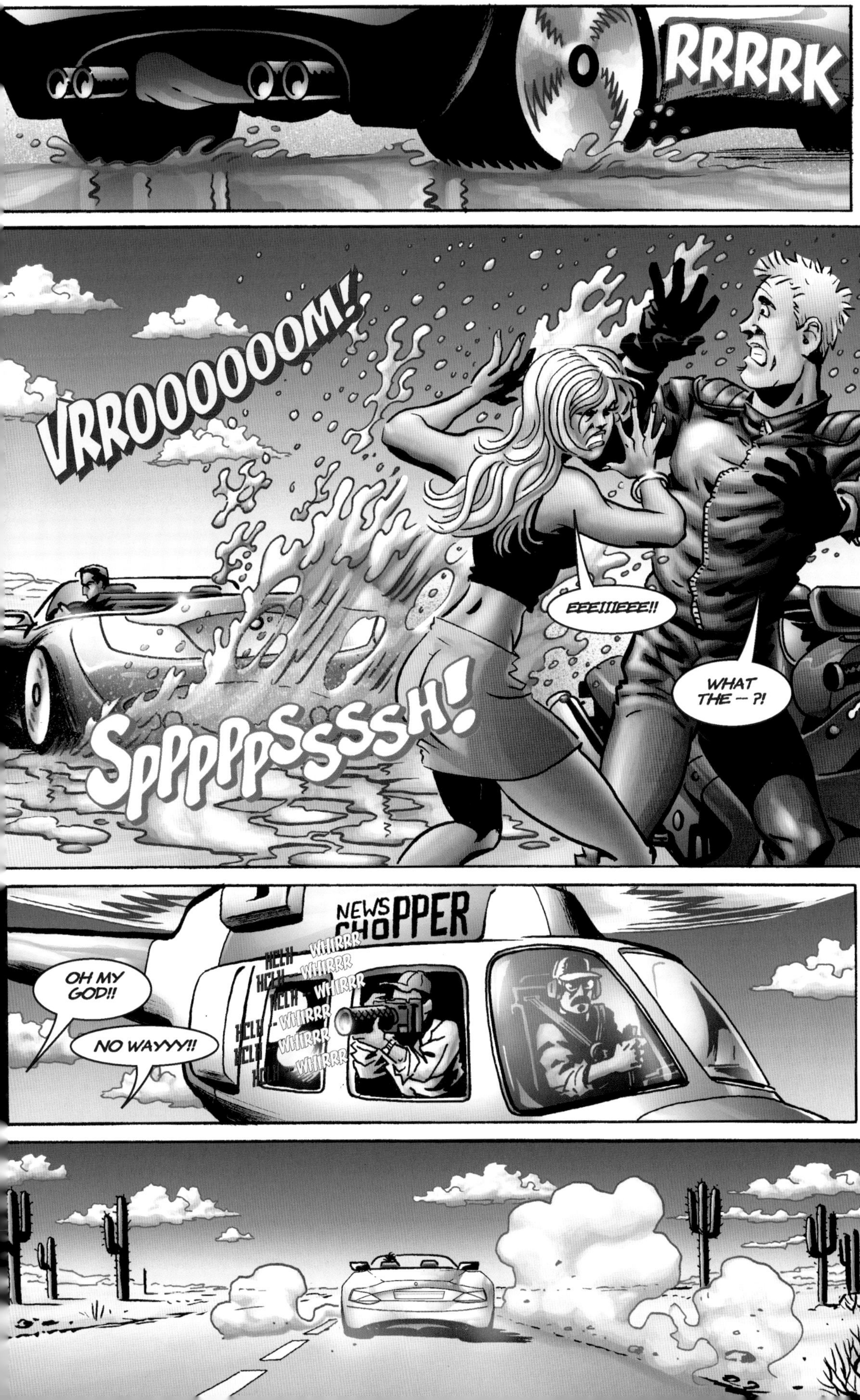
RRRRK
VRROOOOOOM!
EEEIIIEEE!!
WHAT THE -- ?!
SPPPPPSSSSSH!
NEWS CHOPPER
WHIRRR
OH MY GOD!!
NO WAYYY!!

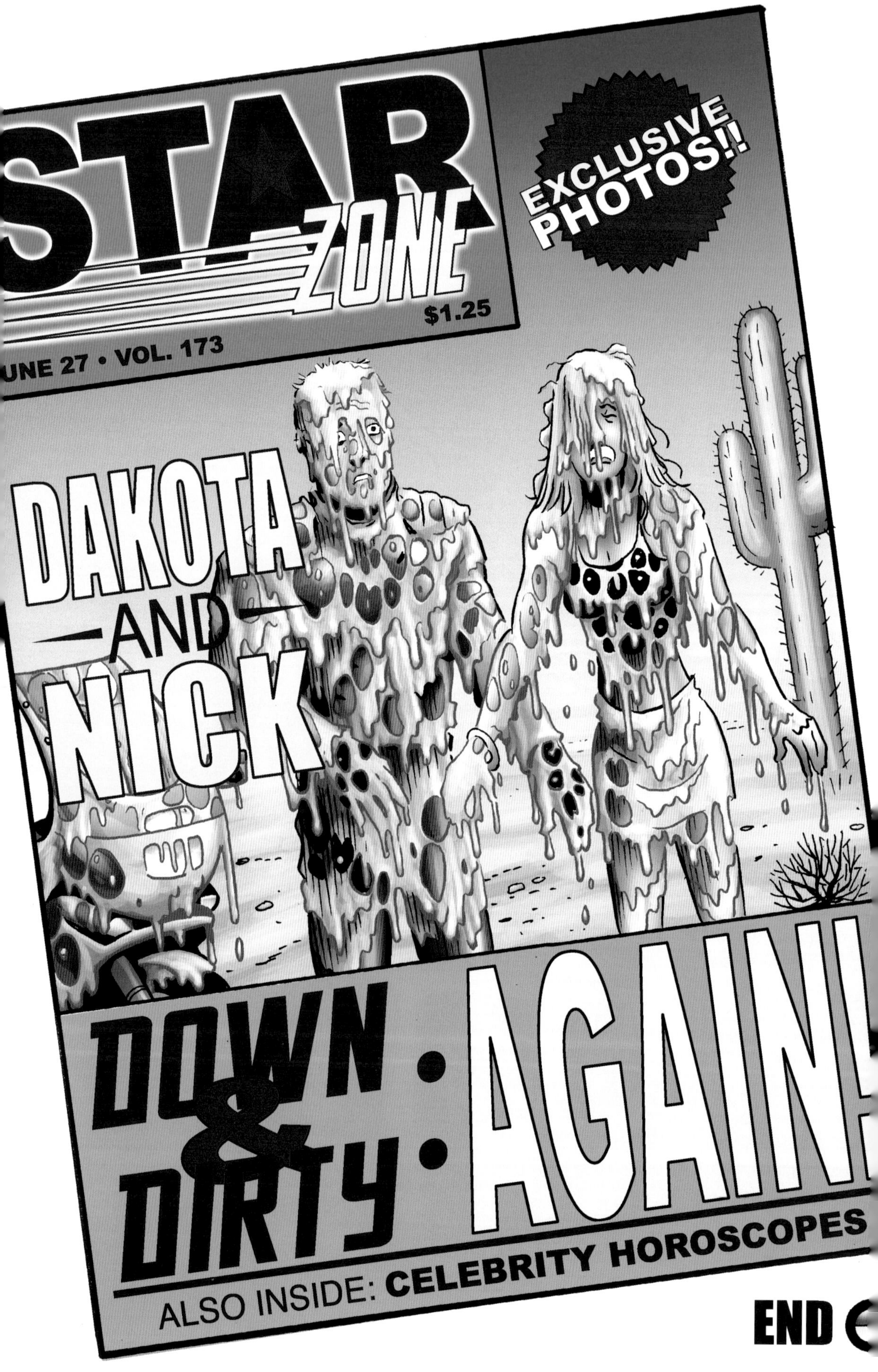
STAR ZONE
$1.25
EXCLUSIVE PHOTOS!!
UNE 27 • VOL. 173
DAKOTA AND NICK
DOWN & DIRTY • AGAIN!
ALSO INSIDE: CELEBRITY HOROSCOPES
END

PRECIOUS CARGO

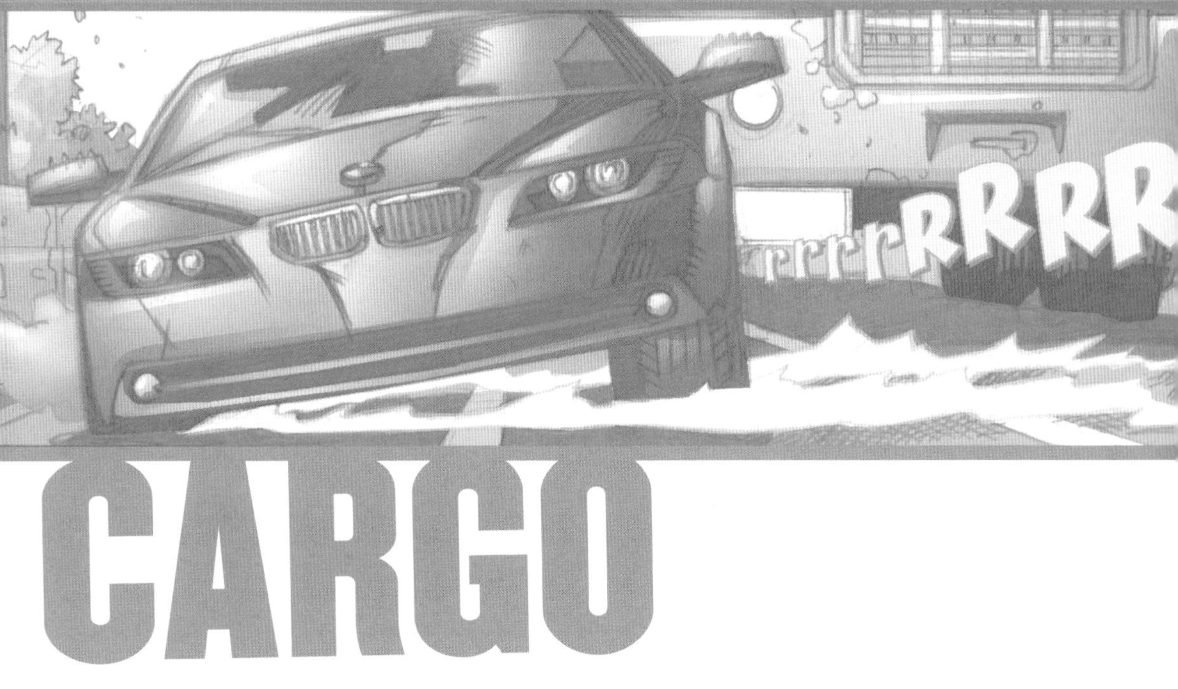
rrrrrRRRR

SCRIPT **BRUCE CAMPBELL** ART **KILIAN PLUNKETT** COLORS **SNO CONE STUDIOS**

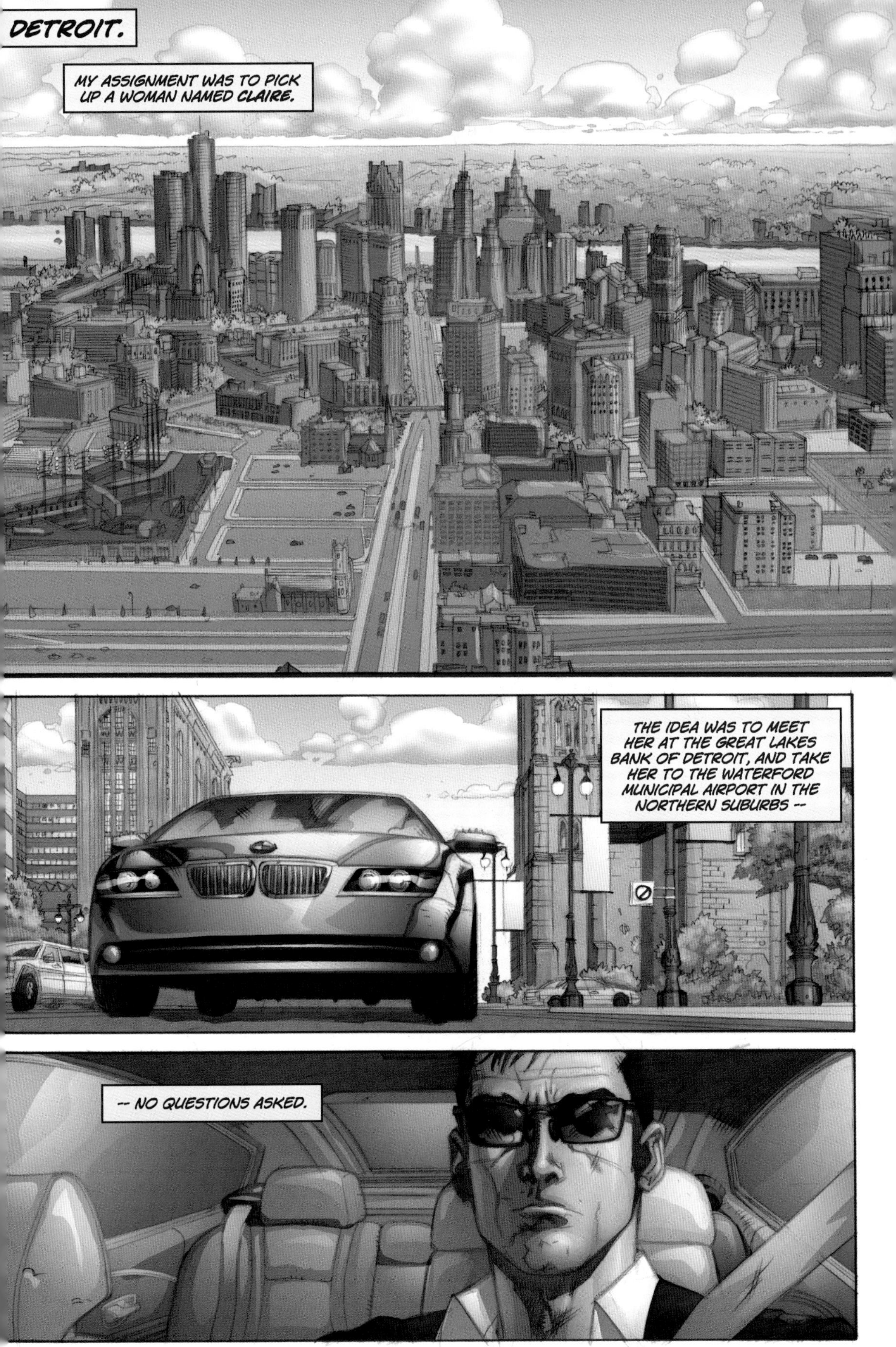
DETROIT.
MY ASSIGNMENT WAS TO PICK UP A WOMAN NAMED CLAIRE.
THE IDEA WAS TO MEET HER AT THE GREAT LAKES BANK OF DETROIT, AND TAKE HER TO THE WATERFORD MUNICIPAL AIRPORT IN THE NORTHERN SUBURBS --
-- NO QUESTIONS ASKED.

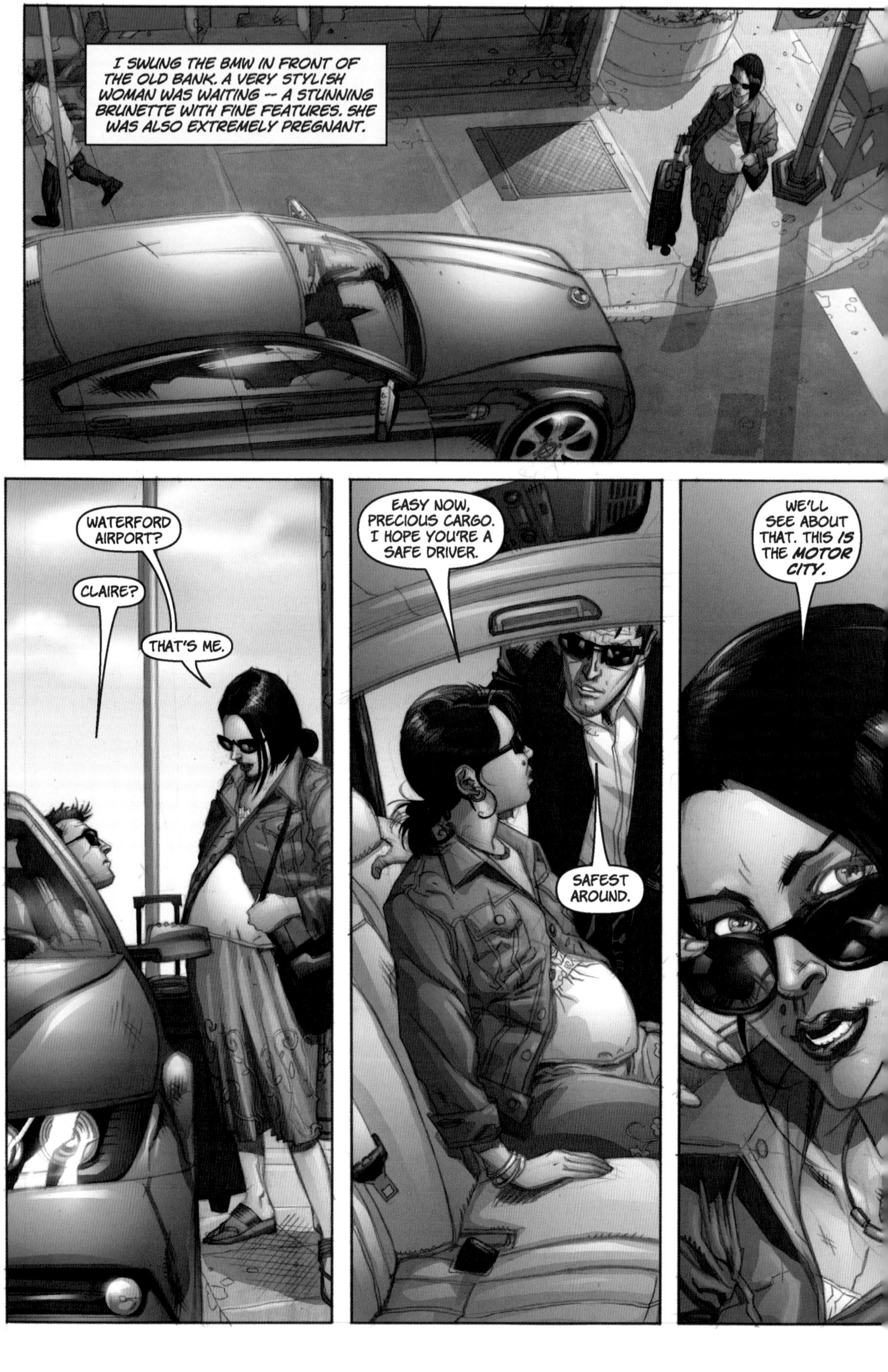
I SWUNG THE BMW IN FRONT OF THE OLD BANK. A VERY STYLISH WOMAN WAS WAITING -- A STUNNING BRUNETTE WITH FINE FEATURES. SHE WAS ALSO EXTREMELY PREGNANT.
WATERFORD AIRPORT?
CLAIRE?
THAT'S ME.
EASY NOW, PRECIOUS CARGO. I HOPE YOU'RE A SAFE DRIVER.
SAFEST AROUND.
WE'LL SEE ABOUT THAT. THIS IS THE MOTOR CITY.

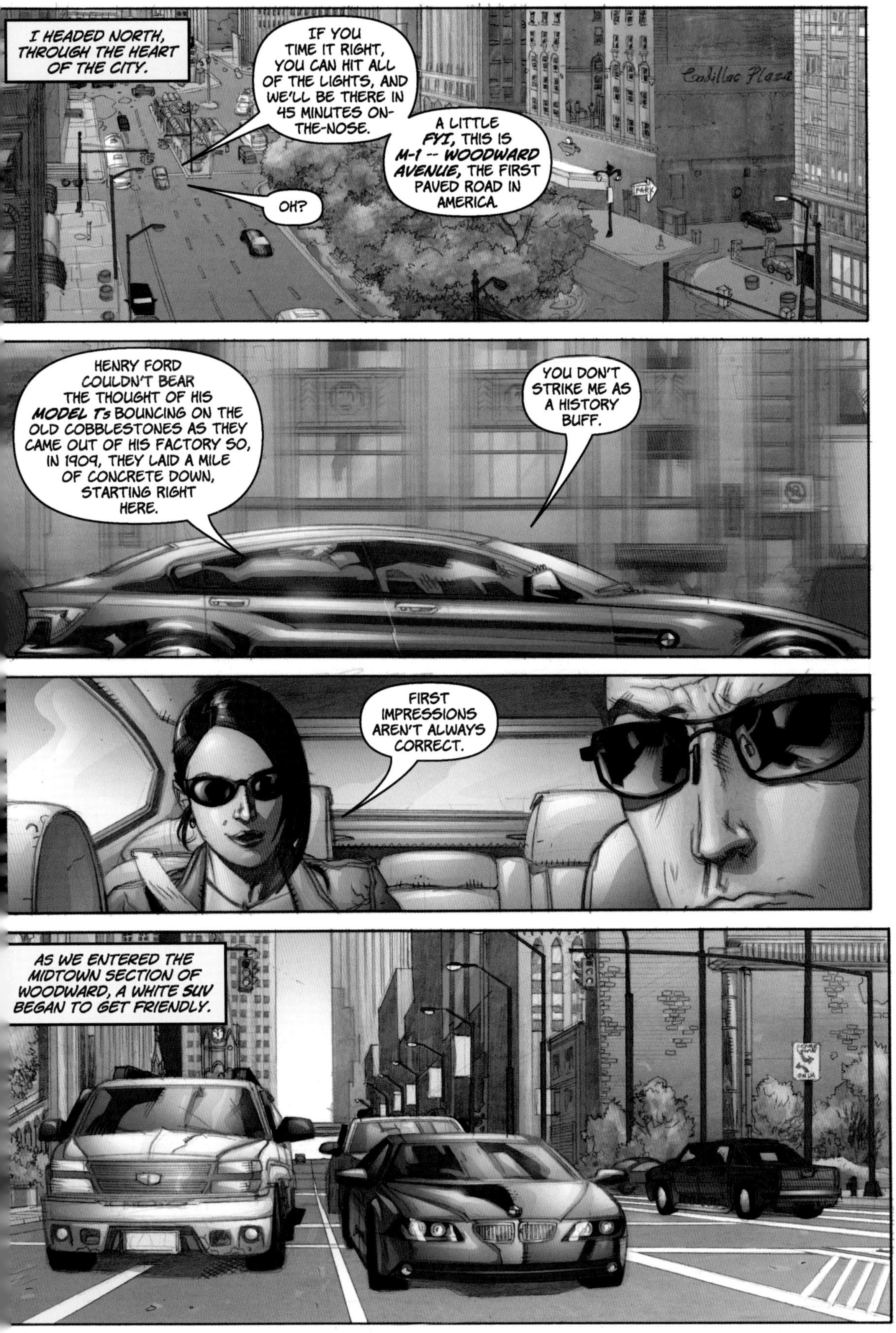
I HEADED NORTH, THROUGH THE HEART OF THE CITY.
IF YOU TIME IT RIGHT, YOU CAN HIT ALL OF THE LIGHTS, AND WE'LL BE THERE IN 45 MINUTES ON-THE-NOSE.
OH?
A LITTLE FYI, THIS IS M-1 -- WOODWARD AVENUE, THE FIRST PAVED ROAD IN AMERICA.
Cadillac Plaza
PARK
HENRY FORD COULDN'T BEAR THE THOUGHT OF HIS MODEL Ts BOUNCING ON THE OLD COBBLESTONES AS THEY CAME OUT OF HIS FACTORY SO, IN 1909, THEY LAID A MILE OF CONCRETE DOWN, STARTING RIGHT HERE.
YOU DON'T STRIKE ME AS A HISTORY BUFF.
FIRST IMPRESSIONS AREN'T ALWAYS CORRECT.
AS WE ENTERED THE MIDTOWN SECTION OF WOODWARD, A WHITE SUV BEGAN TO GET FRIENDLY.

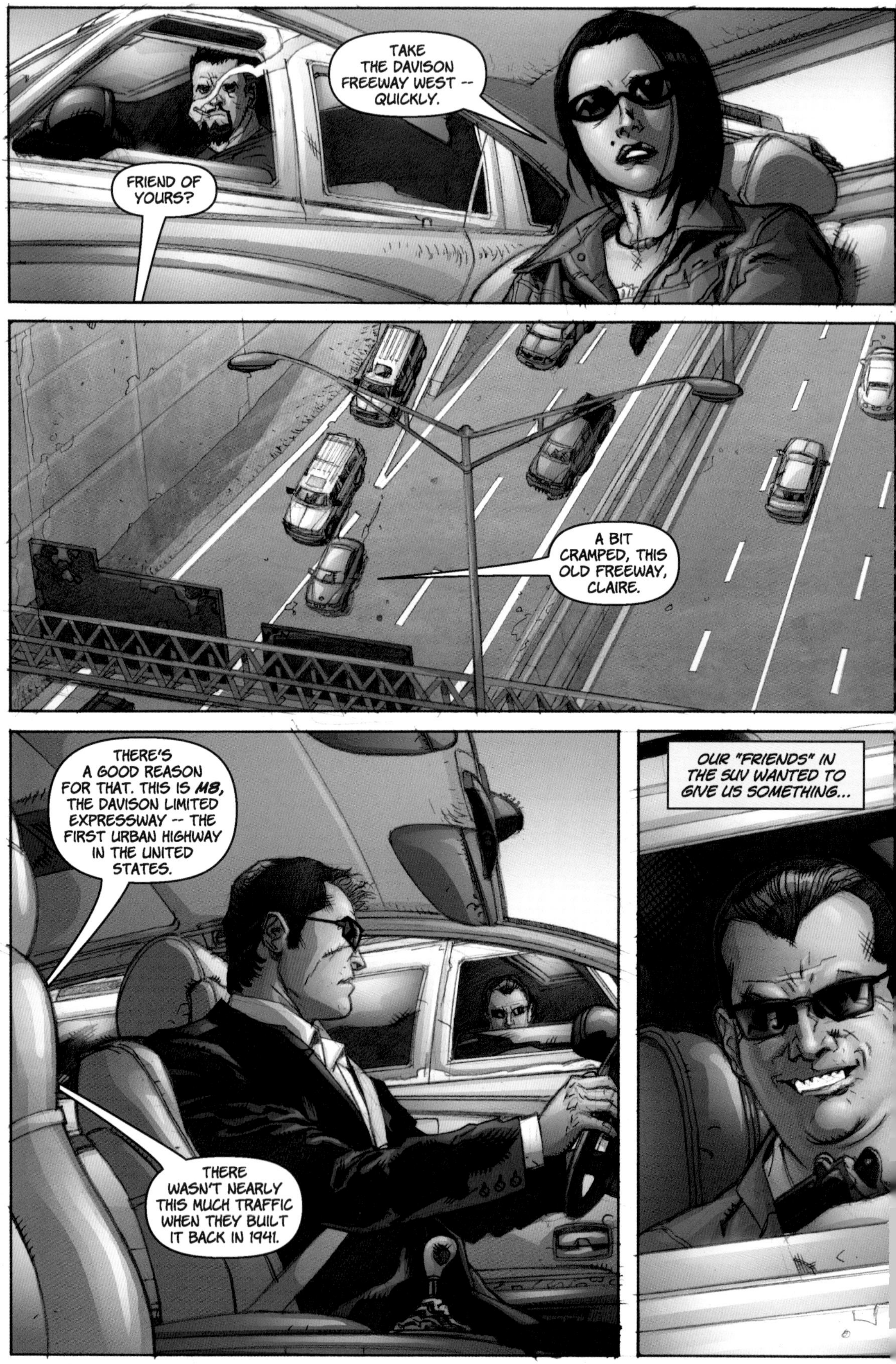
TAKE THE DAVISON FREEWAY WEST -- QUICKLY.
FRIEND OF YOURS?
A BIT CRAMPED, THIS OLD FREEWAY, CLAIRE.
THERE'S A GOOD REASON FOR THAT. THIS IS M8, THE DAVISON LIMITED EXPRESSWAY -- THE FIRST URBAN HIGHWAY IN THE UNITED STATES.
THERE WASN'T NEARLY THIS MUCH TRAFFIC WHEN THEY BUILT IT BACK IN 1941.
OUR "FRIENDS" IN THE SUV WANTED TO GIVE US SOMETHING...

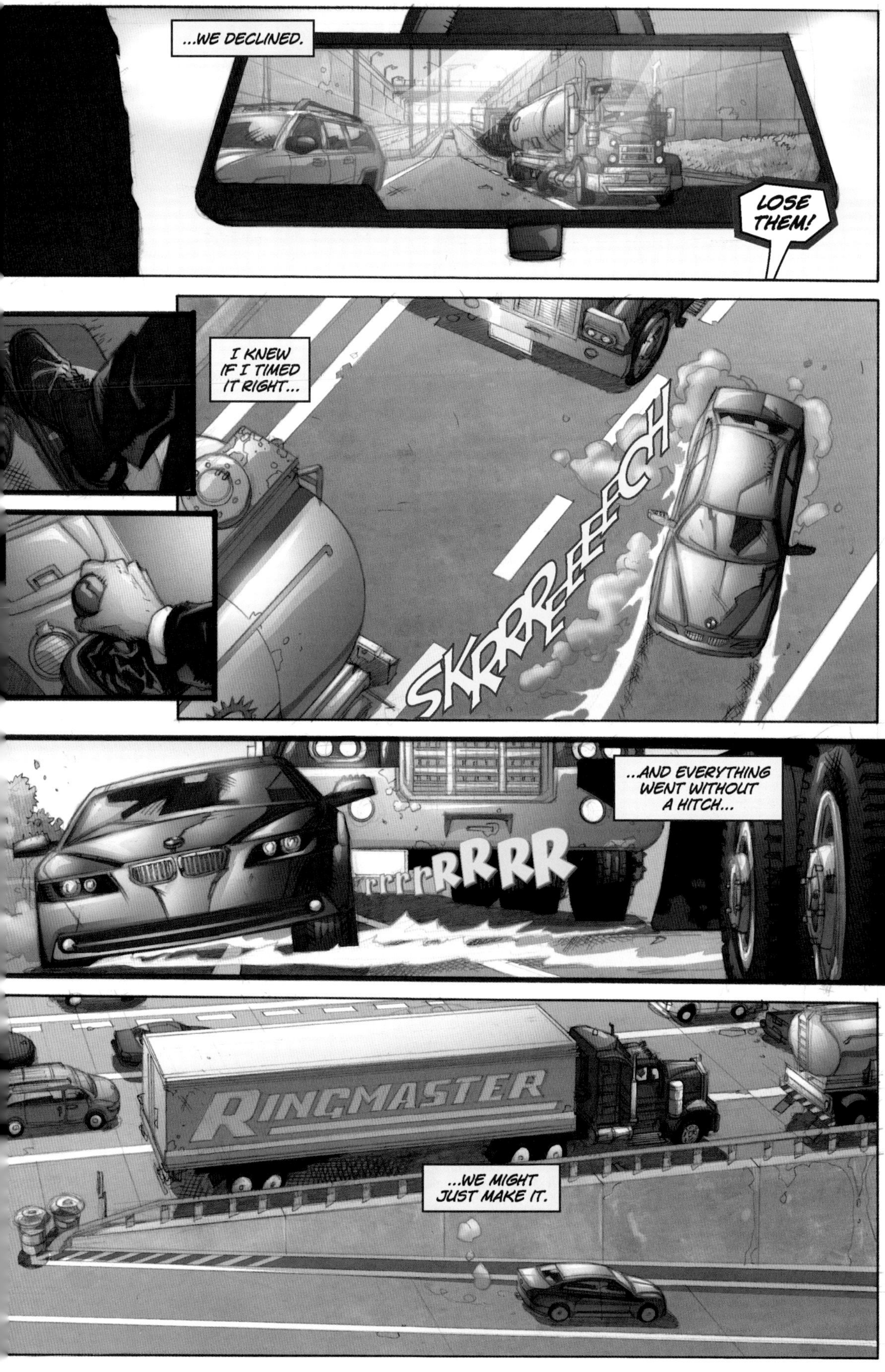
...WE DECLINED.
LOSE THEM!
I KNEW IF I TIMED IT RIGHT...
SKRRRREEEECH
...AND EVERYTHING WENT WITHOUT A HITCH...
rrrrrRRRR
RINGMASTER
...WE MIGHT JUST MAKE IT.

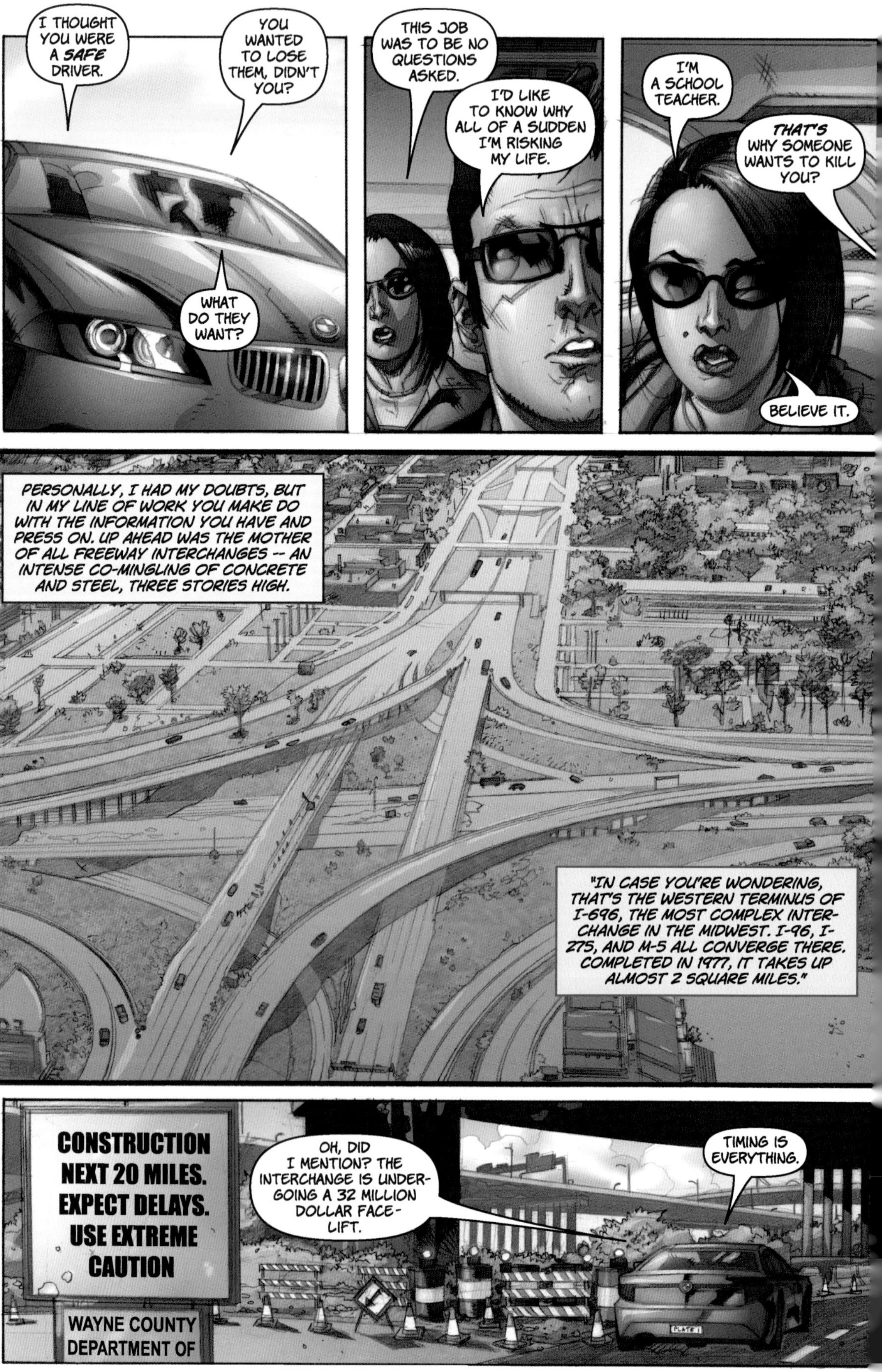
I THOUGHT YOU WERE A SAFE DRIVER.
YOU WANTED TO LOSE THEM, DIDN'T YOU?
WHAT DO THEY WANT?
THIS JOB WAS TO BE NO QUESTIONS ASKED.
I'D LIKE TO KNOW WHY ALL OF A SUDDEN I'M RISKING MY LIFE.
I'M A SCHOOL TEACHER.
THAT'S WHY SOMEONE WANTS TO KILL YOU?
BELIEVE IT.
PERSONALLY, I HAD MY DOUBTS, BUT IN MY LINE OF WORK YOU MAKE DO WITH THE INFORMATION YOU HAVE AND PRESS ON. UP AHEAD WAS THE MOTHER OF ALL FREEWAY INTERCHANGES -- AN INTENSE CO-MINGLING OF CONCRETE AND STEEL, THREE STORIES HIGH.
"IN CASE YOU'RE WONDERING, THAT'S THE WESTERN TERMINUS OF I-696, THE MOST COMPLEX INTER-CHANGE IN THE MIDWEST. I-96, I-275, AND M-5 ALL CONVERGE THERE. COMPLETED IN 1977, IT TAKES UP ALMOST 2 SQUARE MILES."
CONSTRUCTION NEXT 20 MILES. EXPECT DELAYS. USE EXTREME CAUTION
WAYNE COUNTY DEPARTMENT OF
OH, DID I MENTION? THE INTERCHANGE IS UNDER-GOING A 32 MILLION DOLLAR FACE-LIFT.
TIMING IS EVERYTHING.

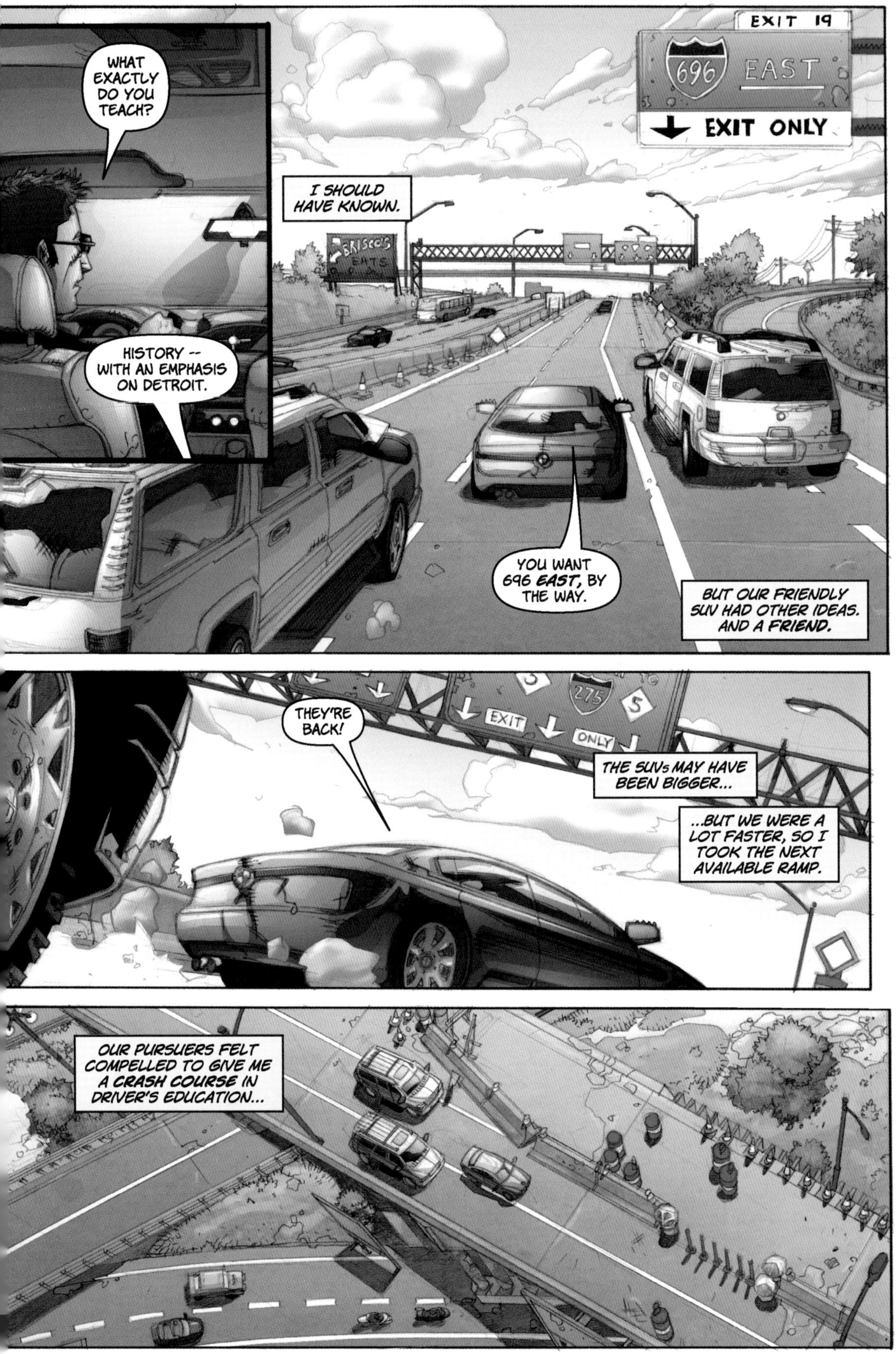

EXIT 19
696 EAST
EXIT ONLY
WHAT EXACTLY DO YOU TEACH?
HISTORY -- WITH AN EMPHASIS ON DETROIT.
I SHOULD HAVE KNOWN.
BRISCO'S EATS
YOU WANT 696 EAST, BY THE WAY.
BUT OUR FRIENDLY SUV HAD OTHER IDEAS. AND A FRIEND.
275
EXIT ONLY
THEY'RE BACK!
THE SUVs MAY HAVE BEEN BIGGER...
...BUT WE WERE A LOT FASTER, SO I TOOK THE NEXT AVAILABLE RAMP.
OUR PURSUERS FELT COMPELLED TO GIVE ME A CRASH COURSE IN DRIVER'S EDUCATION...

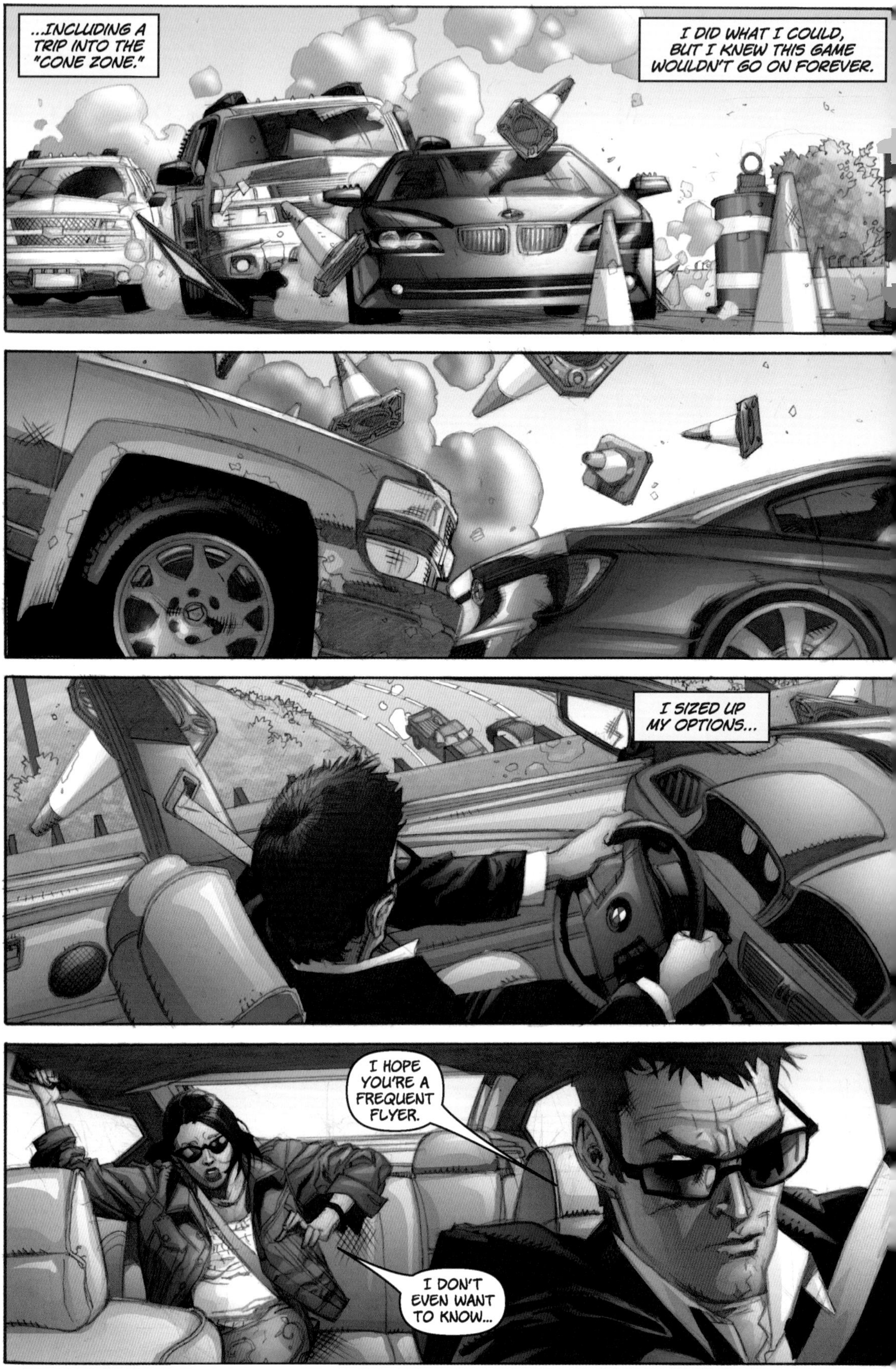
...INCLUDING A TRIP INTO THE "CONE ZONE."
I DID WHAT I COULD, BUT I KNEW THIS GAME WOULDN'T GO ON FOREVER.
I SIZED UP MY OPTIONS...
I HOPE YOU'RE A FREQUENT FLYER.
I DON'T EVEN WANT TO KNOW...

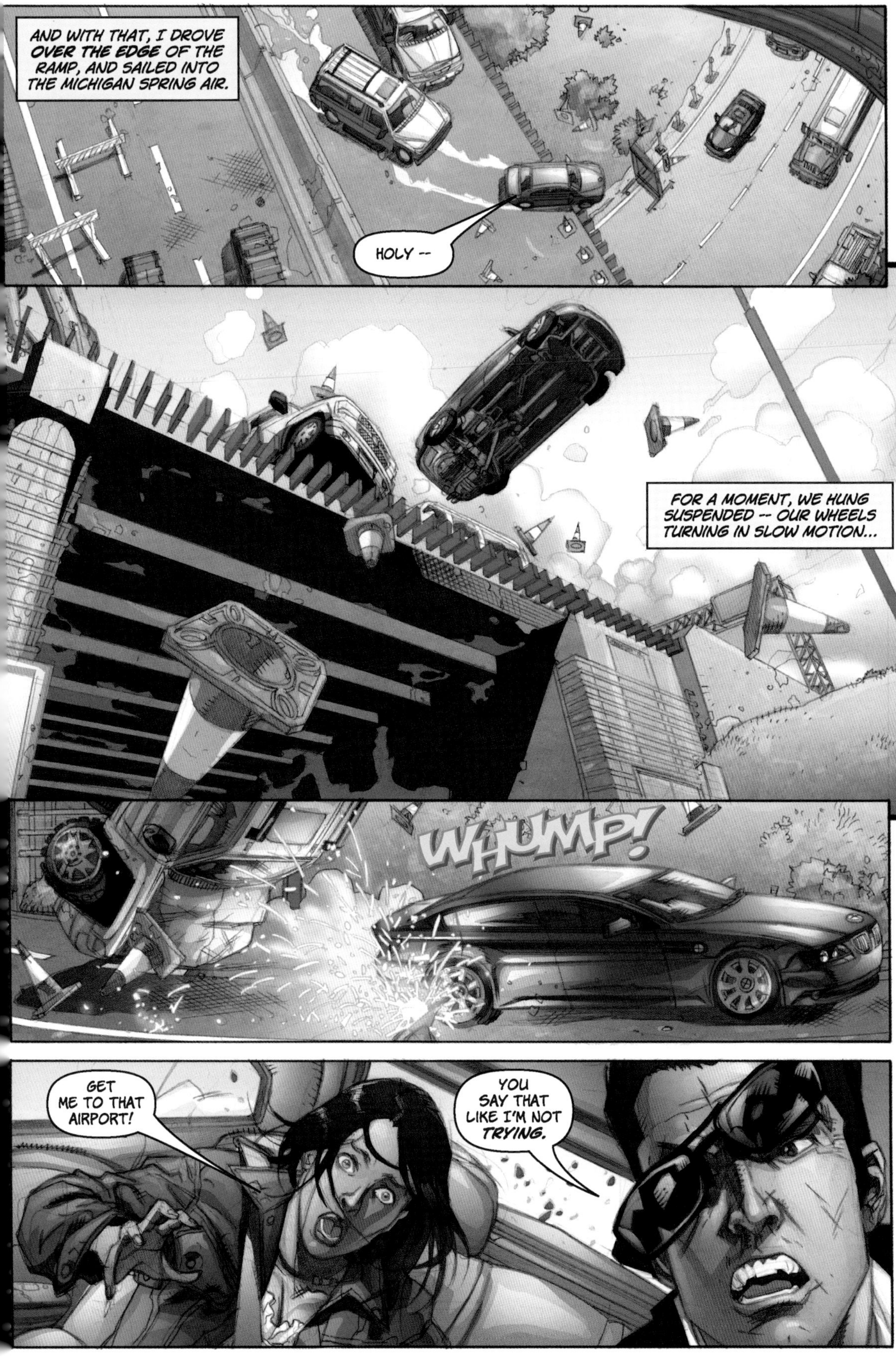
AND WITH THAT, I DROVE OVER THE EDGE OF THE RAMP, AND SAILED INTO THE MICHIGAN SPRING AIR.
HOLY --
FOR A MOMENT, WE HUNG SUSPENDED -- OUR WHEELS TURNING IN SLOW MOTION...
WHUMP!
GET ME TO THAT AIRPORT!
YOU SAY THAT LIKE I'M NOT TRYING.

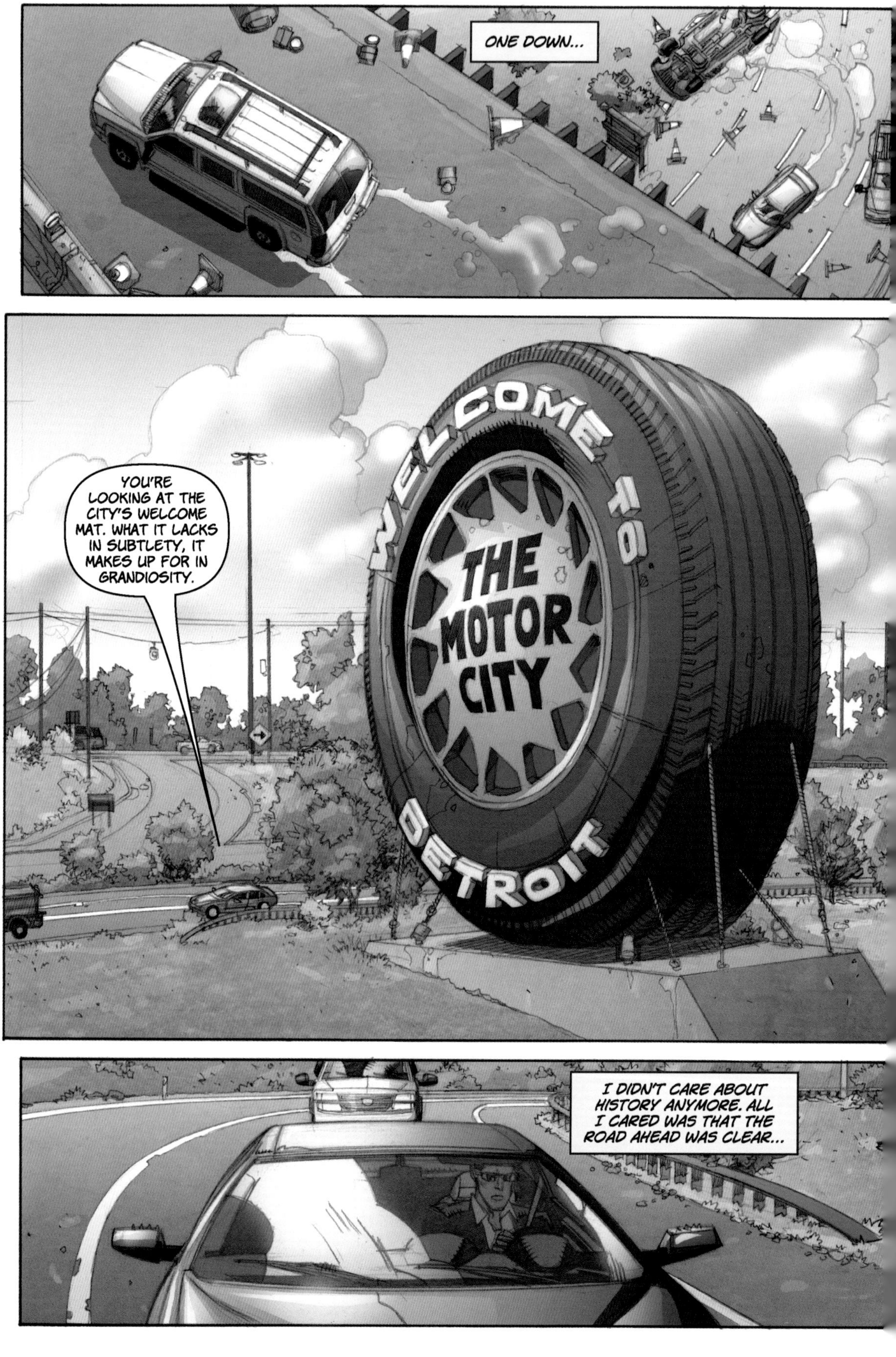
ONE DOWN...
YOU'RE LOOKING AT THE CITY'S WELCOME MAT. WHAT IT LACKS IN SUBTLETY, IT MAKES UP FOR IN GRANDIOSITY.
WELCOME TO
THE MOTOR CITY
DETROIT
I DIDN'T CARE ABOUT HISTORY ANYMORE. ALL I CARED WAS THAT THE ROAD AHEAD WAS CLEAR...

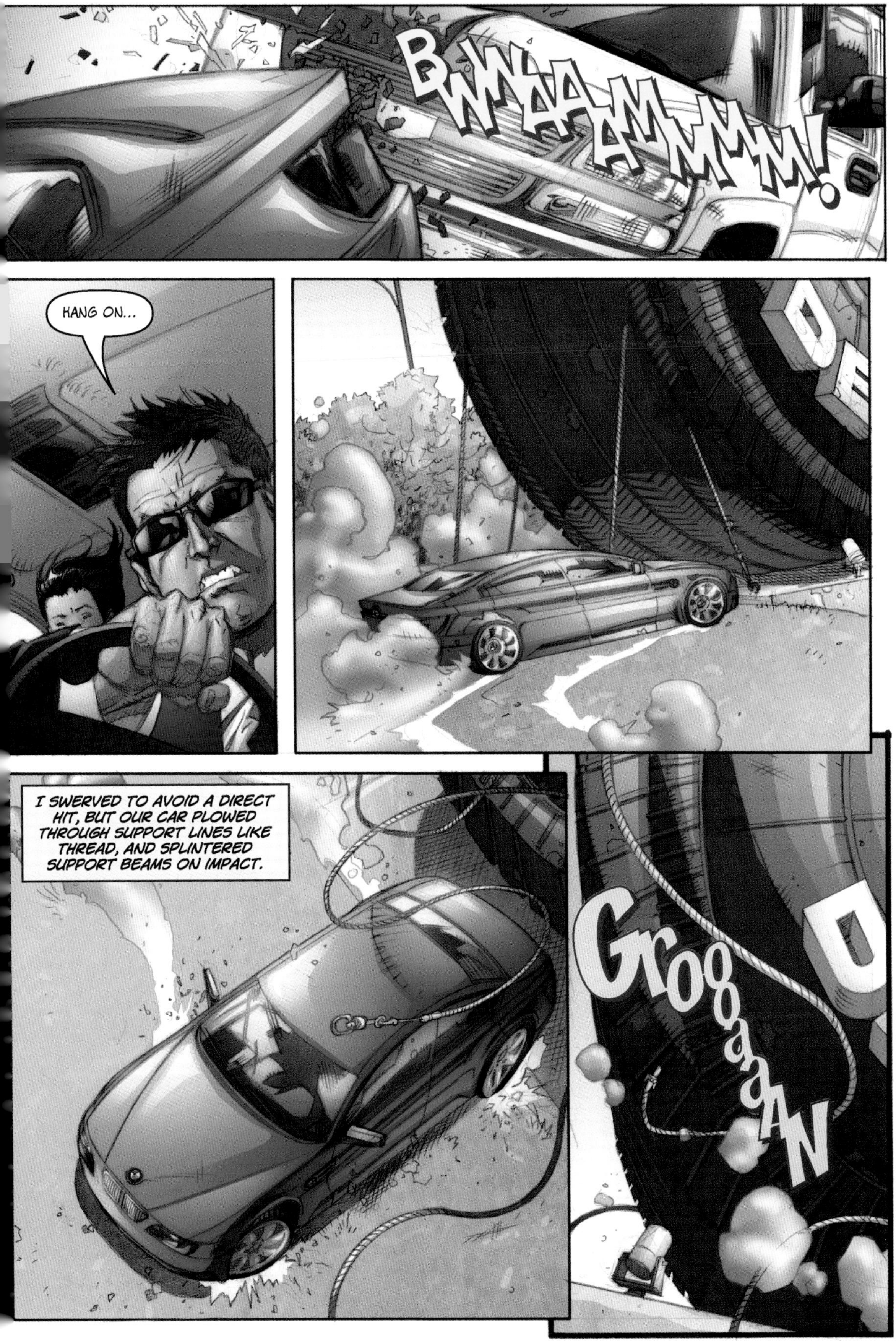
BWAAAMMMM!
HANG ON...
I SWERVED TO AVOID A DIRECT HIT, BUT OUR CAR PLOWED THROUGH SUPPORT LINES LIKE THREAD, AND SPLINTERED SUPPORT BEAMS ON IMPACT.
GROOAAAN

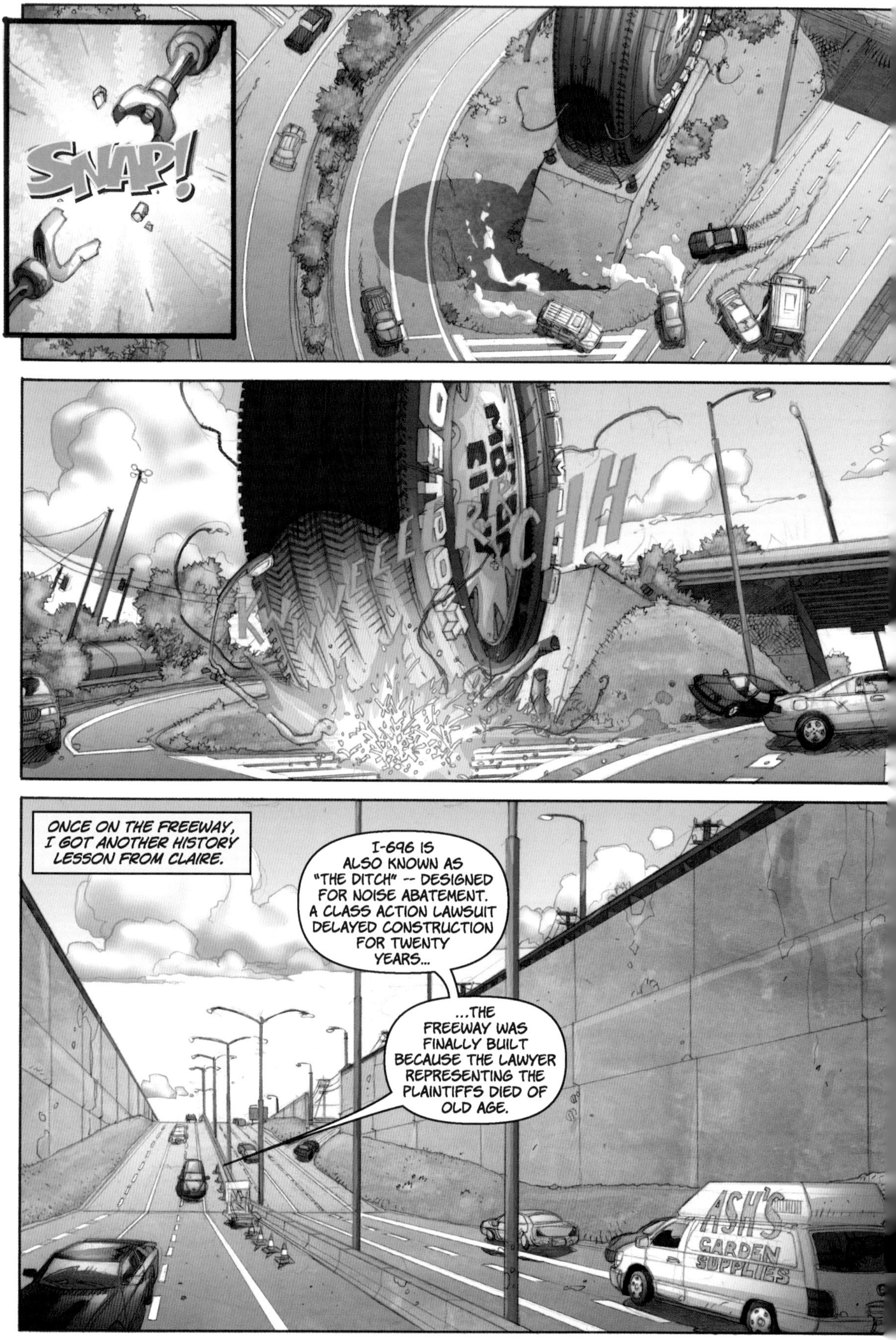
SNAP!
ONCE ON THE FREEWAY, I GOT ANOTHER HISTORY LESSON FROM CLAIRE.
I-696 IS ALSO KNOWN AS "THE DITCH" -- DESIGNED FOR NOISE ABATEMENT. A CLASS ACTION LAWSUIT DELAYED CONSTRUCTION FOR TWENTY YEARS...
...THE FREEWAY WAS FINALLY BUILT BECAUSE THE LAWYER REPRESENTING THE PLAINTIFFS DIED OF OLD AGE.
ASH'S GARDEN SUPPLIES

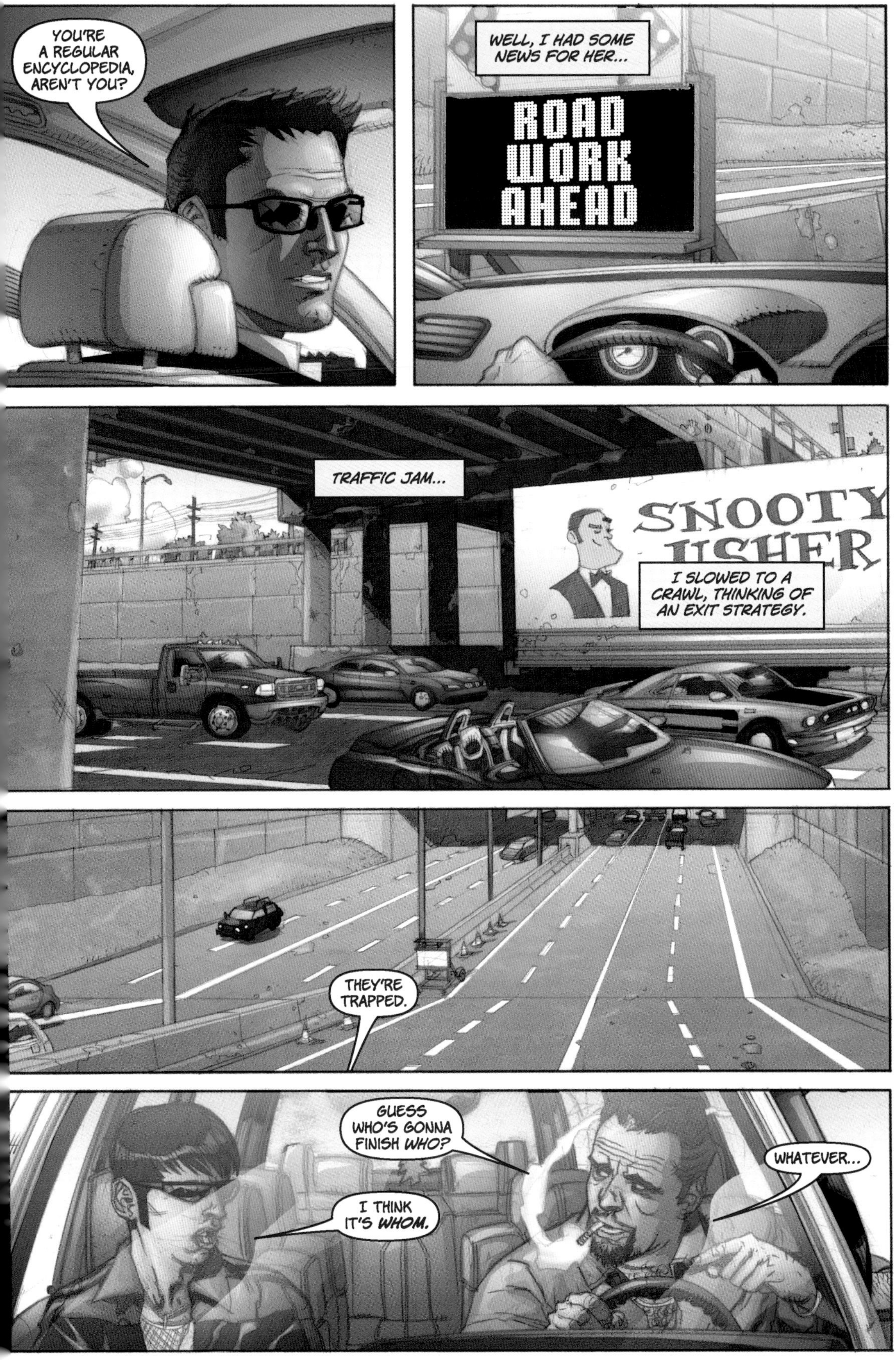
YOU'RE A REGULAR ENCYCLOPEDIA, AREN'T YOU?
WELL, I HAD SOME NEWS FOR HER...
ROAD WORK AHEAD
TRAFFIC JAM...
SNOOTY USHER
I SLOWED TO A CRAWL, THINKING OF AN EXIT STRATEGY.
THEY'RE TRAPPED.
GUESS WHO'S GONNA FINISH *WHO*?
I THINK IT'S *WHOM*.
WHATEVER...

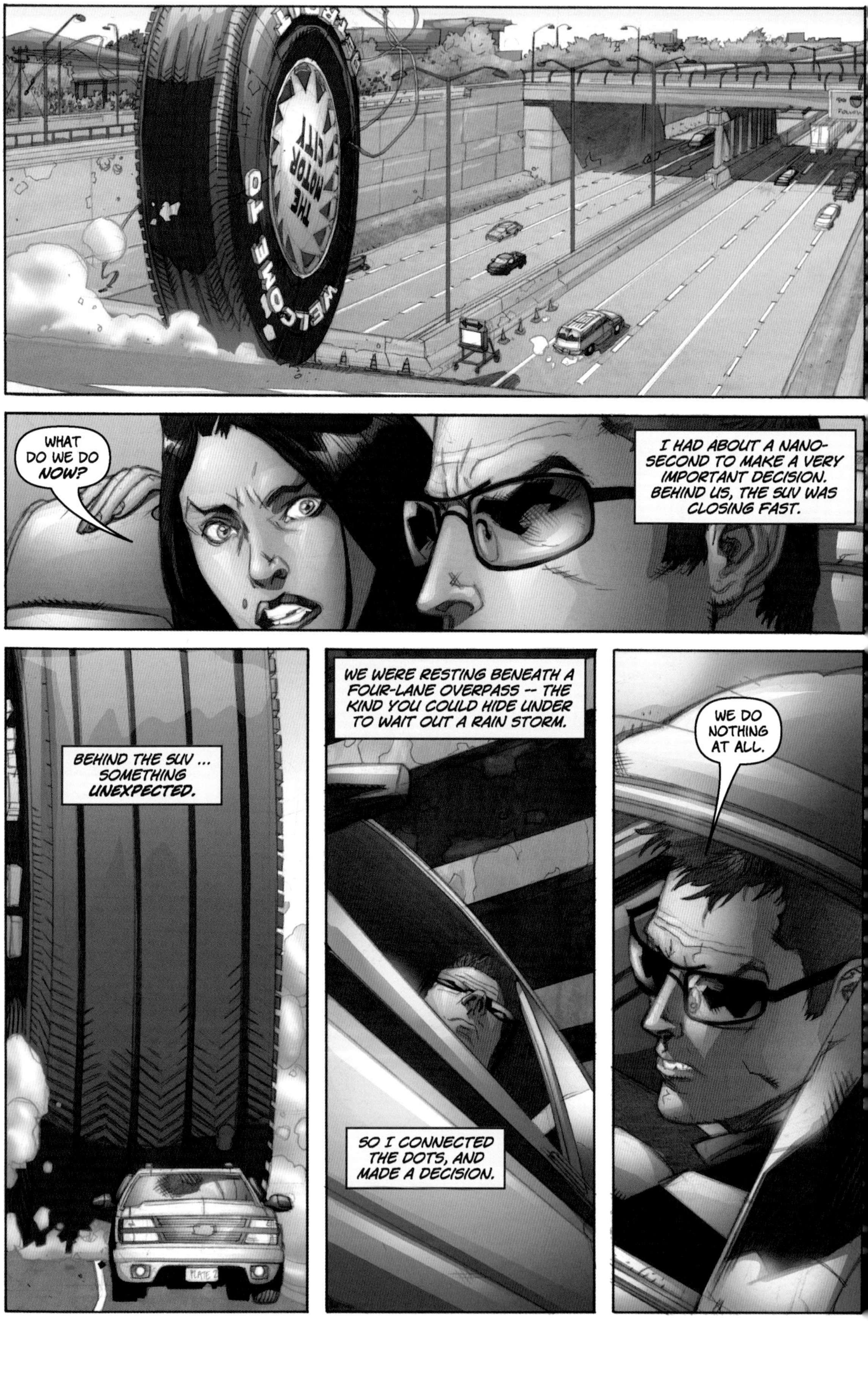
WELCOME TO THE MOTOR CITY
WHAT DO WE DO NOW?
I HAD ABOUT A NANO-SECOND TO MAKE A VERY IMPORTANT DECISION. BEHIND US, THE SUV WAS CLOSING FAST.
BEHIND THE SUV ... SOMETHING UNEXPECTED.
WE WERE RESTING BENEATH A FOUR-LANE OVERPASS -- THE KIND YOU COULD HIDE UNDER TO WAIT OUT A RAIN STORM.
SO I CONNECTED THE DOTS, AND MADE A DECISION.
WE DO NOTHING AT ALL.

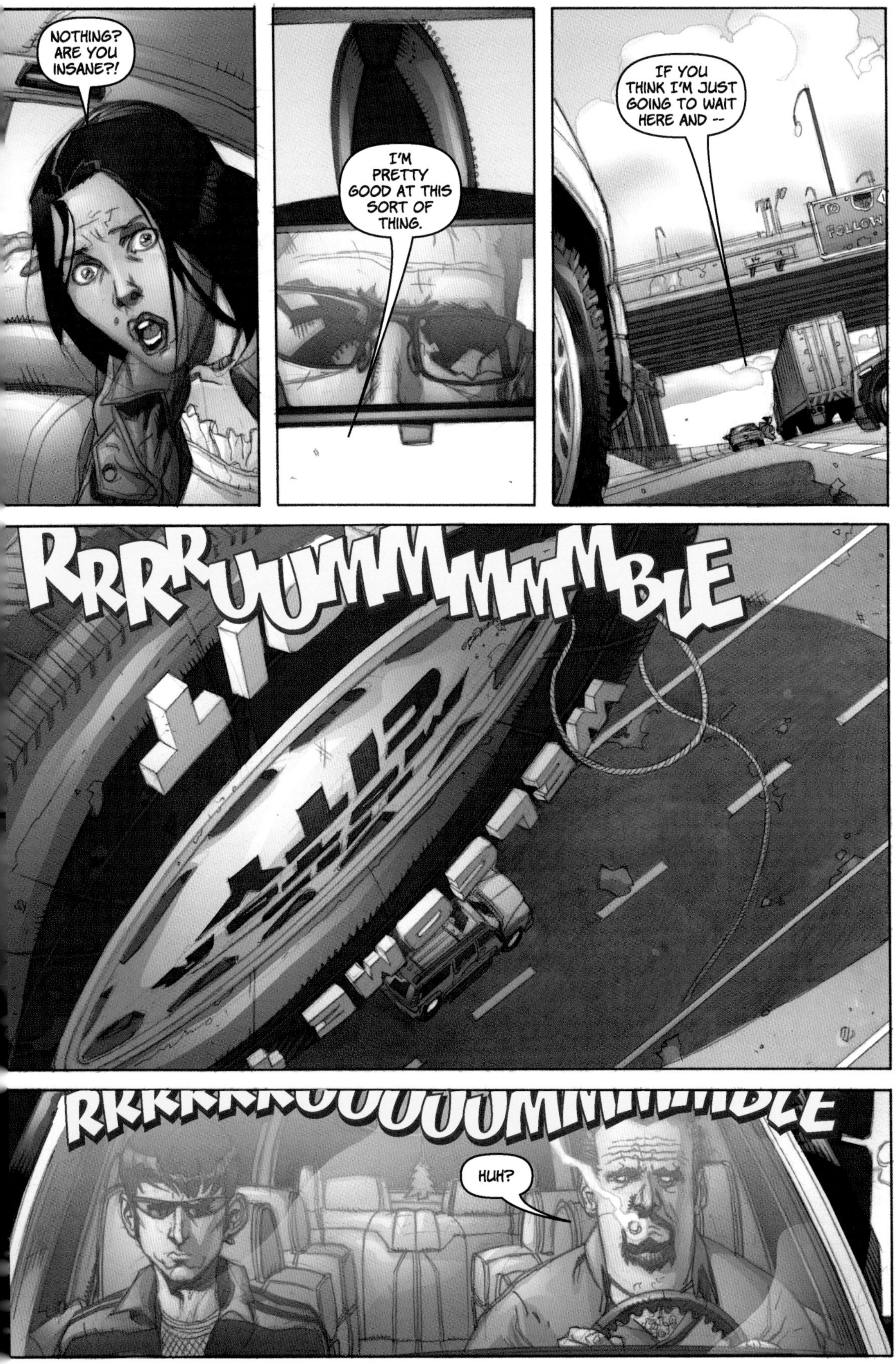
NOTHING? ARE YOU INSANE?!
I'M PRETTY GOOD AT THIS SORT OF THING.
IF YOU THINK I'M JUST GOING TO WAIT HERE AND --
TO FOLLOW
RRRRUUMMMMMMBLE
RKKKKKROOOOOOMMMMMBLE
HUH?

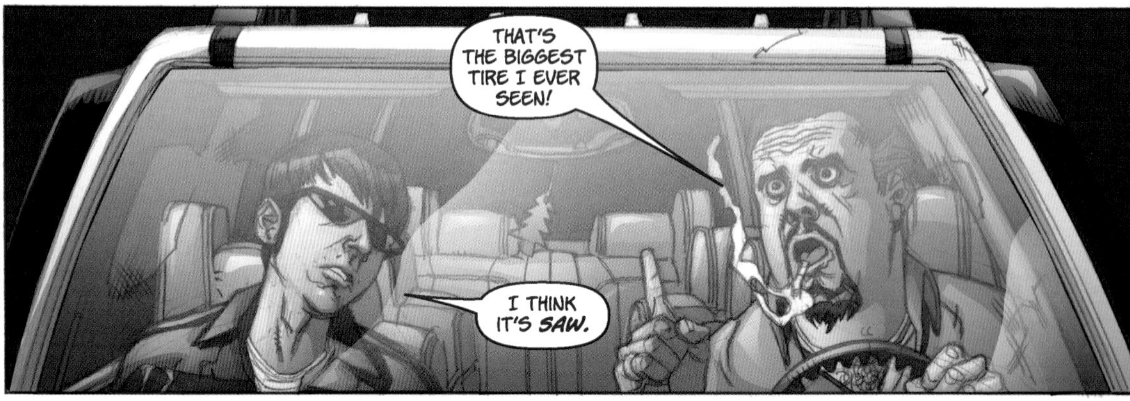
THAT'S THE BIGGEST TIRE I EVER SEEN!
I THINK IT'S SAW.

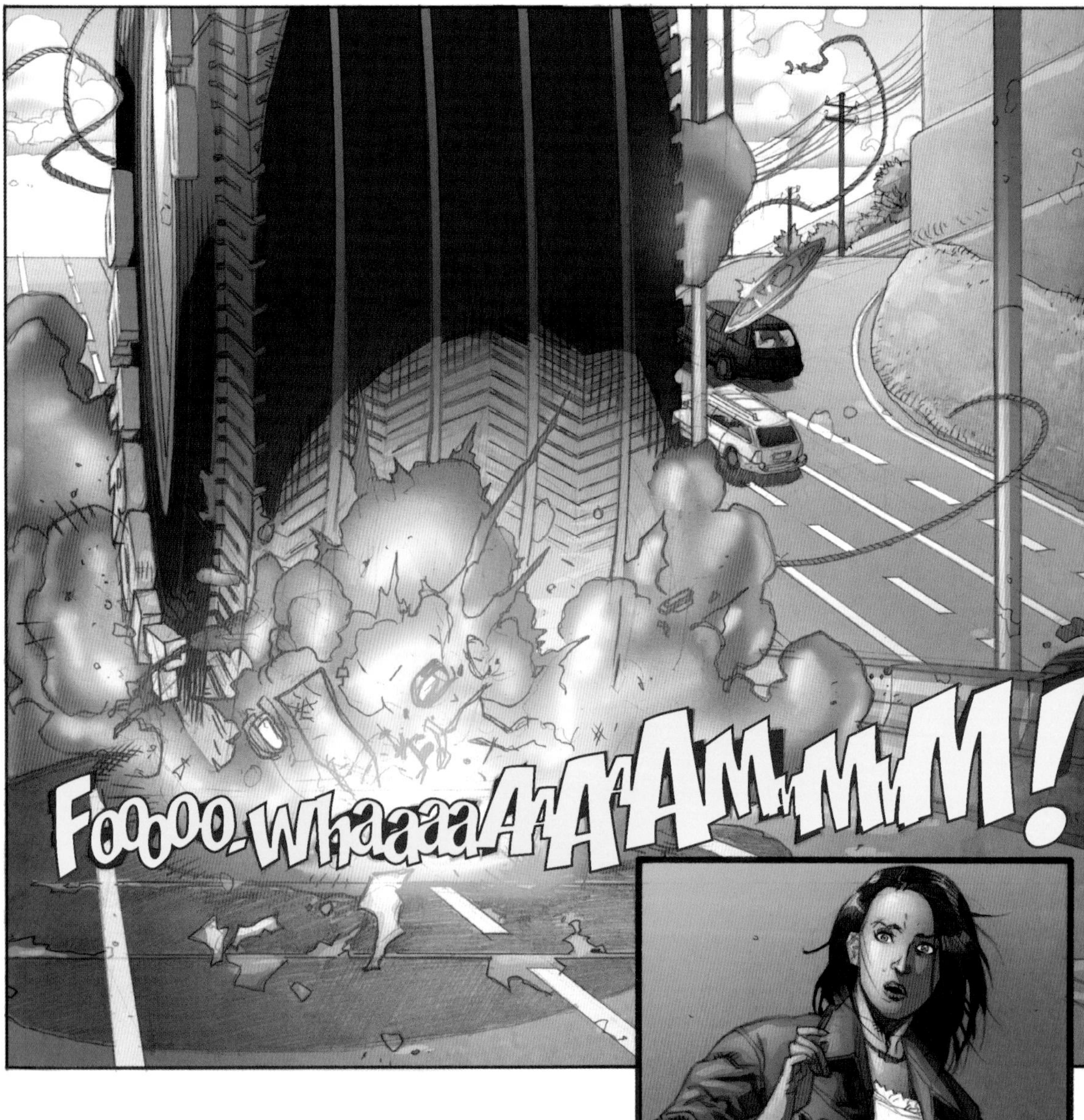
Foooo-whaaaaAAAAMMMM!

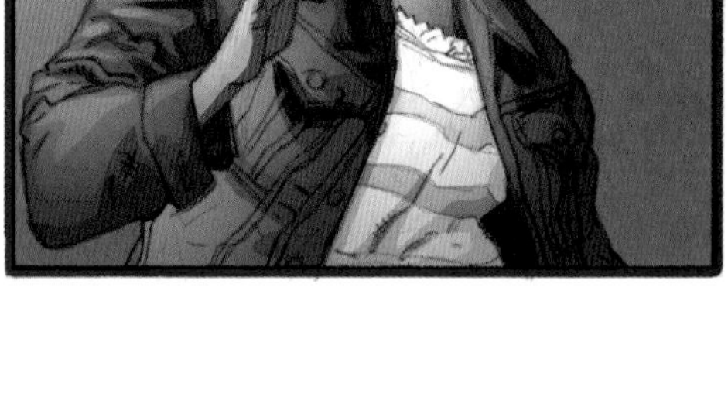

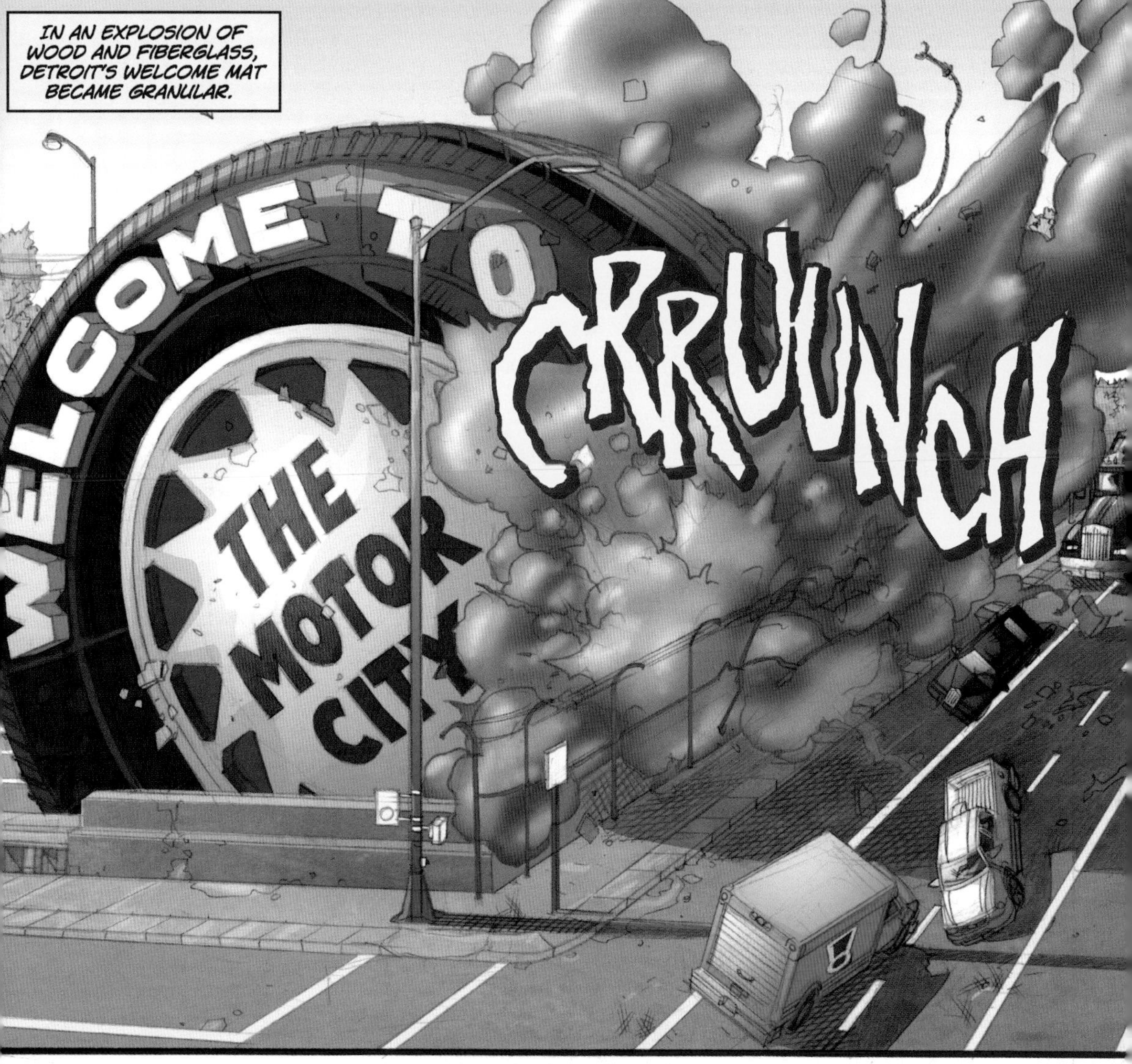
IN AN EXPLOSION OF WOOD AND FIBERGLASS, DETROIT'S WELCOME MAT BECAME GRANULAR.
WELCOME TO
THE MOTOR CITY
CRRUUNCH

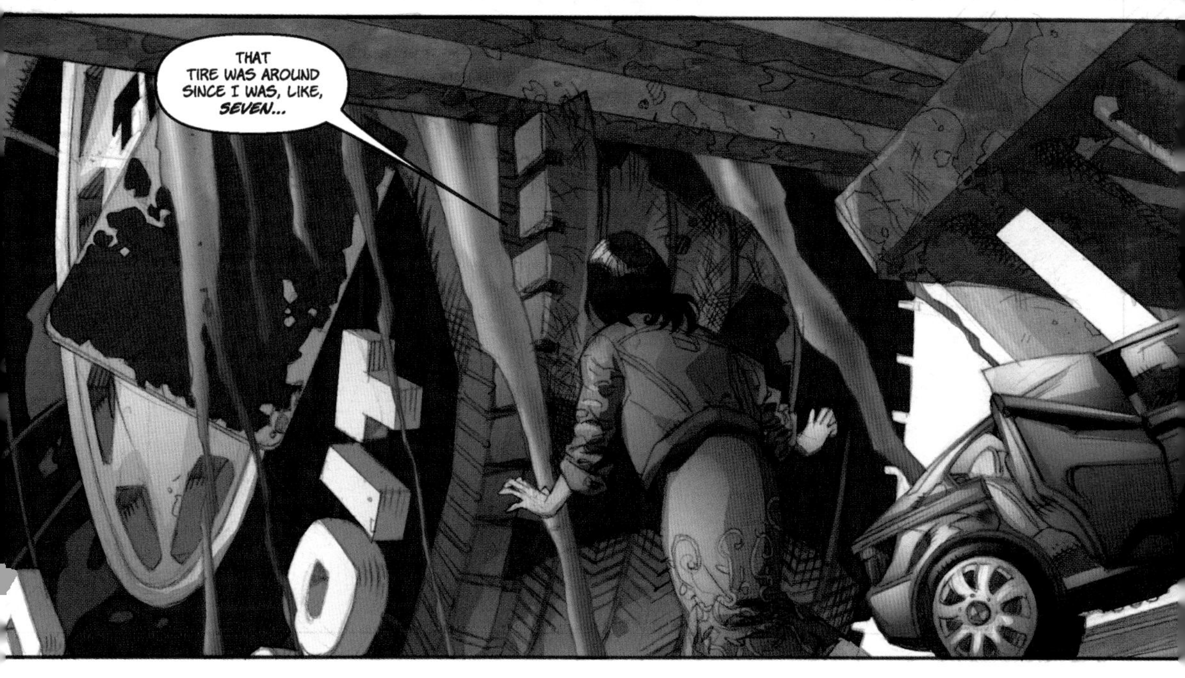
THAT TIRE WAS AROUND SINCE I WAS, LIKE, *SEVEN*...

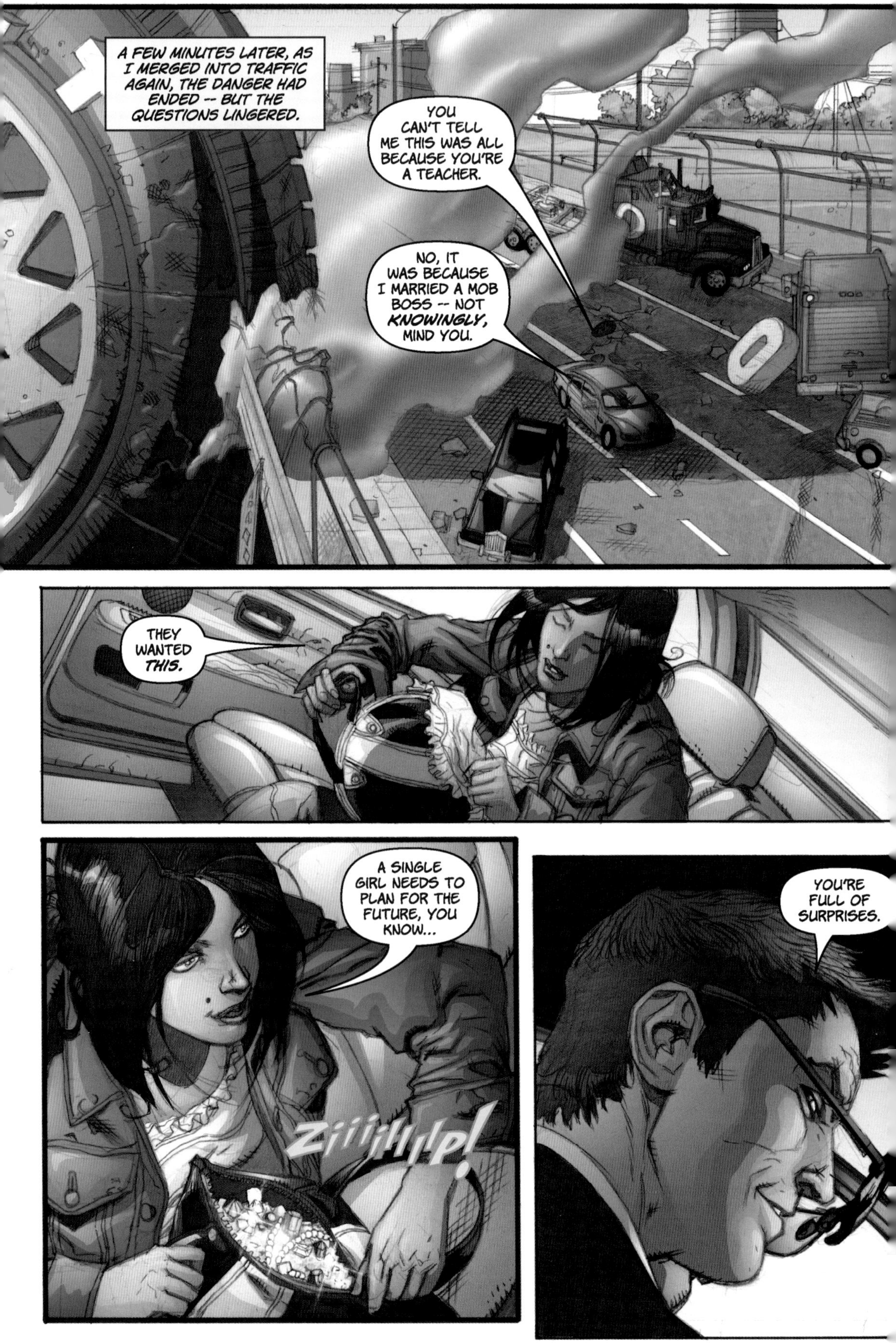
A FEW MINUTES LATER, AS I MERGED INTO TRAFFIC AGAIN, THE DANGER HAD ENDED -- BUT THE QUESTIONS LINGERED.
YOU CAN'T TELL ME THIS WAS ALL BECAUSE YOU'RE A TEACHER.
NO, IT WAS BECAUSE I MARRIED A MOB BOSS -- NOT KNOWINGLY, MIND YOU.
THEY WANTED THIS.
A SINGLE GIRL NEEDS TO PLAN FOR THE FUTURE, YOU KNOW...
ZIIIIIIIP!
YOU'RE FULL OF SURPRISES.

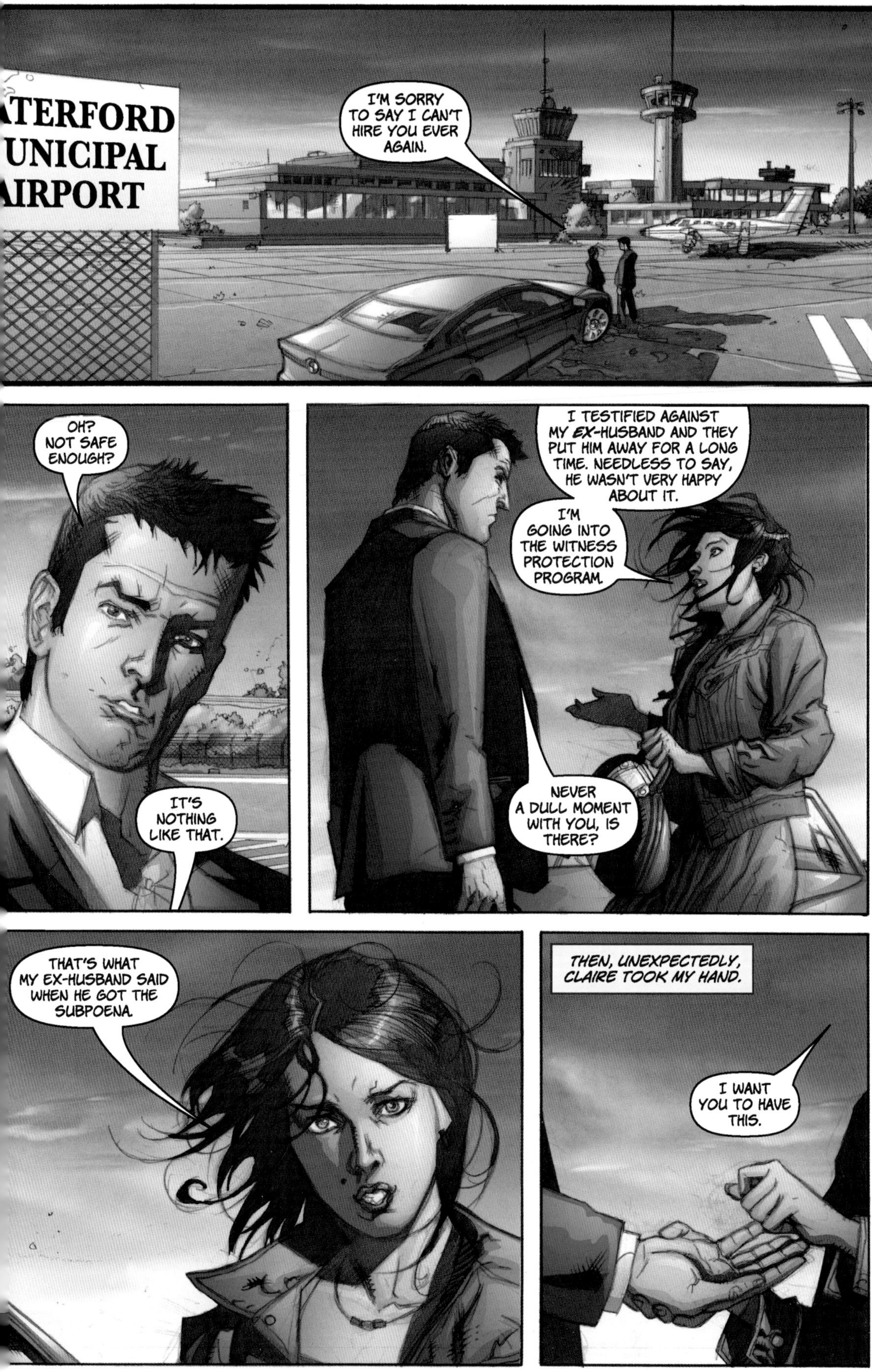
ATERFORD
UNICIPAL
AIRPORT
I'M SORRY TO SAY I CAN'T HIRE YOU EVER AGAIN.
OH? NOT SAFE ENOUGH?
IT'S NOTHING LIKE THAT.
I TESTIFIED AGAINST MY *EX*-HUSBAND AND THEY PUT HIM AWAY FOR A LONG TIME. NEEDLESS TO SAY, HE WASN'T VERY HAPPY ABOUT IT.
I'M GOING INTO THE WITNESS PROTECTION PROGRAM.
NEVER A DULL MOMENT WITH YOU, IS THERE?
THAT'S WHAT MY EX-HUSBAND SAID WHEN HE GOT THE SUBPOENA.
THEN, UNEXPECTEDLY, CLAIRE TOOK MY HAND.
I WANT YOU TO HAVE THIS.

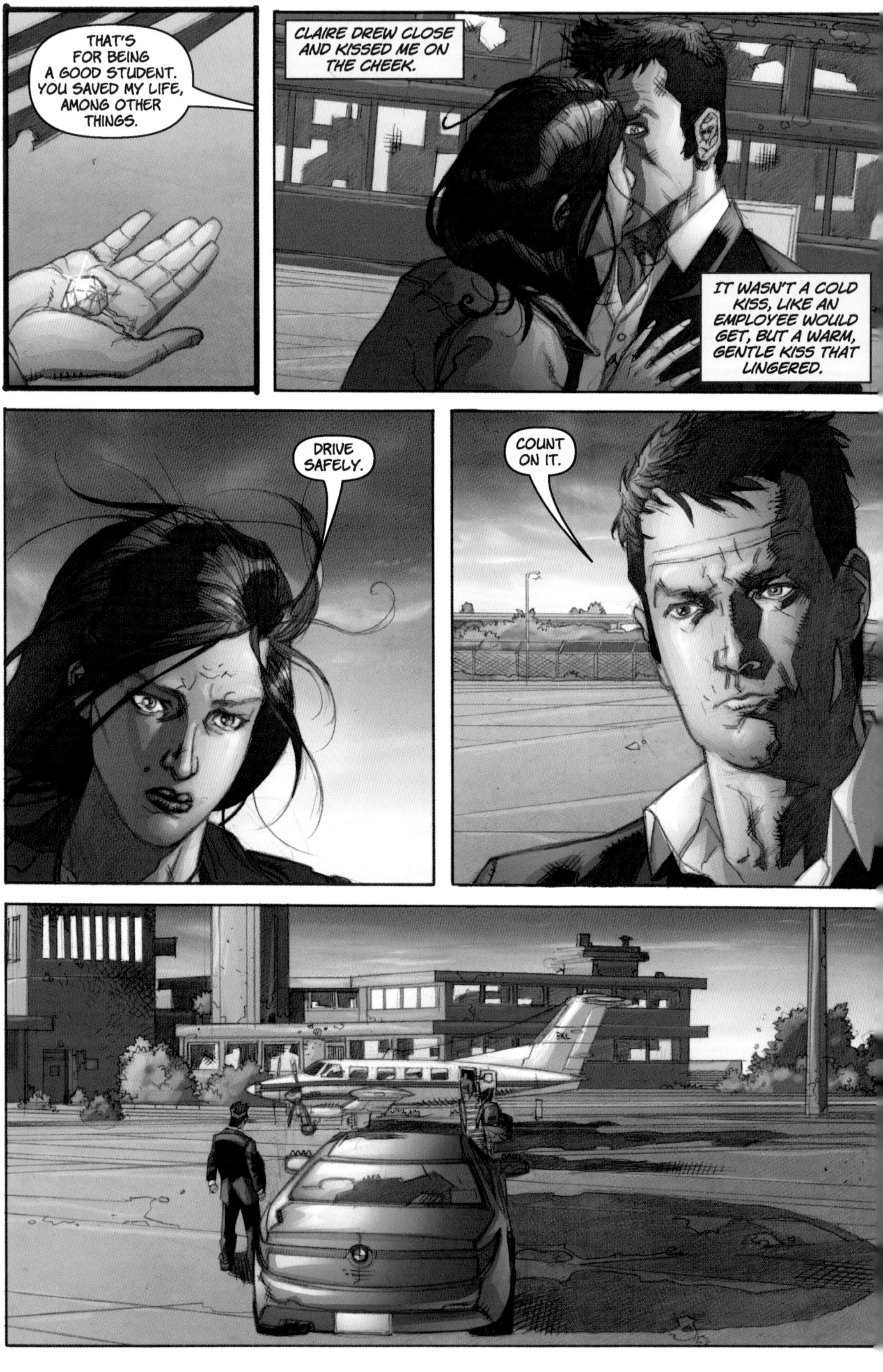
THAT'S FOR BEING A GOOD STUDENT. YOU SAVED MY LIFE, AMONG OTHER THINGS.
CLAIRE DREW CLOSE AND KISSED ME ON THE CHEEK.
IT WASN'T A COLD KISS, LIKE AN EMPLOYEE WOULD GET, BUT A WARM, GENTLE KISS THAT LINGERED.
DRIVE SAFELY.
COUNT ON IT.

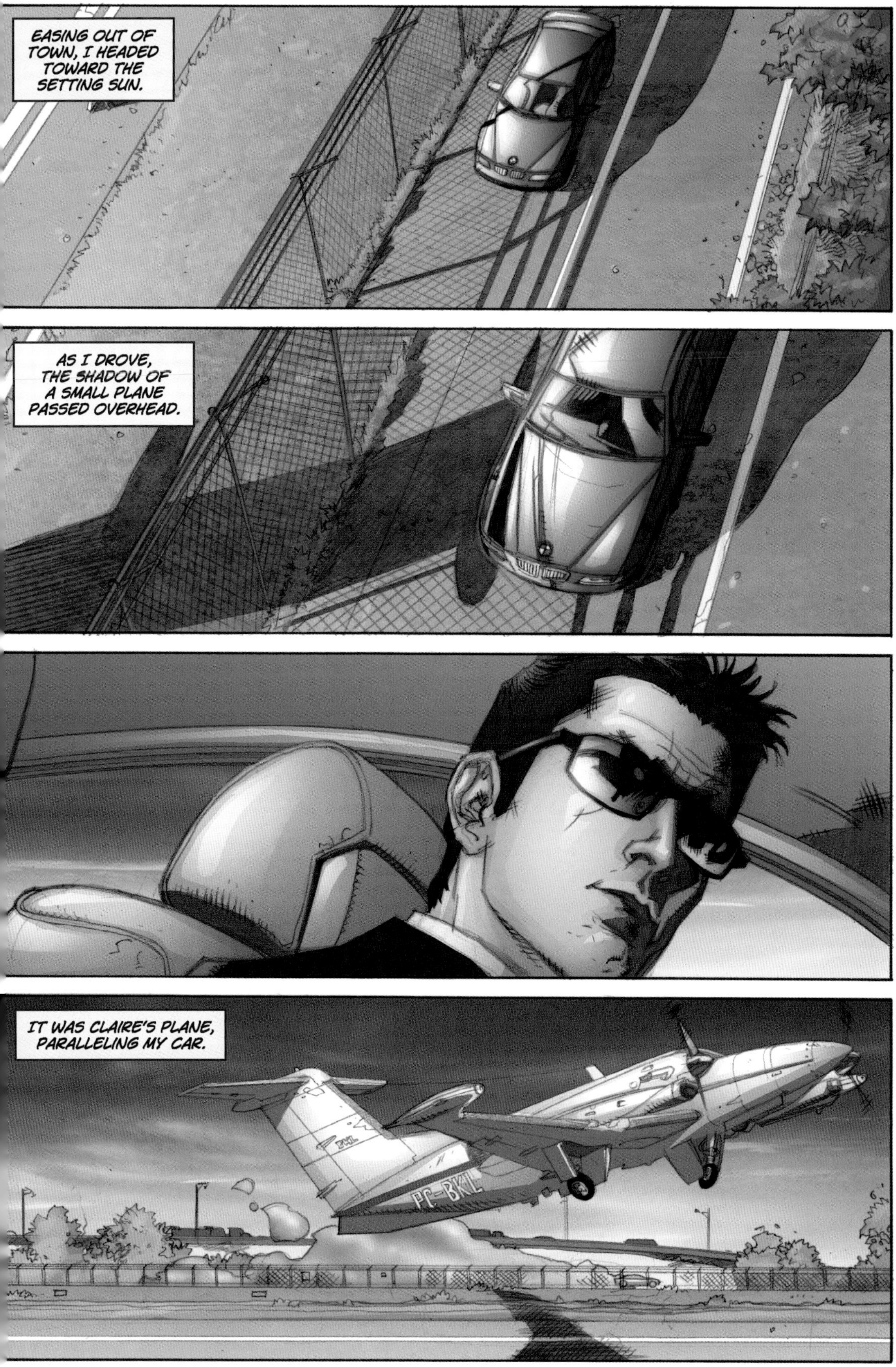
EASING OUT OF TOWN, I HEADED TOWARD THE SETTING SUN.
AS I DROVE, THE SHADOW OF A SMALL PLANE PASSED OVERHEAD.
IT WAS CLAIRE'S PLANE, PARALLELING MY CAR.
PC-BKL

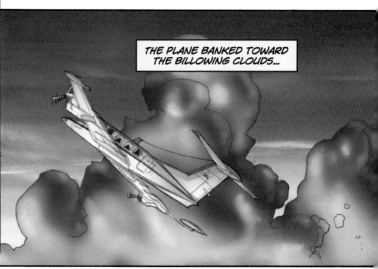

THE PLANE BANKED TOWARD THE BILLOWING CLOUDS...

...AND I NEVER SAW HER AGAIN...

I MADE MY WAY ACROSS TOWN AND HEADED HOME WITH A POCKET FULL OF MOTOR CITY MEMORIES.

THE END

HIJACKED

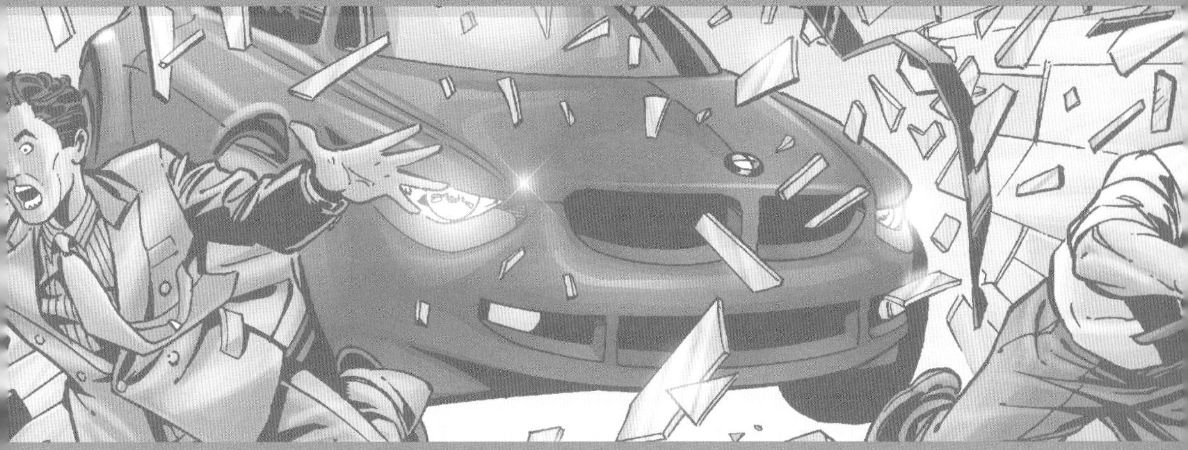

SCRIPT **MARK WAID** ART **CLAUDE ST. AUBIN** COLORS **WIL GLASS**

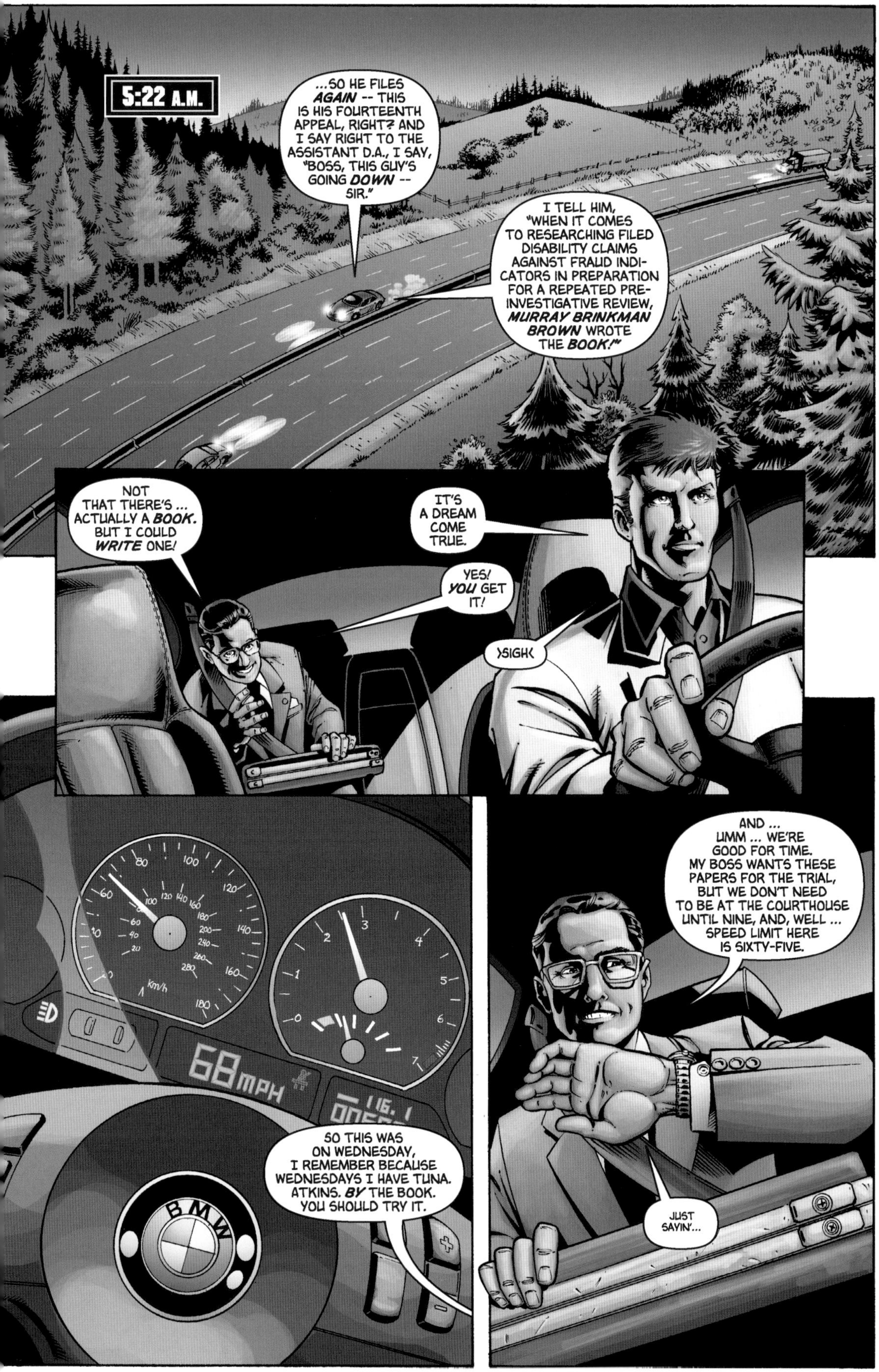
5:22 A.M.
...SO HE FILES AGAIN -- THIS IS HIS FOURTEENTH APPEAL, RIGHT? AND I SAY RIGHT TO THE ASSISTANT D.A., I SAY, "BOSS, THIS GUY'S GOING DOWN -- SIR."
I TELL HIM, "WHEN IT COMES TO RESEARCHING FILED DISABILITY CLAIMS AGAINST FRAUD INDICATORS IN PREPARATION FOR A REPEATED PRE-INVESTIGATIVE REVIEW, MURRAY BRINKMAN BROWN WROTE THE BOOK!"
NOT THAT THERE'S ... ACTUALLY A BOOK. BUT I COULD WRITE ONE!
IT'S A DREAM COME TRUE.
YES! YOU GET IT!
>SIGH<
68 MPH
SO THIS WAS ON WEDNESDAY, I REMEMBER BECAUSE WEDNESDAYS I HAVE TUNA. ATKINS. BY THE BOOK. YOU SHOULD TRY IT.
BMW
AND ... UMM ... WE'RE GOOD FOR TIME. MY BOSS WANTS THESE PAPERS FOR THE TRIAL, BUT WE DON'T NEED TO BE AT THE COURTHOUSE UNTIL NINE, AND, WELL ... SPEED LIMIT HERE IS SIXTY-FIVE.
JUST SAYIN'...

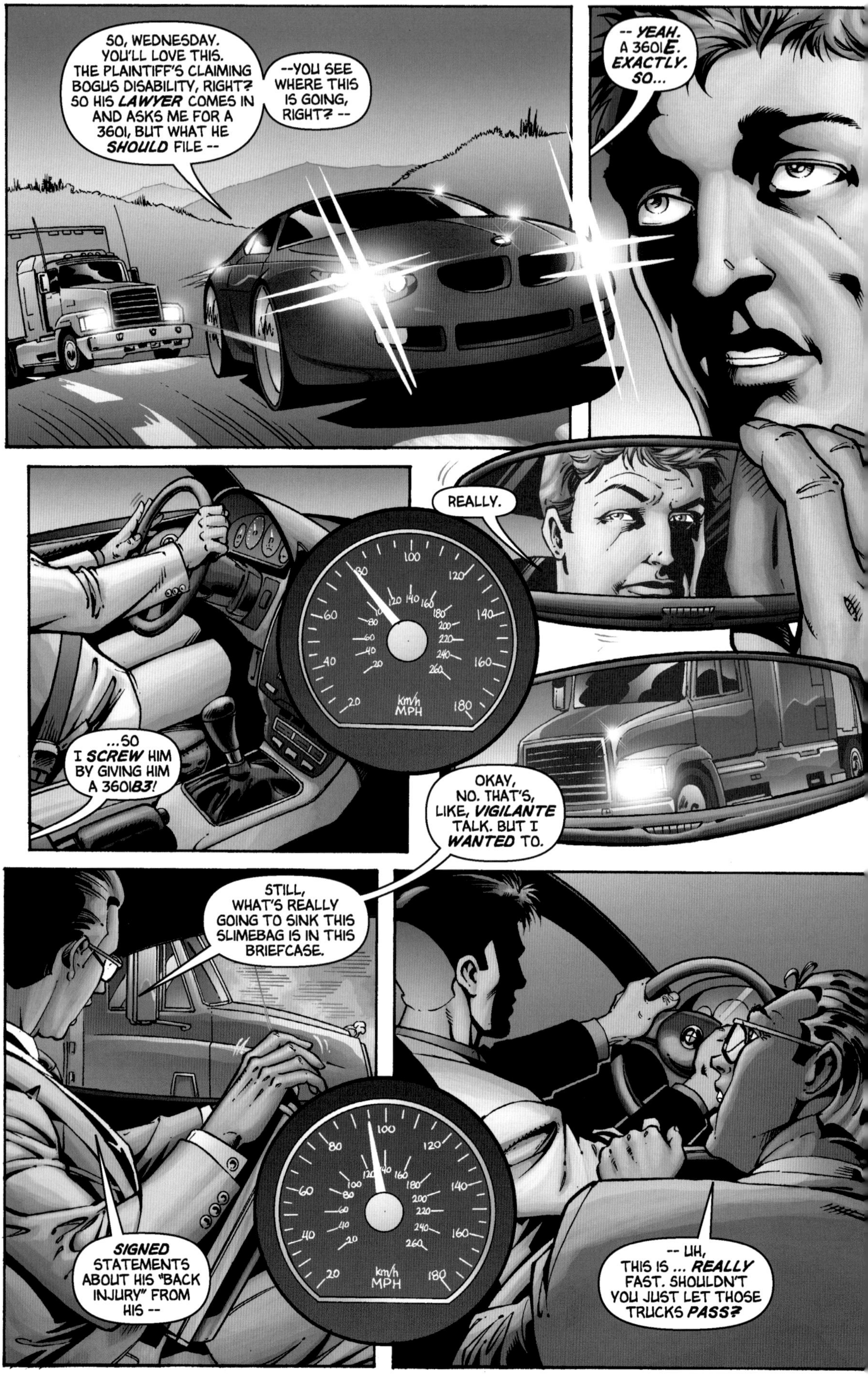
SO, WEDNESDAY. YOU'LL LOVE THIS. THE PLAINTIFF'S CLAIMING BOGUS DISABILITY, RIGHT? SO HIS LAWYER COMES IN AND ASKS ME FOR A 3601, BUT WHAT HE SHOULD FILE --
--YOU SEE WHERE THIS IS GOING, RIGHT? --
-- YEAH. A 3601E. EXACTLY. SO...
REALLY.
...SO I SCREW HIM BY GIVING HIM A 3601B3!
OKAY, NO. THAT'S, LIKE, VIGILANTE TALK. BUT I WANTED TO.
STILL, WHAT'S REALLY GOING TO SINK THIS SLIMEBAG IS IN THIS BRIEFCASE.
SIGNED STATEMENTS ABOUT HIS "BACK INJURY" FROM HIS --
-- UH, THIS IS ... REALLY FAST. SHOULDN'T YOU JUST LET THOSE TRUCKS PASS?

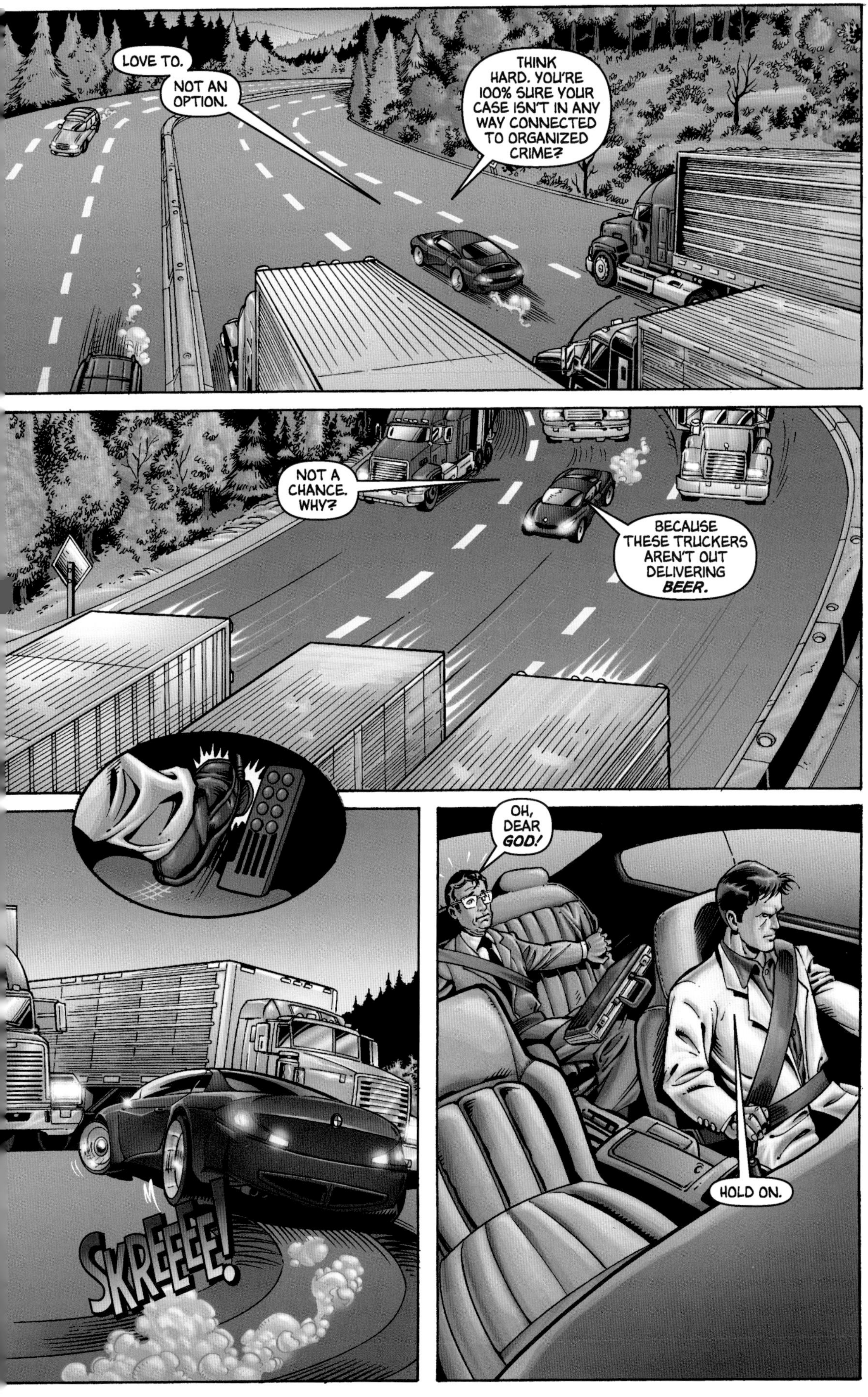
LOVE TO.
NOT AN OPTION.
THINK HARD. YOU'RE 100% SURE YOUR CASE ISN'T IN ANY WAY CONNECTED TO ORGANIZED CRIME?
NOT A CHANCE. WHY?
BECAUSE THESE TRUCKERS AREN'T OUT DELIVERING *BEER.*
SKREEEE!
OH, DEAR *GOD!*
HOLD ON.

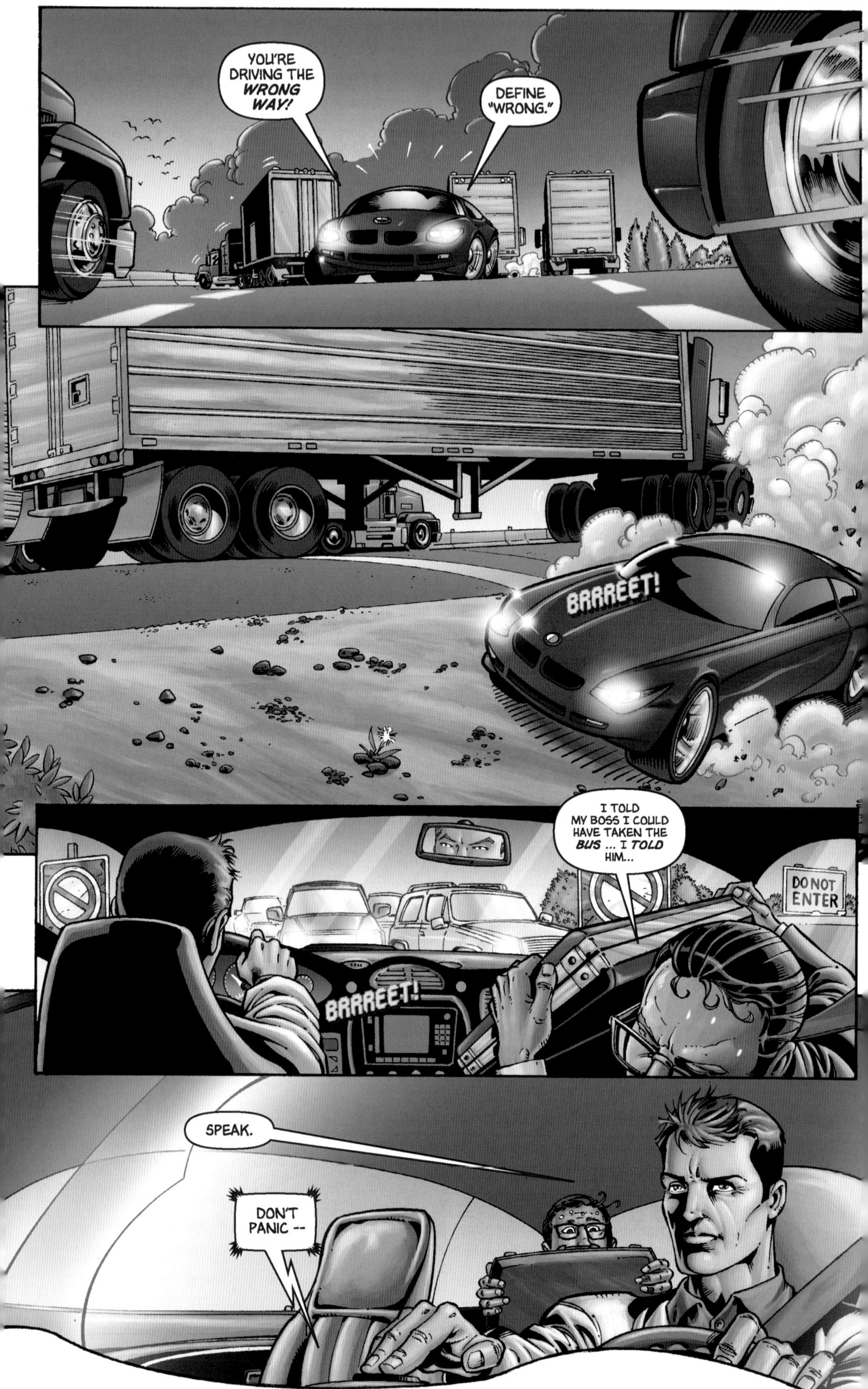
YOU'RE DRIVING THE *WRONG WAY!*
DEFINE "WRONG."
BRRREET!
I TOLD MY BOSS I COULD HAVE TAKEN THE *BUS* ... I *TOLD* HIM...
DO NOT ENTER
BRRREET!
SPEAK.
DON'T PANIC --

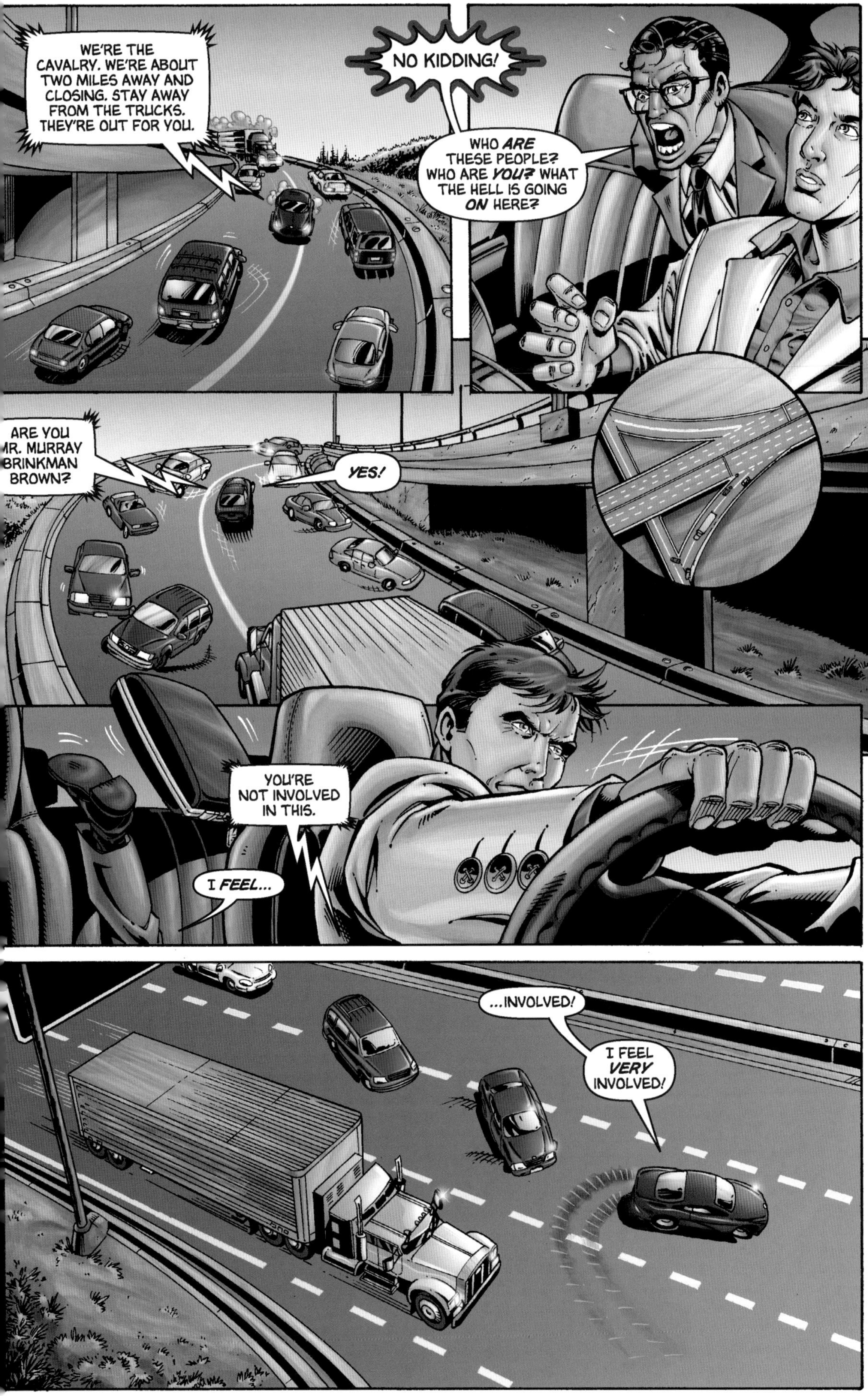
WE'RE THE CAVALRY. WE'RE ABOUT TWO MILES AWAY AND CLOSING. STAY AWAY FROM THE TRUCKS. THEY'RE OUT FOR YOU.
NO KIDDING!
WHO *ARE* THESE PEOPLE? WHO ARE *YOU?* WHAT THE HELL IS GOING *ON* HERE?
ARE YOU MR. MURRAY BRINKMAN BROWN?
YES!
YOU'RE NOT INVOLVED IN THIS.
I *FEEL*...
...INVOLVED!
I FEEL *VERY* INVOLVED!

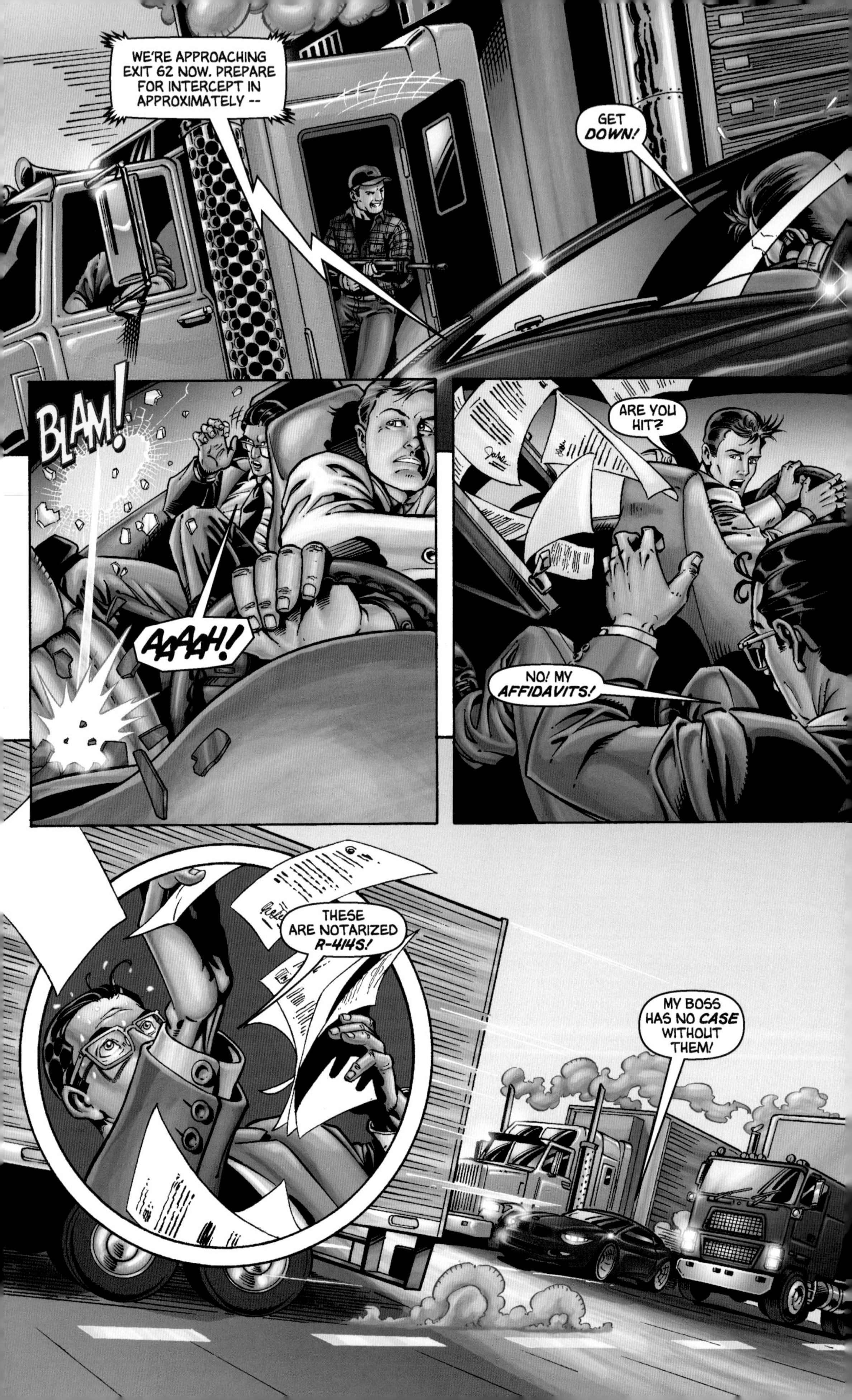
WE'RE APPROACHING EXIT 62 NOW. PREPARE FOR INTERCEPT IN APPROXIMATELY --
GET DOWN!
BLAM!
AAAAH!
ARE YOU HIT?
NO! MY AFFIDAVITS!
THESE ARE NOTARIZED R-414S!
MY BOSS HAS NO CASE WITHOUT THEM!

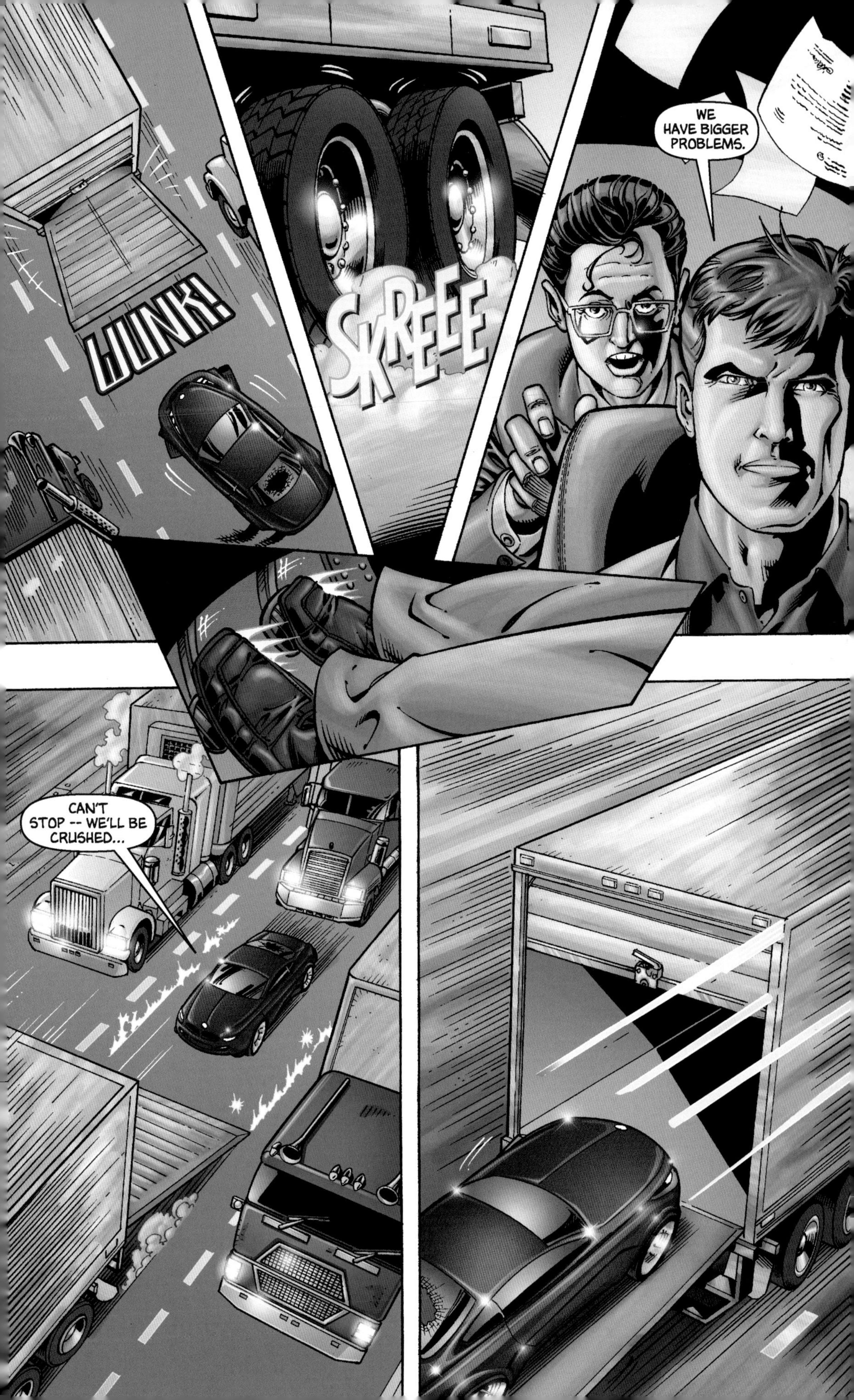
WUNK!
SKREEE
WE HAVE BIGGER PROBLEMS.
CAN'T STOP -- WE'LL BE CRUSHED...

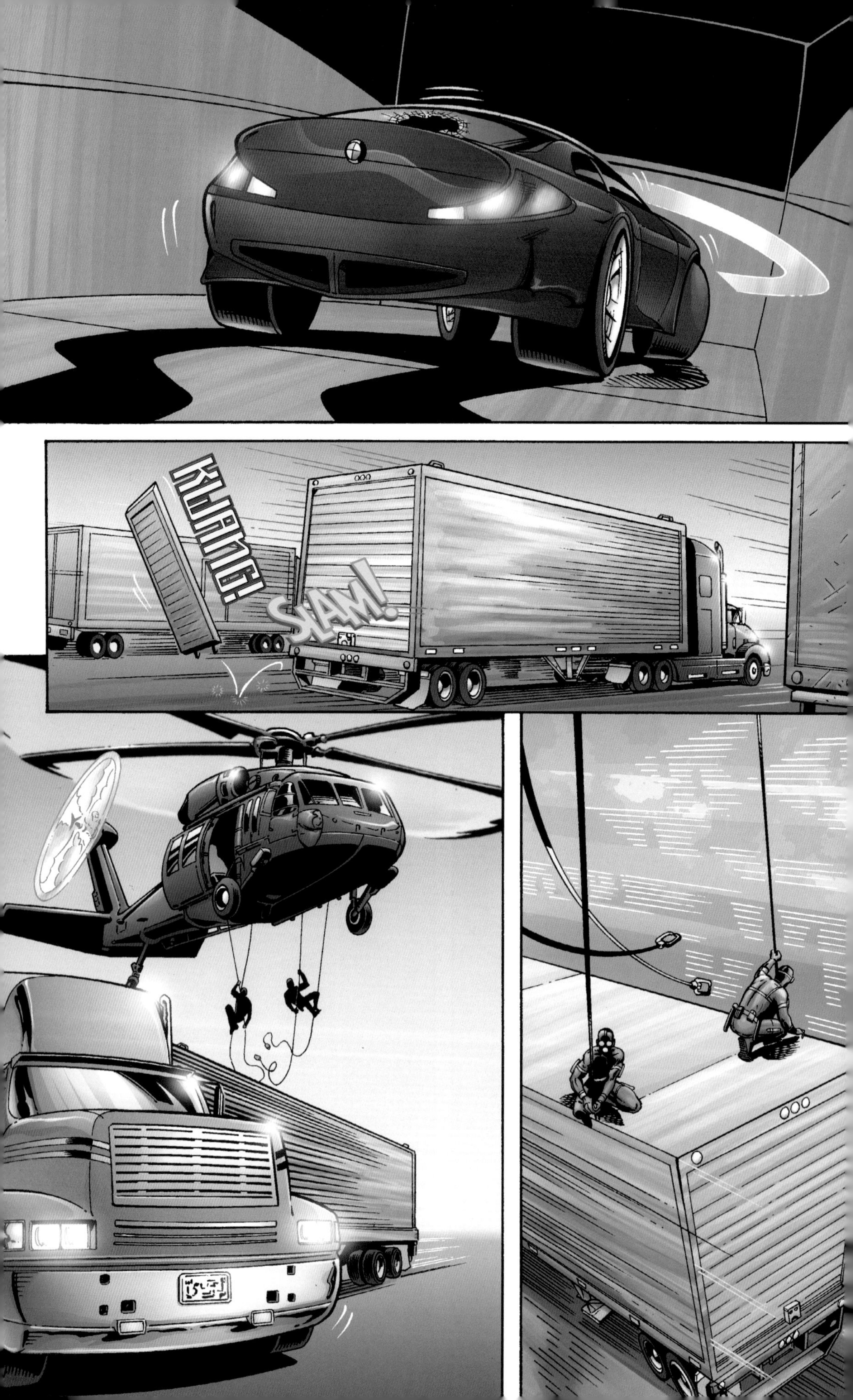
KLUANG!
SLAM!

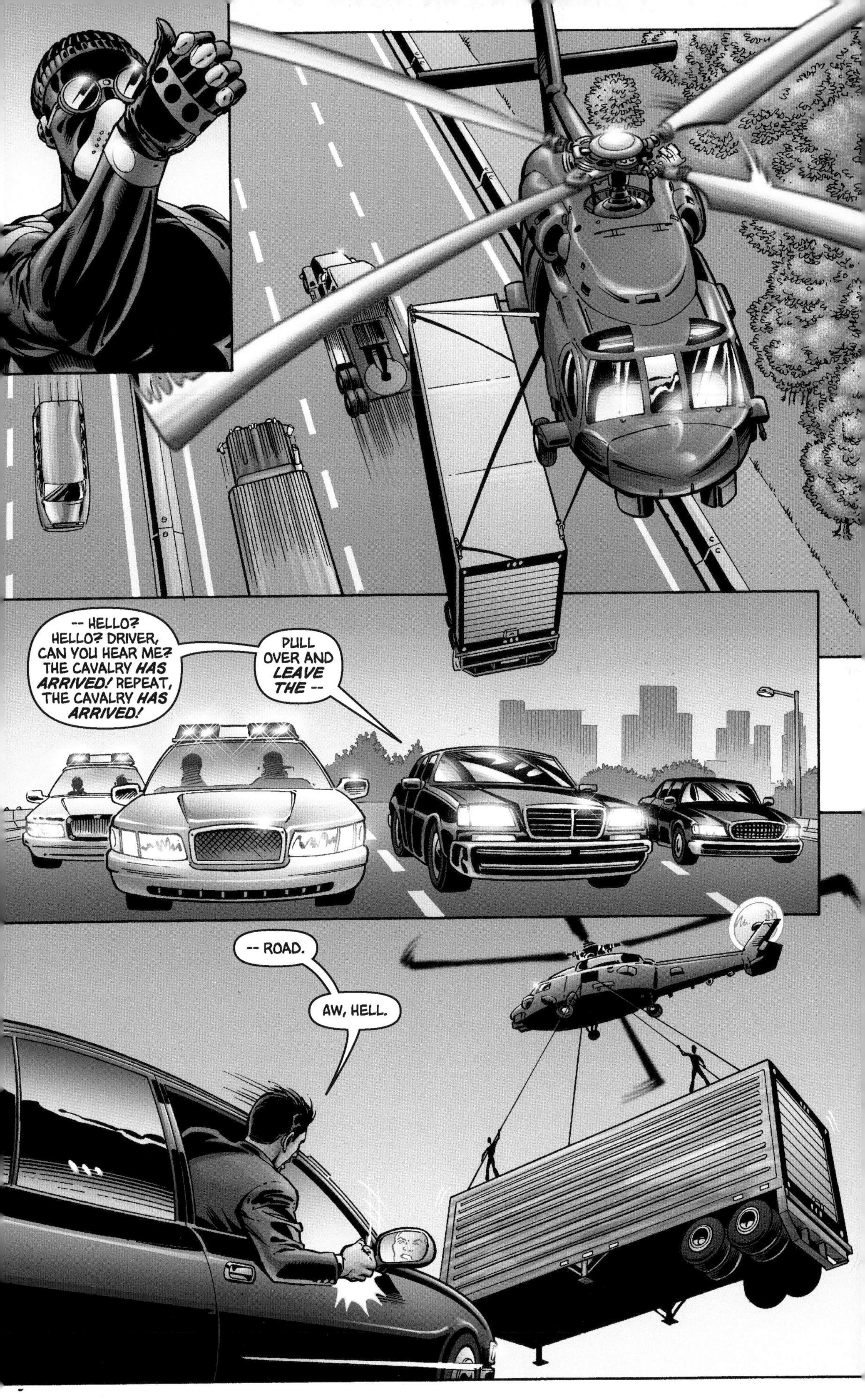
-- HELLO? HELLO? DRIVER, CAN YOU HEAR ME? THE CAVALRY *HAS ARRIVED!* REPEAT, THE CAVALRY *HAS ARRIVED!*
PULL OVER AND *LEAVE THE* --
-- ROAD.
AW, HELL.

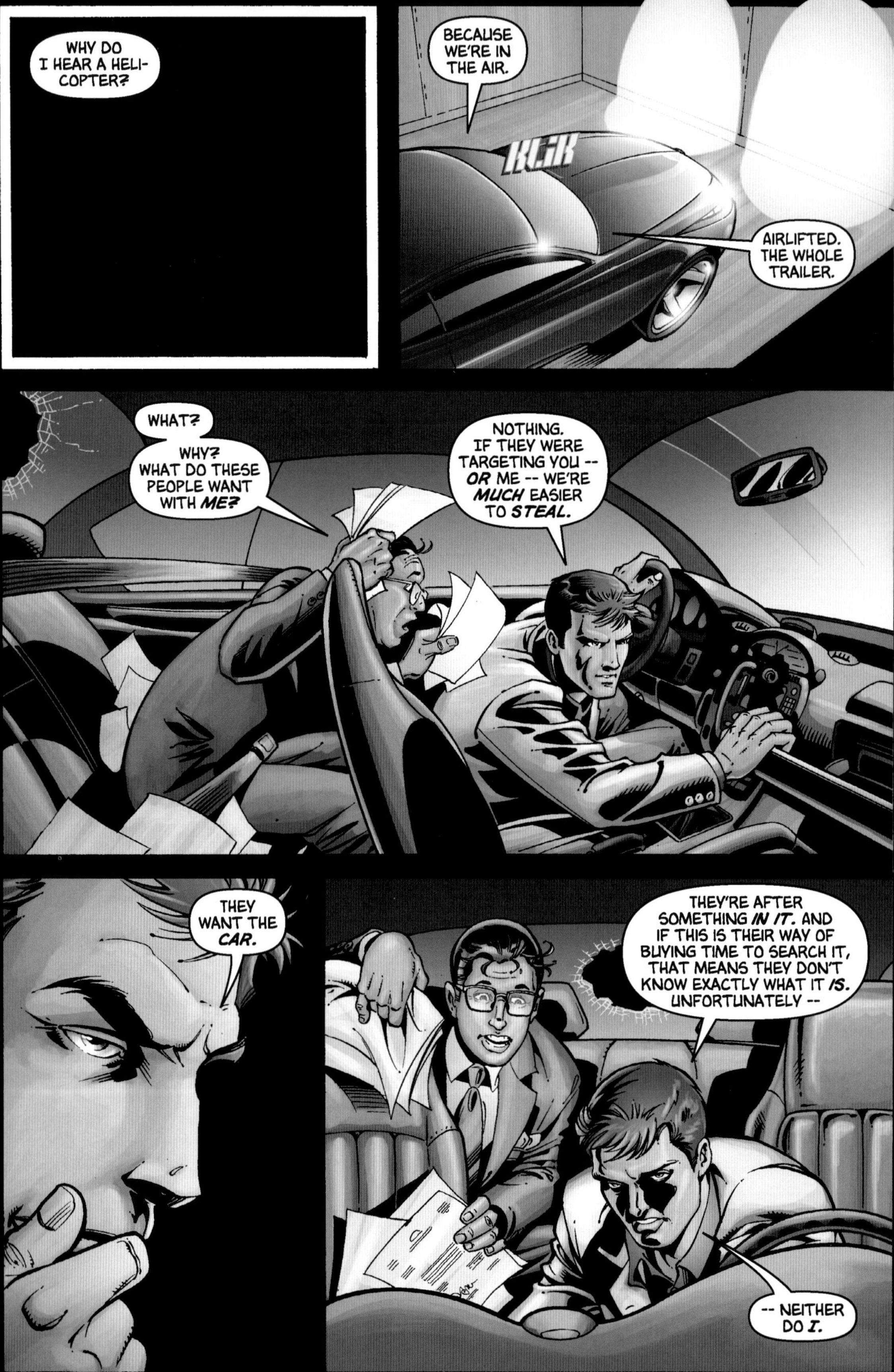

WHY DO I HEAR A HELI-COPTER?
BECAUSE WE'RE IN THE AIR.
AIRLIFTED. THE WHOLE TRAILER.
WHAT?
WHY? WHAT DO THESE PEOPLE WANT WITH *ME?*
NOTHING. IF THEY WERE TARGETING YOU -- *OR* ME -- WE'RE *MUCH* EASIER TO *STEAL.*
THEY WANT THE *CAR.*
THEY'RE AFTER SOMETHING *IN IT.* AND IF THIS IS THEIR WAY OF BUYING TIME TO SEARCH IT, THAT MEANS THEY DON'T KNOW EXACTLY WHAT IT *IS.* UNFORTUNATELY --
-- NEITHER DO *I.*

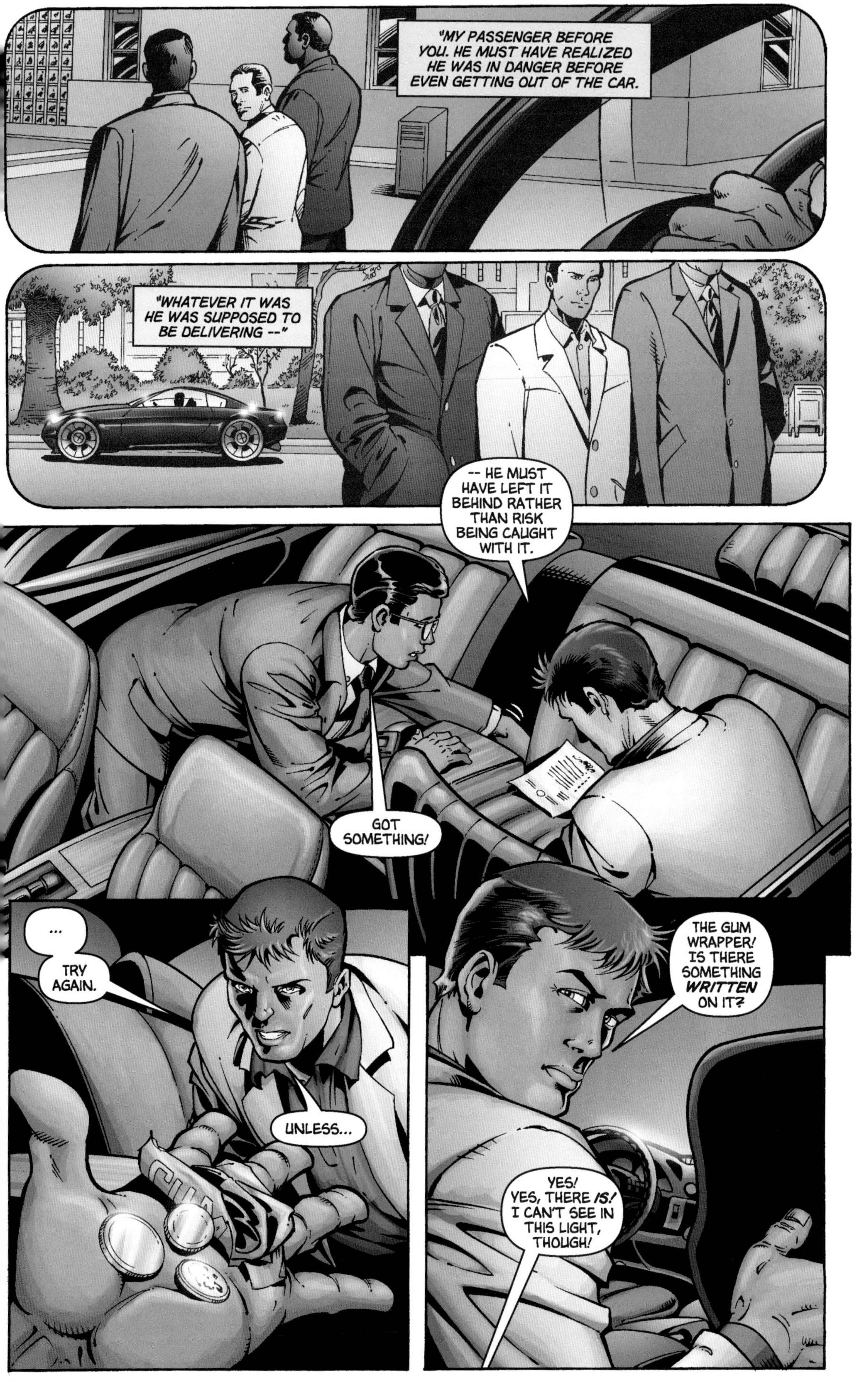
"MY PASSENGER BEFORE YOU. HE MUST HAVE REALIZED HE WAS IN DANGER BEFORE EVEN GETTING OUT OF THE CAR.
"WHATEVER IT WAS HE WAS SUPPOSED TO BE DELIVERING --"
-- HE MUST HAVE LEFT IT BEHIND RATHER THAN RISK BEING CAUGHT WITH IT.
GOT SOMETHING!
...
TRY AGAIN.
UNLESS...
THE GUM WRAPPER! IS THERE SOMETHING *WRITTEN* ON IT?
YES! YES, THERE *IS*! I CAN'T SEE IN THIS LIGHT, THOUGH!

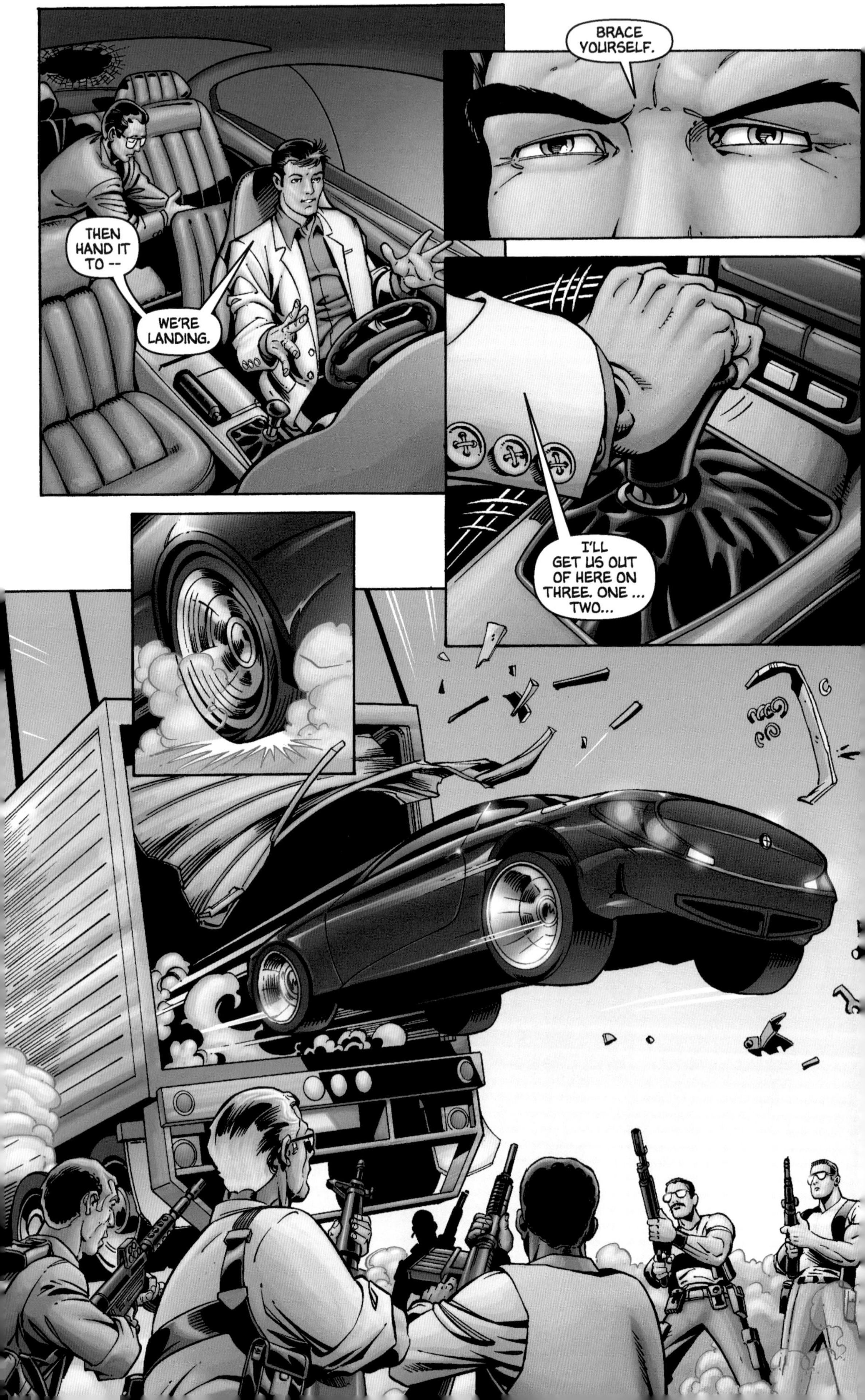
THEN HAND IT TO --
WE'RE LANDING.
BRACE YOURSELF.
I'LL GET US OUT OF HERE ON THREE. ONE ... TWO...

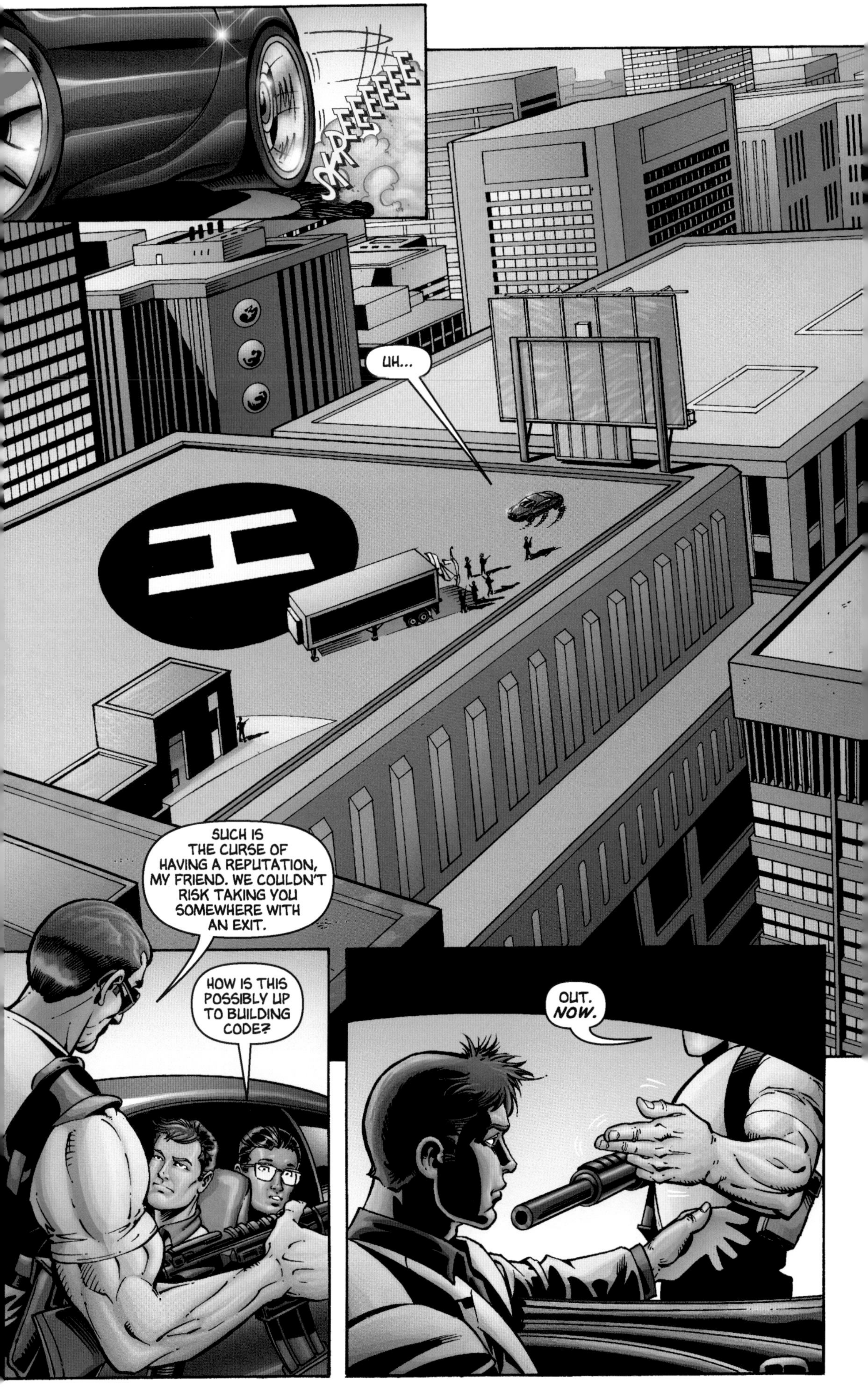
SKREEEEEE
UH...
SUCH IS THE CURSE OF HAVING A REPUTATION, MY FRIEND. WE COULDN'T RISK TAKING YOU SOMEWHERE WITH AN EXIT.
HOW IS THIS POSSIBLY UP TO BUILDING CODE?
OUT. *NOW.*

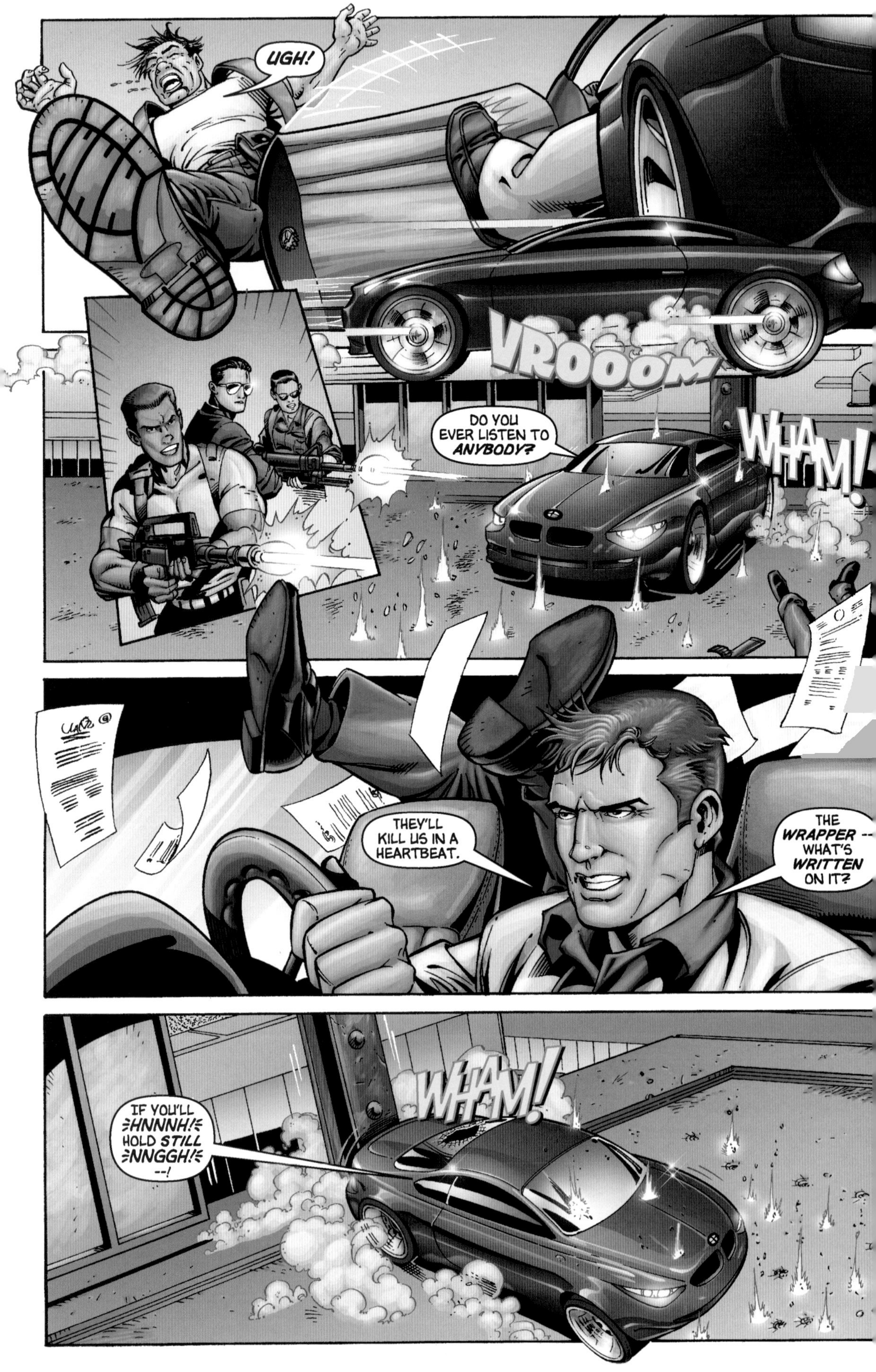
UGH!
VROOOM
DO YOU EVER LISTEN TO ANYBODY?
WHAM!
THEY'LL KILL US IN A HEARTBEAT.
THE WRAPPER -- WHAT'S WRITTEN ON IT?
WHAM!
IF YOU'LL =HNNNH!= HOLD STILL =NNGGH!= --!

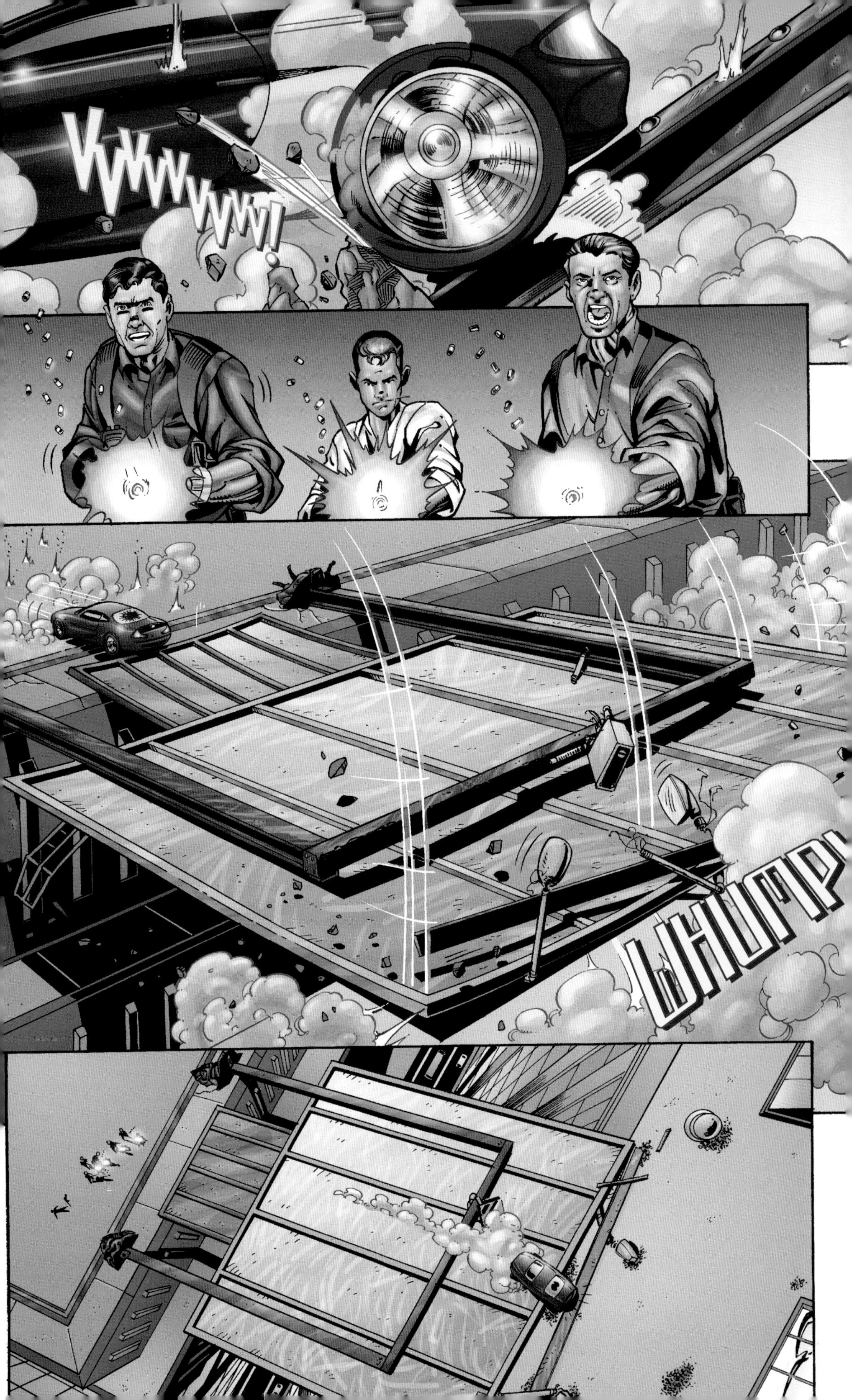
WHUMP

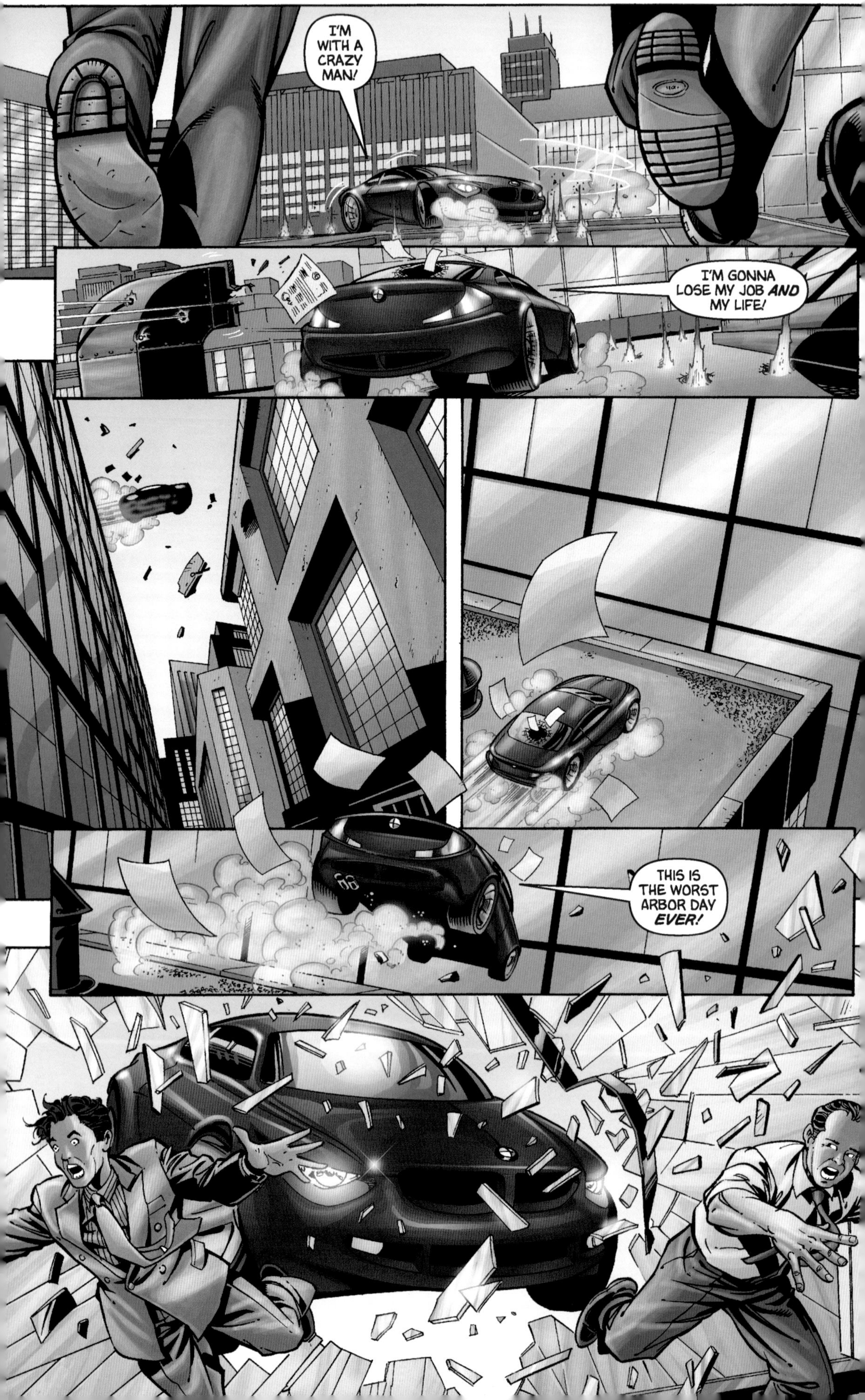
I'M WITH A CRAZY MAN!
I'M GONNA LOSE MY JOB *AND* MY LIFE!
THIS IS THE WORST ARBOR DAY *EVER!*

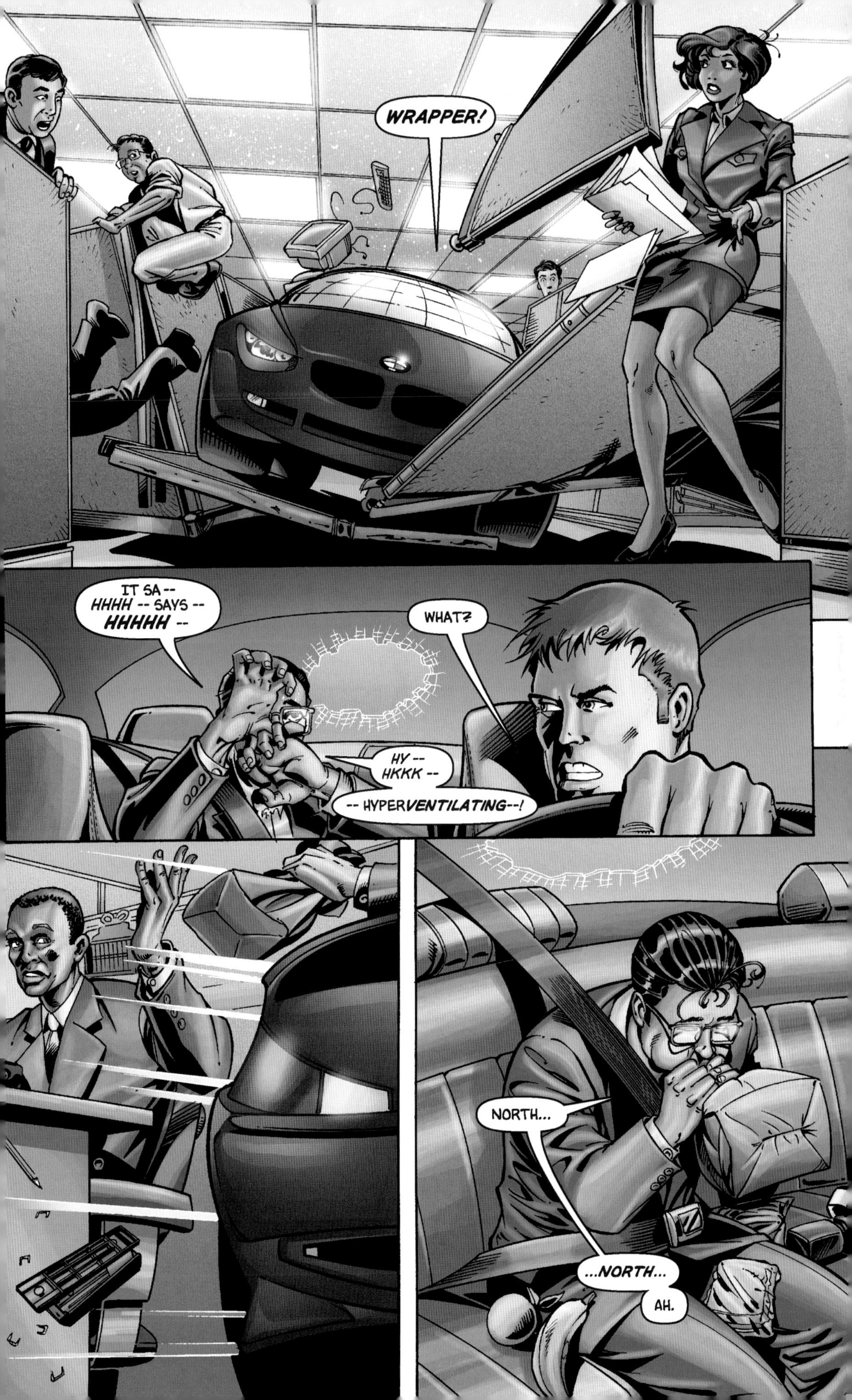

WRAPPER!
IT SA -- HHHH -- SAYS -- HHHHH --
WHAT?
HY -- HKKK --
-- HYPERVENTILATING--!
NORTH...
...NORTH...
AH.

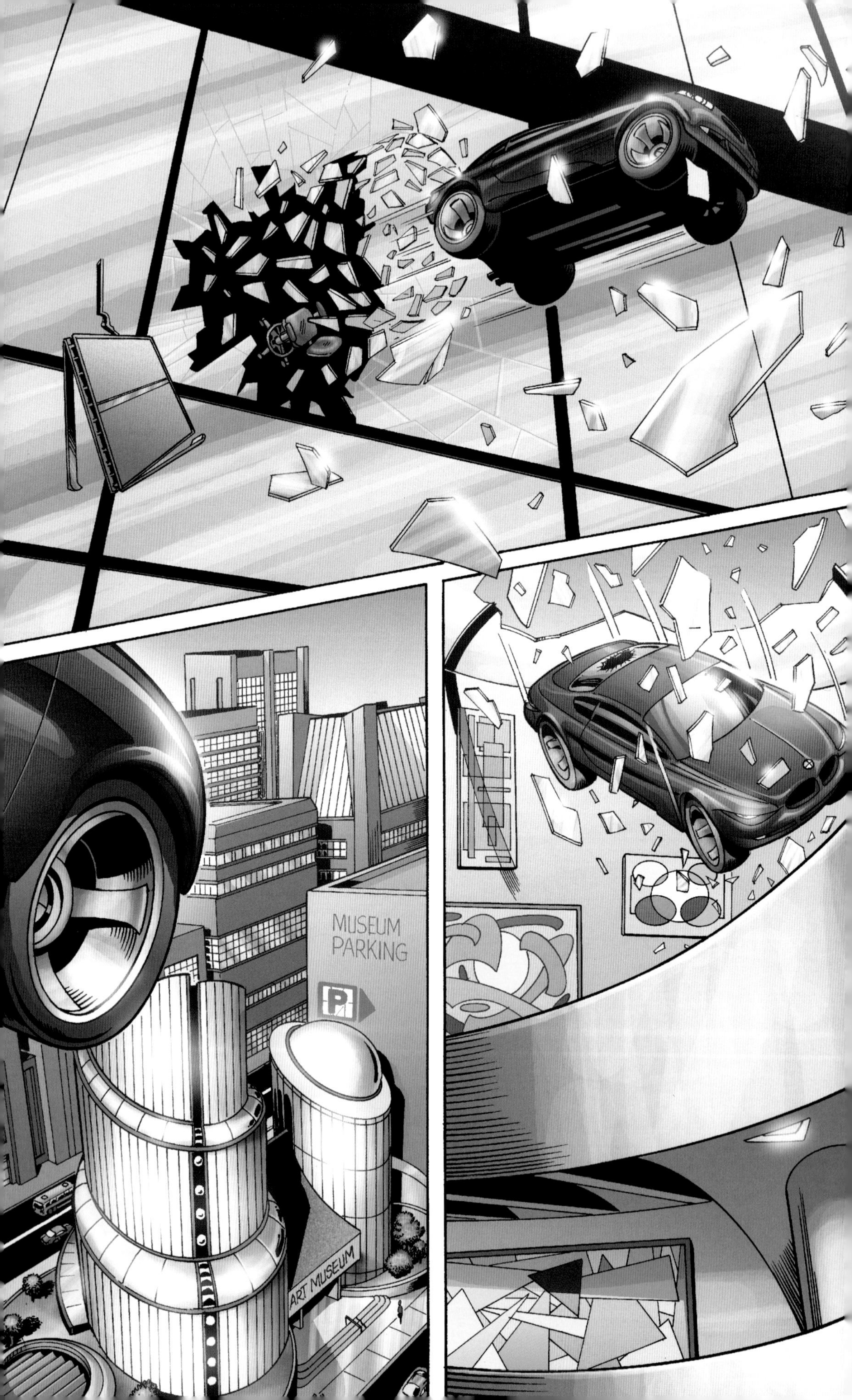
MUSEUM PARKING
P
ART MUSEUM

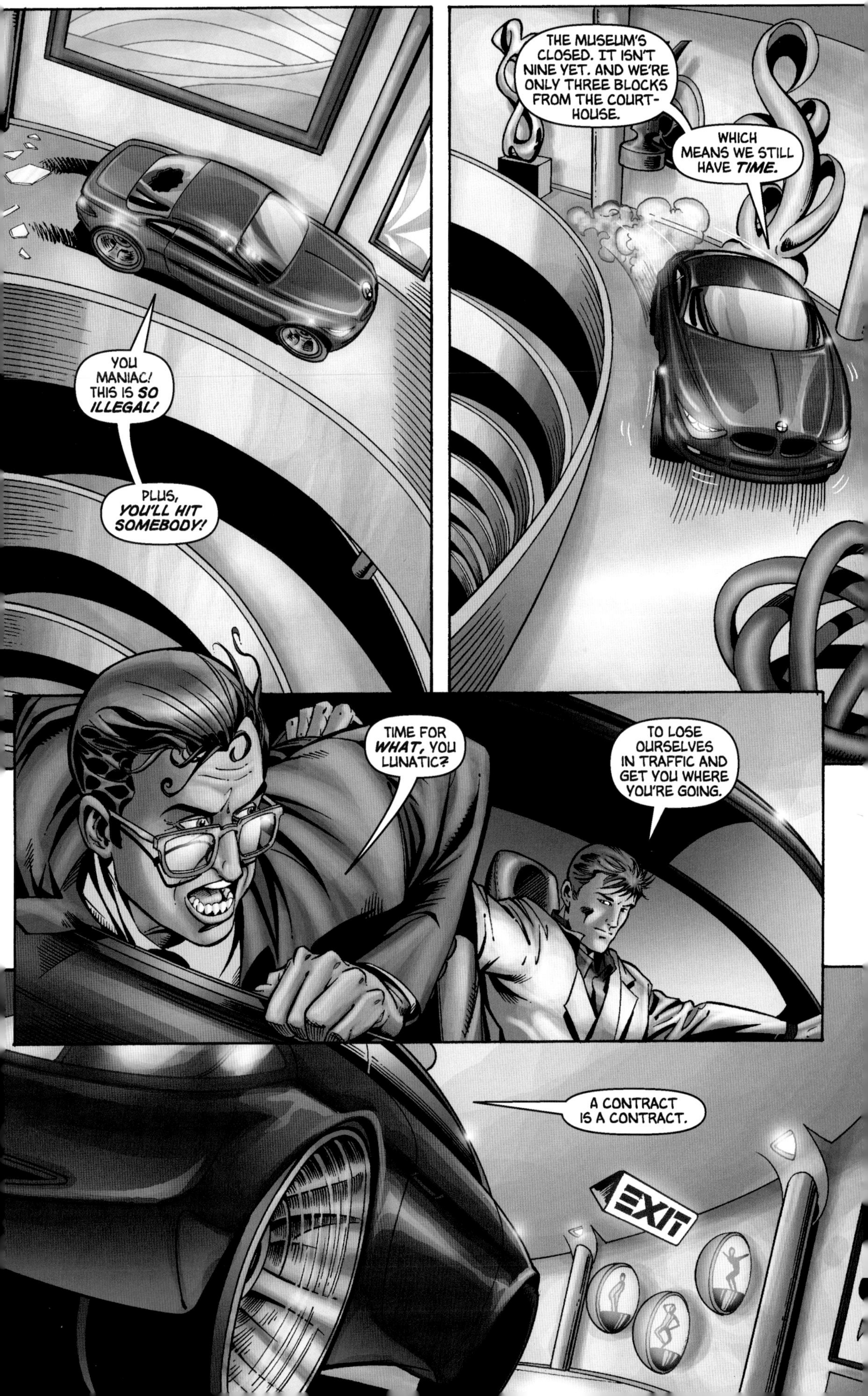
YOU MANIAC! THIS IS SO ILLEGAL!
PLUS, YOU'LL HIT SOMEBODY!
THE MUSEUM'S CLOSED. IT ISN'T NINE YET. AND WE'RE ONLY THREE BLOCKS FROM THE COURT-HOUSE.
WHICH MEANS WE STILL HAVE TIME.
TIME FOR WHAT, YOU LUNATIC?
TO LOSE OURSELVES IN TRAFFIC AND GET YOU WHERE YOU'RE GOING.
A CONTRACT IS A CONTRACT.
EXIT

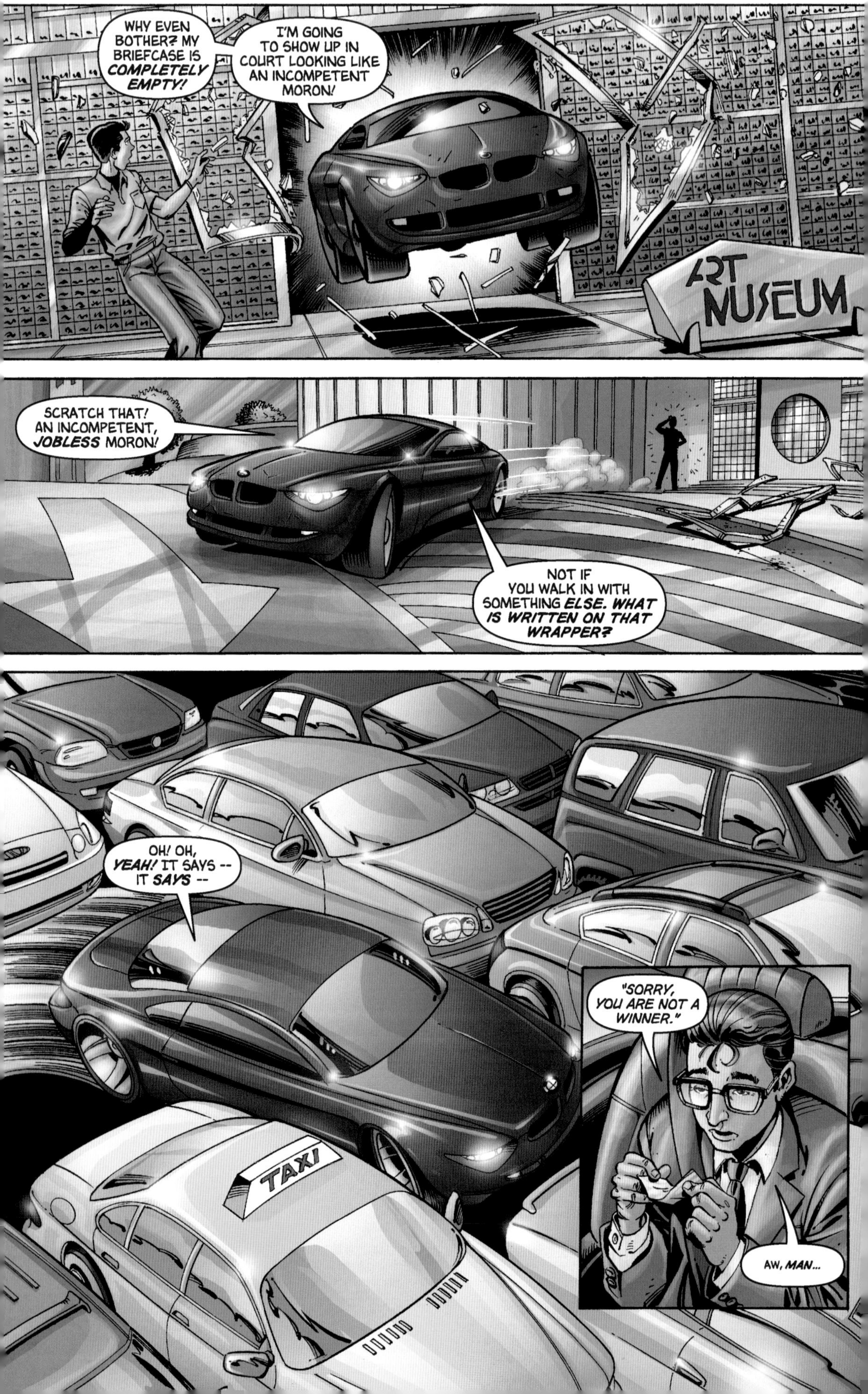
WHY EVEN BOTHER? MY BRIEFCASE IS COMPLETELY EMPTY!
I'M GOING TO SHOW UP IN COURT LOOKING LIKE AN INCOMPETENT MORON!
ART MUSEUM
SCRATCH THAT! AN INCOMPETENT, JOBLESS MORON!
NOT IF YOU WALK IN WITH SOMETHING ELSE. WHAT IS WRITTEN ON THAT WRAPPER?
OH! OH, YEAH! IT SAYS -- IT SAYS --
TAXI
"SORRY, YOU ARE NOT A WINNER."
AW, MAN...

8:58 A.M.

COURT OF JUSTICE

YOU JUST FOUND A PARKING SPOT IN MIDTOWN.

YOU *ARE* GOOD.

WELL ... THANKS. I GUESS. Y'KNOW, EXCEPT FOR THE WHOLE "GETTING ME SHOT AT" PART.

CURBSIDE'S A BUCK AN HOUR. YOU WANT TO COME IN TO COLLECT YOUR FEE, I'LL POP FOR FIFTEEN MINUTES. I NEED THE REST OF MY MONEY FOR CAB FARE TO THE *UNEMPLOYMENT OFFICE.*

I KNOW, I KNOW ... THERE'S NO METER MAIDS AROUND...

...BUT THE LAW IS THE L--

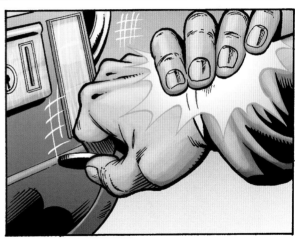

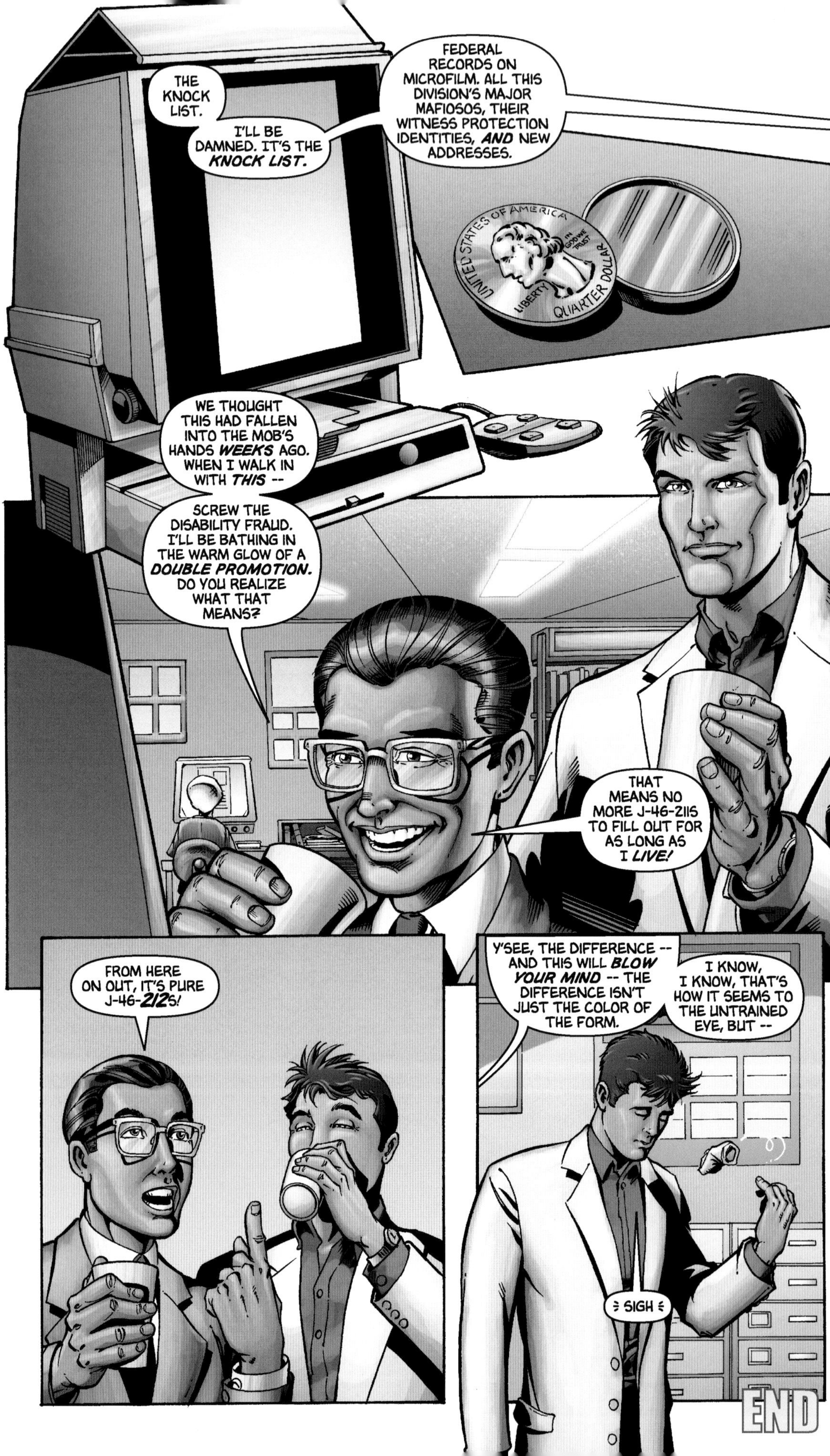
THE KNOCK LIST.
I'LL BE DAMNED. IT'S THE KNOCK LIST.
FEDERAL RECORDS ON MICROFILM. ALL THIS DIVISION'S MAJOR MAFIOSOS, THEIR WITNESS PROTECTION IDENTITIES, AND NEW ADDRESSES.
UNITED STATES OF AMERICA
IN GOD WE TRUST
LIBERTY
QUARTER DOLLAR
WE THOUGHT THIS HAD FALLEN INTO THE MOB'S HANDS WEEKS AGO. WHEN I WALK IN WITH THIS --
SCREW THE DISABILITY FRAUD. I'LL BE BATHING IN THE WARM GLOW OF A DOUBLE PROMOTION. DO YOU REALIZE WHAT THAT MEANS?
THAT MEANS NO MORE J-46-211S TO FILL OUT FOR AS LONG AS I LIVE!
FROM HERE ON OUT, IT'S PURE J-46-212S!
Y'SEE, THE DIFFERENCE -- AND THIS WILL BLOW YOUR MIND -- THE DIFFERENCE ISN'T JUST THE COLOR OF THE FORM.
I KNOW, I KNOW, THAT'S HOW IT SEEMS TO THE UNTRAINED EYE, BUT --
SIGH
END

TYCOON

SCRIPT **KURT BUSIEK** AND **STEVEN GRANT** ART **FRANCISCO RUIZ VELASCO**
COLORS **FRANCISCO RUIZ VELASCO/STUDIO F**

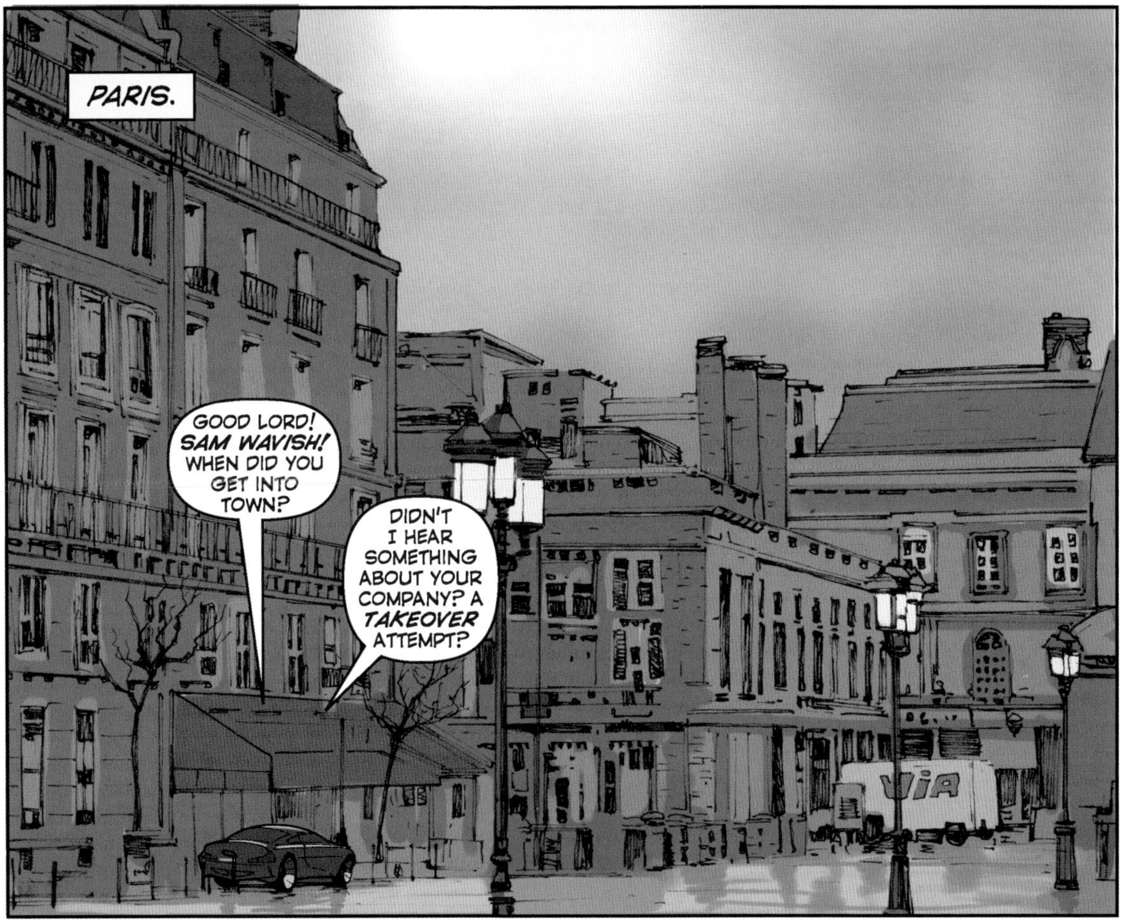
PARIS.
GOOD LORD! SAM WAVISH! WHEN DID YOU GET INTO TOWN?
DIDN'T I HEAR SOMETHING ABOUT YOUR COMPANY? A TAKEOVER ATTEMPT?

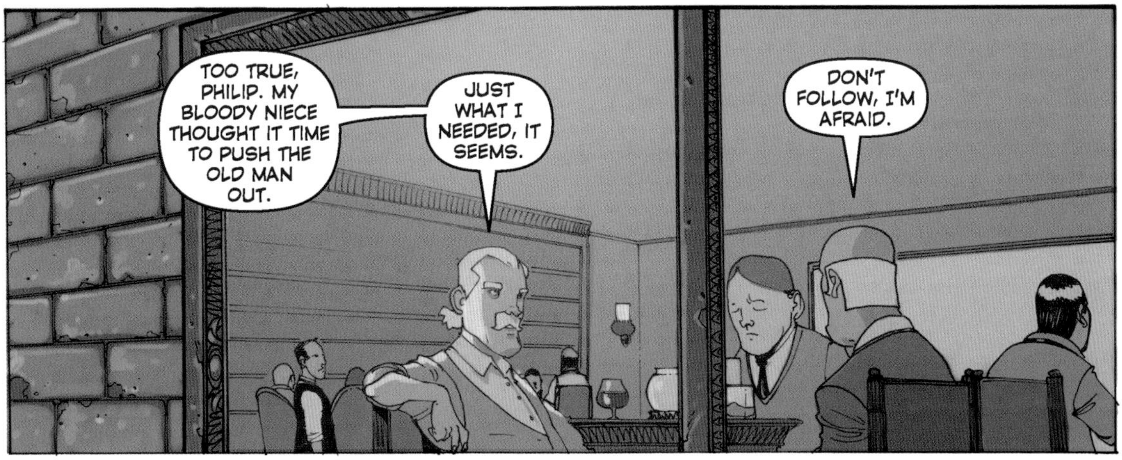
TOO TRUE, PHILIP. MY BLOODY NIECE THOUGHT IT TIME TO PUSH THE OLD MAN OUT.
JUST WHAT I NEEDED, IT SEEMS.
DON'T FOLLOW, I'M AFRAID.

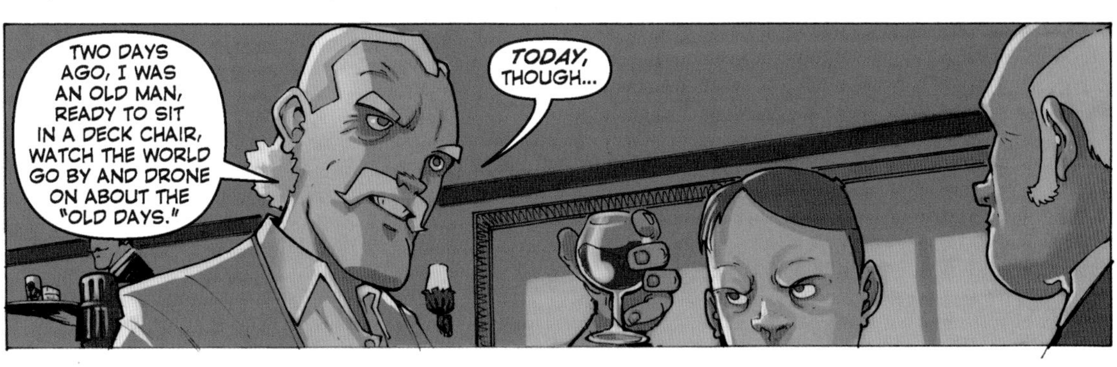
TWO DAYS AGO, I WAS AN OLD MAN, READY TO SIT IN A DECK CHAIR, WATCH THE WORLD GO BY AND DRONE ON ABOUT THE "OLD DAYS."
TODAY, THOUGH...

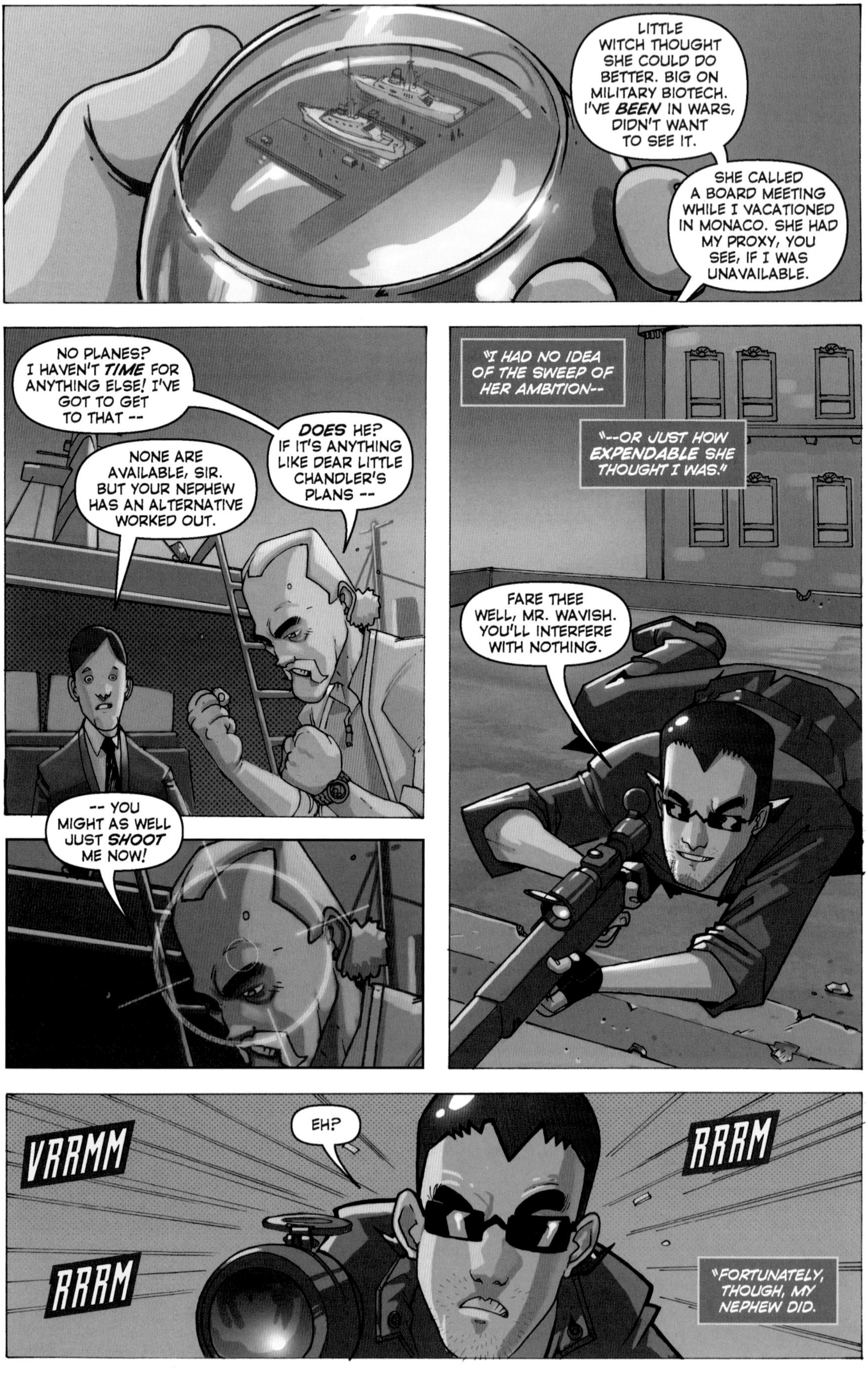
LITTLE WITCH THOUGHT SHE COULD DO BETTER. BIG ON MILITARY BIOTECH. I'VE *BEEN* IN WARS, DIDN'T WANT TO SEE IT.
SHE CALLED A BOARD MEETING WHILE I VACATIONED IN MONACO. SHE HAD MY PROXY, YOU SEE, IF I WAS UNAVAILABLE.
NO PLANES? I HAVEN'T *TIME* FOR ANYTHING ELSE! I'VE GOT TO GET TO THAT --
NONE ARE AVAILABLE, SIR. BUT YOUR NEPHEW HAS AN ALTERNATIVE WORKED OUT.
DOES HE? IF IT'S ANYTHING LIKE DEAR LITTLE CHANDLER'S PLANS --
-- YOU MIGHT AS WELL JUST *SHOOT* ME NOW!
"I HAD NO IDEA OF THE SWEEP OF HER AMBITION--
"--OR JUST HOW *EXPENDABLE* SHE THOUGHT I WAS."
FARE THEE WELL, MR. WAVISH. YOU'LL INTERFERE WITH NOTHING.
VRRMM
EH?
RRRM
RRRM
"FORTUNATELY, THOUGH, MY NEPHEW DID.

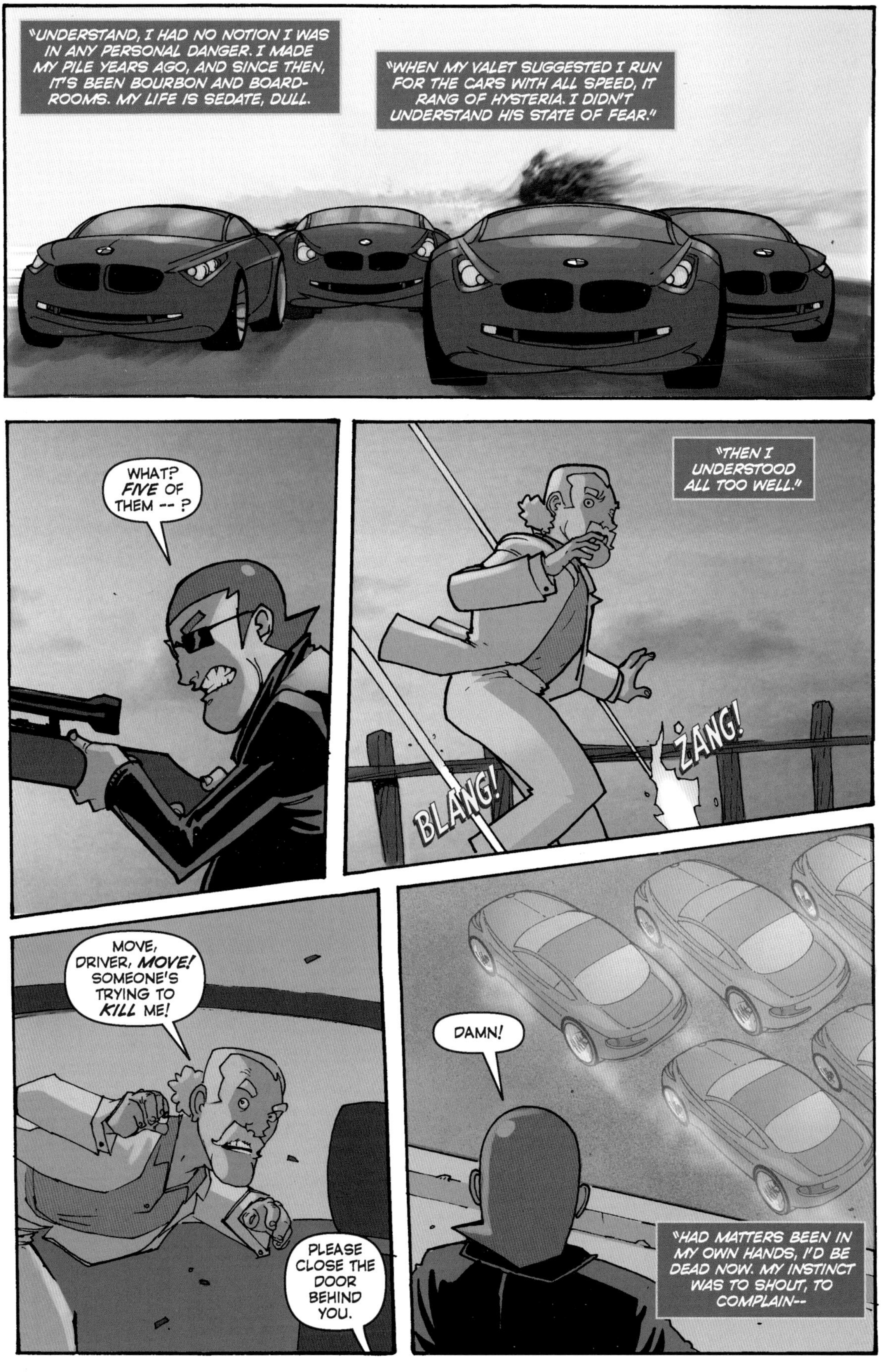
"UNDERSTAND, I HAD NO NOTION I WAS IN ANY PERSONAL DANGER. I MADE MY PILE YEARS AGO, AND SINCE THEN, IT'S BEEN BOURBON AND BOARD-ROOMS. MY LIFE IS SEDATE, DULL.
"WHEN MY VALET SUGGESTED I RUN FOR THE CARS WITH ALL SPEED, IT RANG OF HYSTERIA. I DIDN'T UNDERSTAND HIS STATE OF FEAR."
WHAT? FIVE OF THEM -- ?
"THEN I UNDERSTOOD ALL TOO WELL."
BLANG!
ZANG!
MOVE, DRIVER, MOVE! SOMEONE'S TRYING TO KILL ME!
PLEASE CLOSE THE DOOR BEHIND YOU.
DAMN!
"HAD MATTERS BEEN IN MY OWN HANDS, I'D BE DEAD NOW. MY INSTINCT WAS TO SHOUT, TO COMPLAIN--

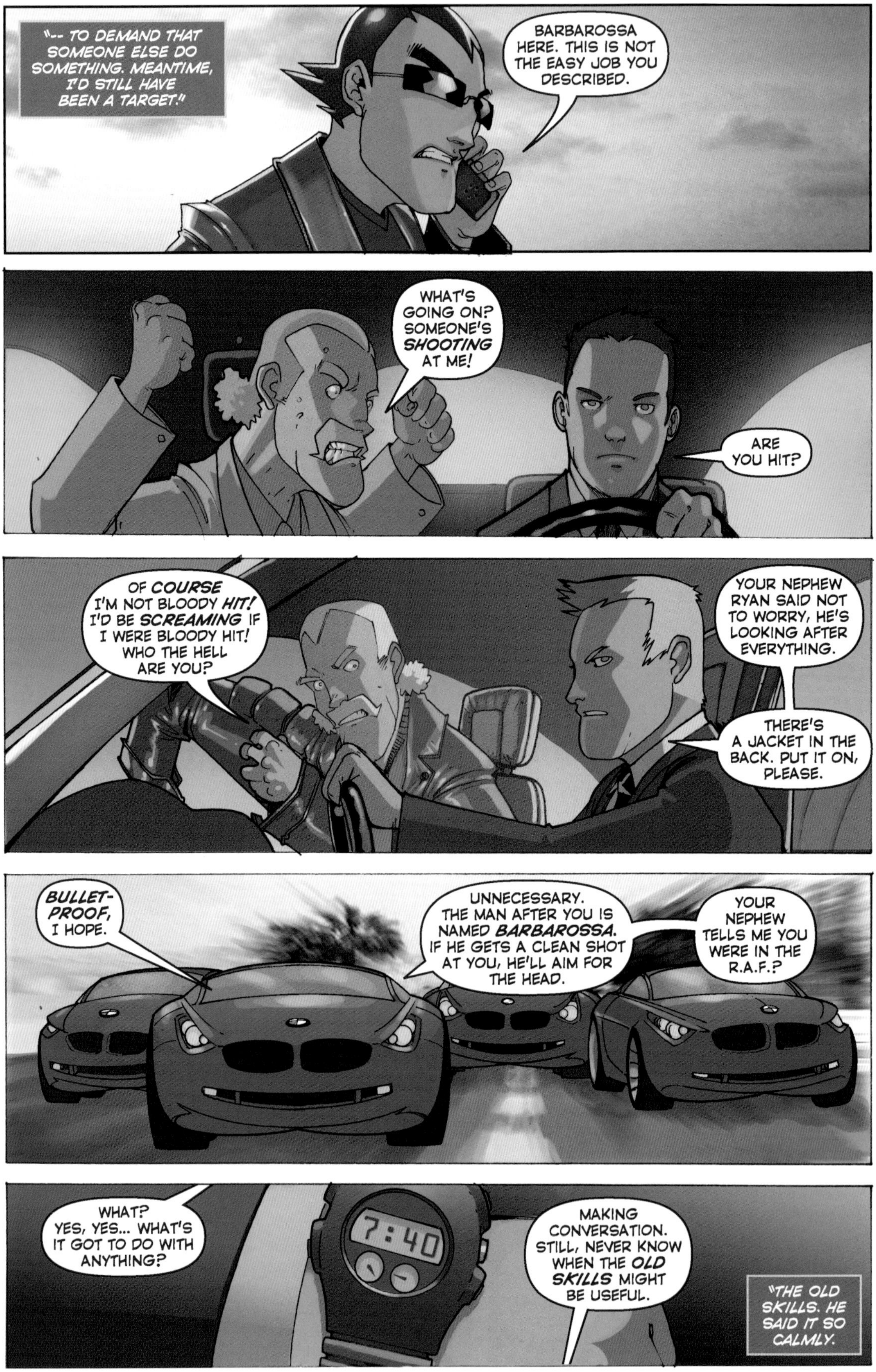

"-- TO DEMAND THAT SOMEONE ELSE DO SOMETHING. MEANTIME, I'D STILL HAVE BEEN A TARGET."
BARBAROSSA HERE. THIS IS NOT THE EASY JOB YOU DESCRIBED.
WHAT'S GOING ON? SOMEONE'S SHOOTING AT ME!
ARE YOU HIT?
OF COURSE I'M NOT BLOODY HIT! I'D BE SCREAMING IF I WERE BLOODY HIT! WHO THE HELL ARE YOU?
YOUR NEPHEW RYAN SAID NOT TO WORRY, HE'S LOOKING AFTER EVERYTHING.
THERE'S A JACKET IN THE BACK. PUT IT ON, PLEASE.
BULLET-PROOF, I HOPE.
UNNECESSARY. THE MAN AFTER YOU IS NAMED BARBAROSSA. IF HE GETS A CLEAN SHOT AT YOU, HE'LL AIM FOR THE HEAD.
YOUR NEPHEW TELLS ME YOU WERE IN THE R.A.F.?
WHAT? YES, YES... WHAT'S IT GOT TO DO WITH ANYTHING?
7:40
MAKING CONVERSATION. STILL, NEVER KNOW WHEN THE OLD SKILLS MIGHT BE USEFUL.
"THE OLD SKILLS. HE SAID IT SO CALMLY.

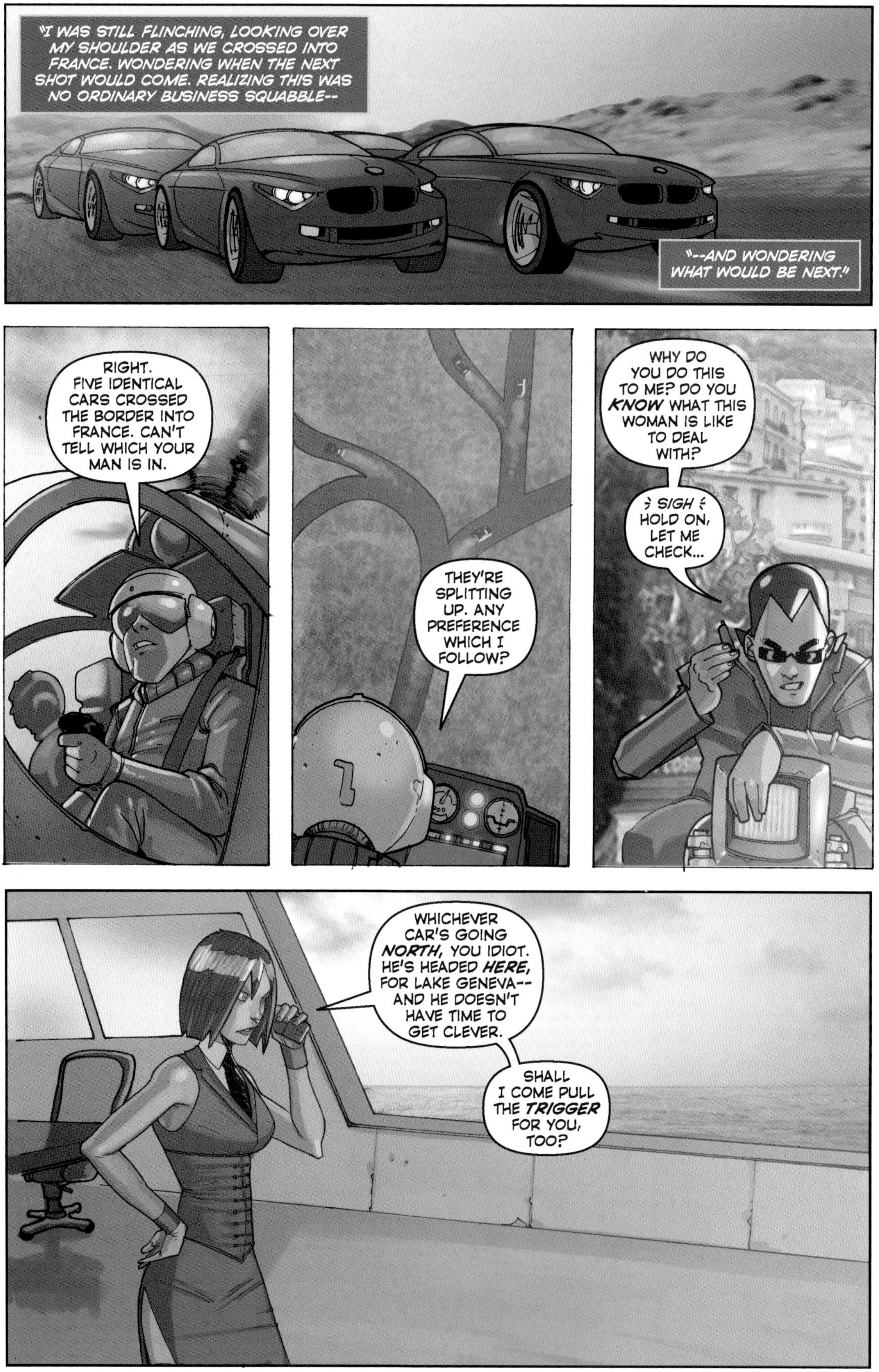
"I WAS STILL FLINCHING, LOOKING OVER MY SHOULDER AS WE CROSSED INTO FRANCE. WONDERING WHEN THE NEXT SHOT WOULD COME. REALIZING THIS WAS NO ORDINARY BUSINESS SQUABBLE--
"--AND WONDERING WHAT WOULD BE NEXT."
RIGHT. FIVE IDENTICAL CARS CROSSED THE BORDER INTO FRANCE. CAN'T TELL WHICH YOUR MAN IS IN.
THEY'RE SPLITTING UP. ANY PREFERENCE WHICH I FOLLOW?
WHY DO YOU DO THIS TO ME? DO YOU *KNOW* WHAT THIS WOMAN IS LIKE TO DEAL WITH?
SIGH HOLD ON, LET ME CHECK...
WHICHEVER CAR'S GOING *NORTH*, YOU IDIOT. HE'S HEADED *HERE*, FOR LAKE GENEVA-- AND HE DOESN'T HAVE TIME TO GET CLEVER.
SHALL I COME PULL THE *TRIGGER* FOR YOU, TOO?

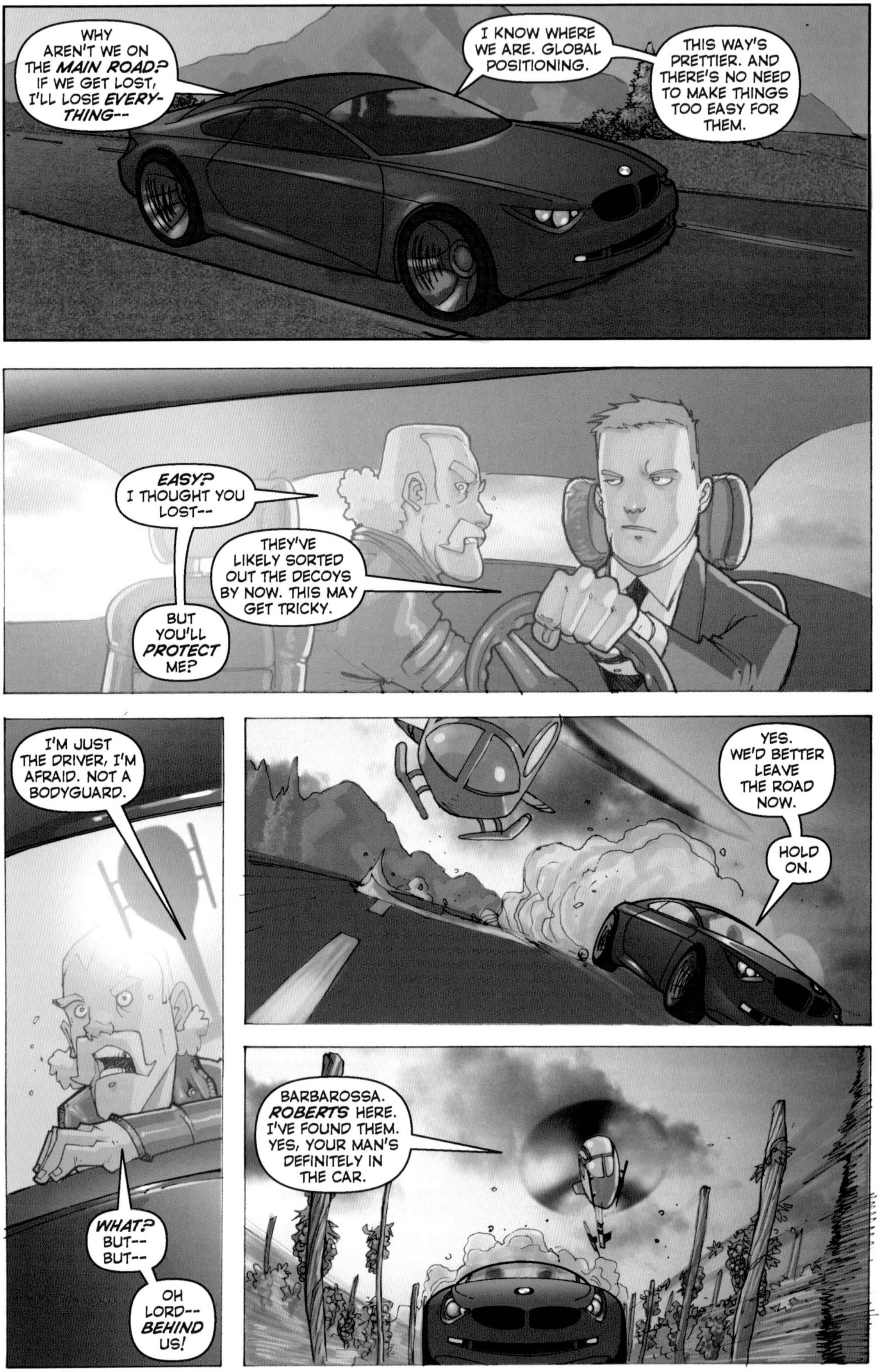
WHY AREN'T WE ON THE MAIN ROAD? IF WE GET LOST, I'LL LOSE EVERY-THING--
I KNOW WHERE WE ARE. GLOBAL POSITIONING.
THIS WAY'S PRETTIER. AND THERE'S NO NEED TO MAKE THINGS TOO EASY FOR THEM.
EASY? I THOUGHT YOU LOST--
THEY'VE LIKELY SORTED OUT THE DECOYS BY NOW. THIS MAY GET TRICKY.
BUT YOU'LL PROTECT ME?
I'M JUST THE DRIVER, I'M AFRAID. NOT A BODYGUARD.
WHAT? BUT-- BUT--
OH LORD-- BEHIND US!
YES. WE'D BETTER LEAVE THE ROAD NOW.
HOLD ON.
BARBAROSSA. ROBERTS HERE. I'VE FOUND THEM. YES, YOUR MAN'S DEFINITELY IN THE CAR.

OH, YES. I CAN KEEP THEM VERY BUSY.

"AGAIN, I'D HAVE BEEN DEAD. I'D HAVE TRIED TO GET AWAY FROM THE EXPLOSION, TUMBLING THE VEHICLE.

"BUT HE SWERVED TOWARD THE BLAST, RIGHTING THE CAR BEFORE IT COULD TIP."

GOOD GOD, THAT WAS DYNAMITE!

I'D NOTICED, YES. NOW LISTEN CAREFULLY...

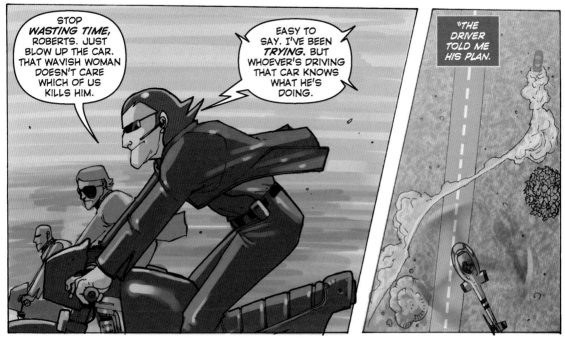

STOP WASTING TIME, ROBERTS. JUST BLOW UP THE CAR. THAT WAVISH WOMAN DOESN'T CARE WHICH OF US KILLS HIM.

EASY TO SAY. I'VE BEEN TRYING. BUT WHOEVER'S DRIVING THAT CAR KNOWS WHAT HE'S DOING.

"THE DRIVER TOLD ME HIS PLAN.

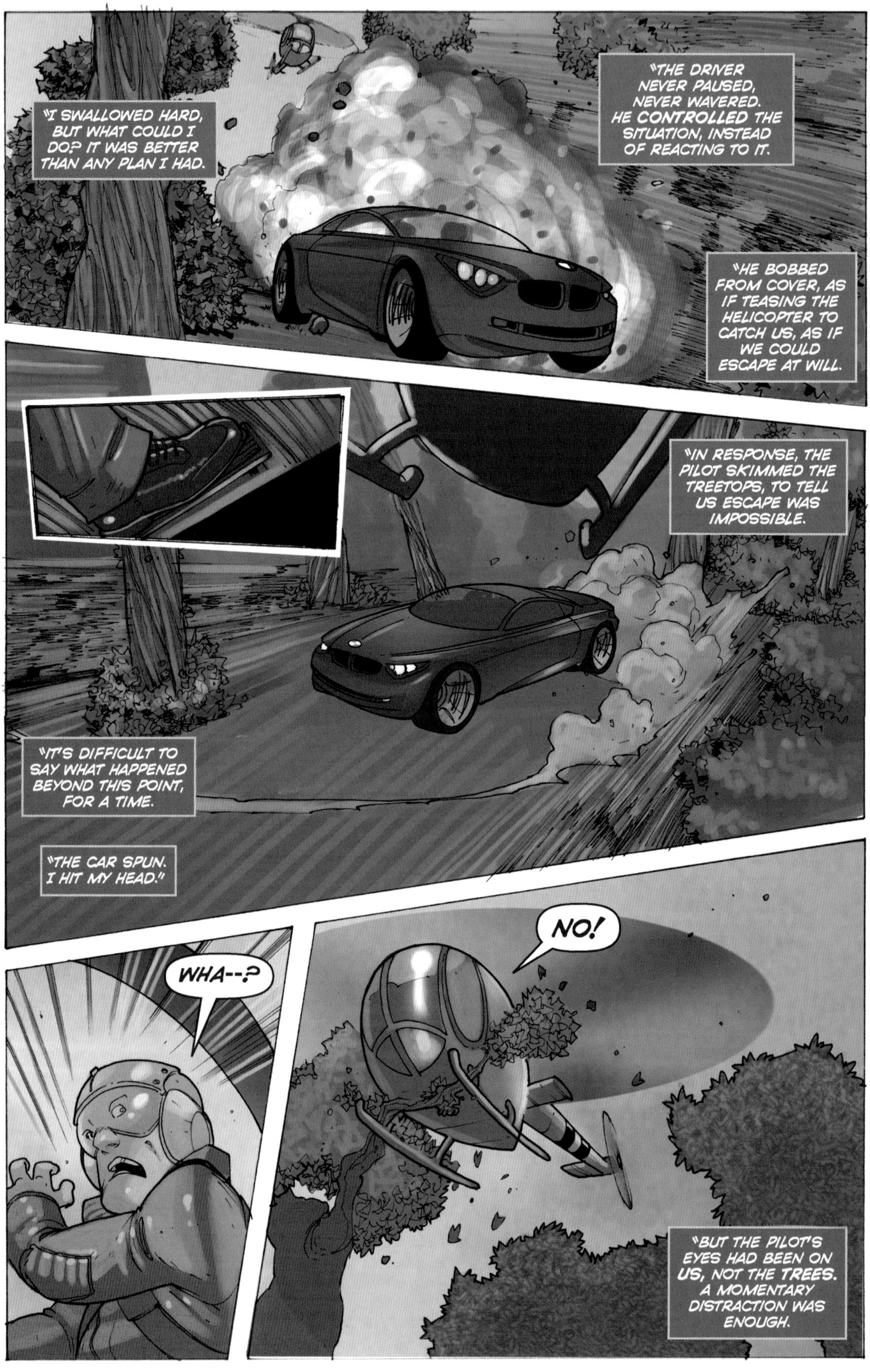
"I SWALLOWED HARD, BUT WHAT COULD I DO? IT WAS BETTER THAN ANY PLAN I HAD.
"THE DRIVER NEVER PAUSED, NEVER WAVERED. HE CONTROLLED THE SITUATION, INSTEAD OF REACTING TO IT.
"HE BOBBED FROM COVER, AS IF TEASING THE HELICOPTER TO CATCH US, AS IF WE COULD ESCAPE AT WILL.
"IN RESPONSE, THE PILOT SKIMMED THE TREETOPS, TO TELL US ESCAPE WAS IMPOSSIBLE.
"IT'S DIFFICULT TO SAY WHAT HAPPENED BEYOND THIS POINT, FOR A TIME.
"THE CAR SPUN. I HIT MY HEAD."
WHA--?
NO!
"BUT THE PILOT'S EYES HAD BEEN ON US, NOT THE TREES. A MOMENTARY DISTRACTION WAS ENOUGH.

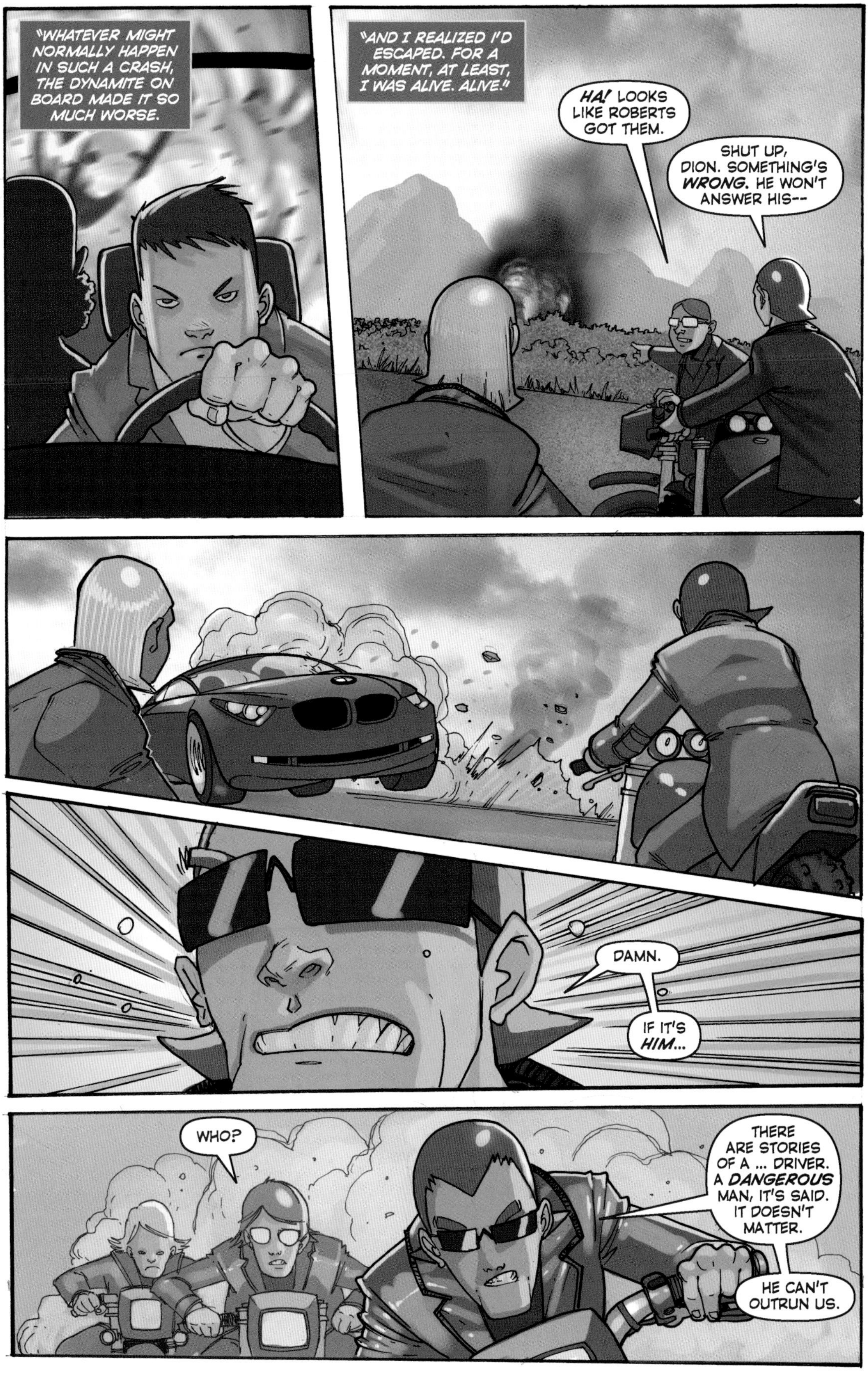

"WHATEVER MIGHT NORMALLY HAPPEN IN SUCH A CRASH, THE DYNAMITE ON BOARD MADE IT SO MUCH WORSE.
"AND I REALIZED I'D ESCAPED. FOR A MOMENT, AT LEAST, I WAS ALIVE. ALIVE."
HA! LOOKS LIKE ROBERTS GOT THEM.
SHUT UP, DION. SOMETHING'S WRONG. HE WON'T ANSWER HIS--
DAMN.
IF IT'S HIM...
WHO?
THERE ARE STORIES OF A ... DRIVER. A DANGEROUS MAN, IT'S SAID. IT DOESN'T MATTER.
HE CAN'T OUTRUN US.

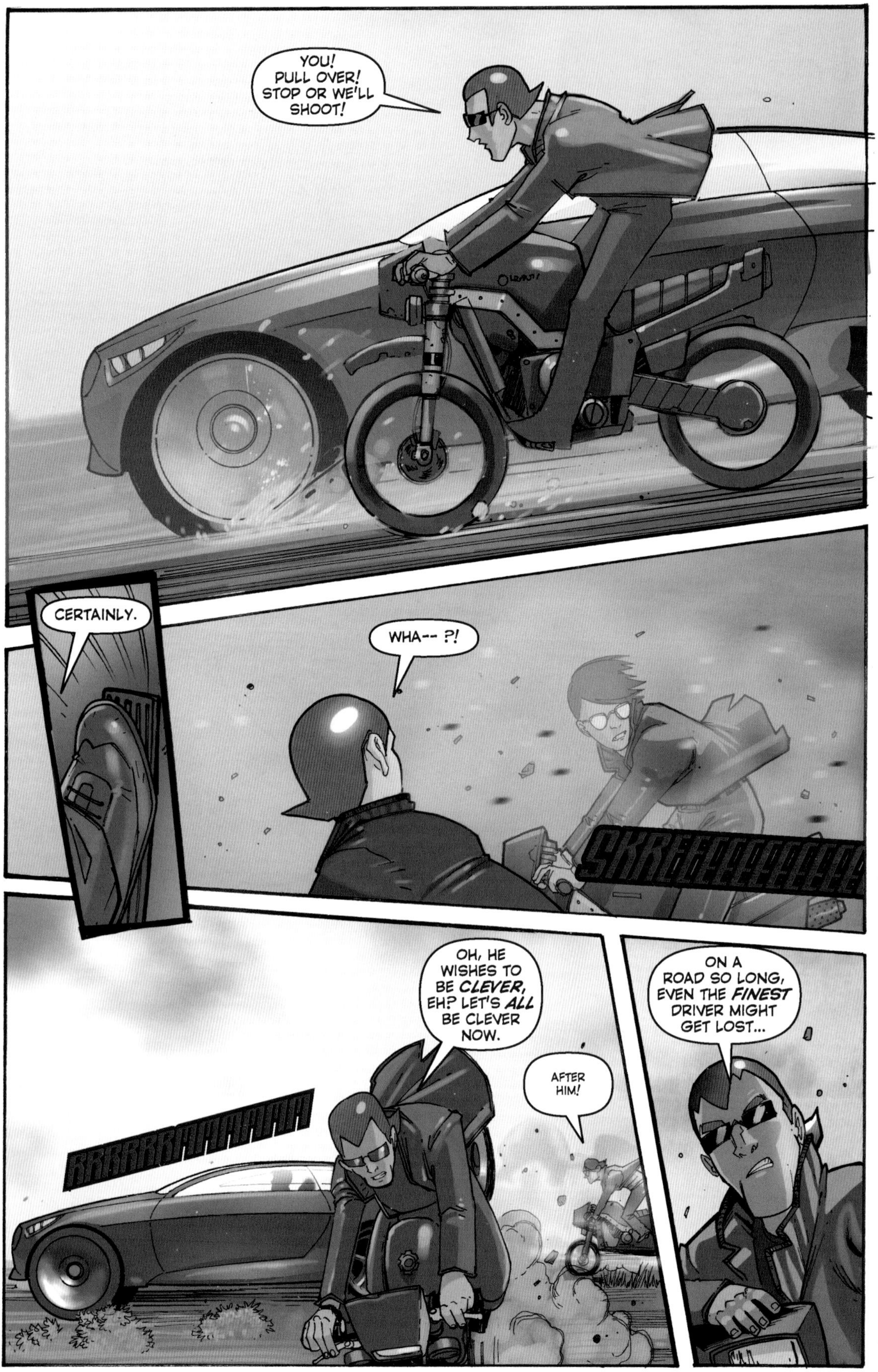
YOU! PULL OVER! STOP OR WE'LL SHOOT!
CERTAINLY.
WHA-- ?!
OH, HE WISHES TO BE *CLEVER*, EH? LET'S *ALL* BE CLEVER NOW.
AFTER HIM!
ON A ROAD SO LONG, EVEN THE *FINEST* DRIVER MIGHT GET LOST...

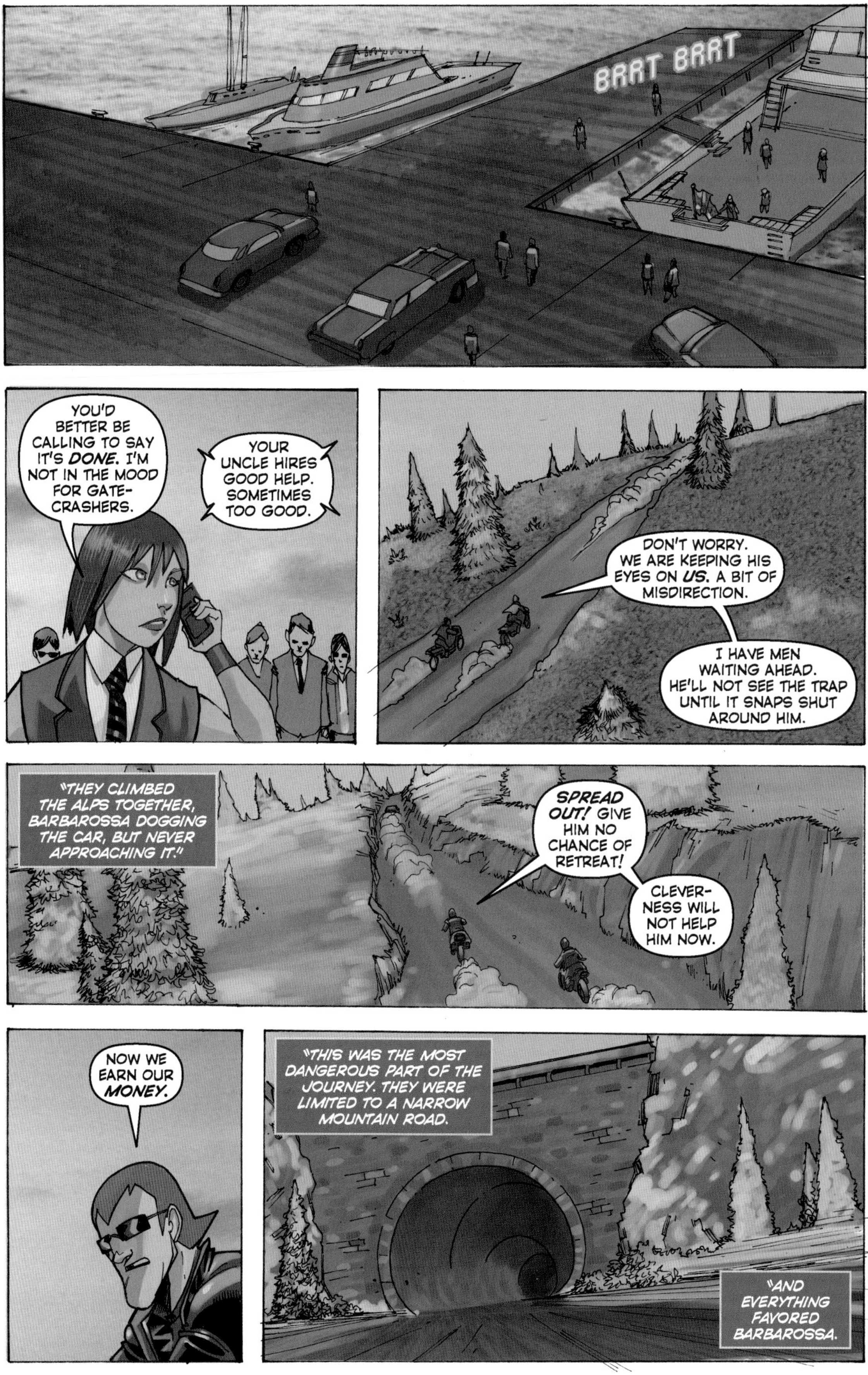
BRRT BRRT
YOU'D BETTER BE CALLING TO SAY IT'S DONE. I'M NOT IN THE MOOD FOR GATE-CRASHERS.
YOUR UNCLE HIRES GOOD HELP. SOMETIMES TOO GOOD.
DON'T WORRY. WE ARE KEEPING HIS EYES ON US. A BIT OF MISDIRECTION.
I HAVE MEN WAITING AHEAD. HE'LL NOT SEE THE TRAP UNTIL IT SNAPS SHUT AROUND HIM.
"THEY CLIMBED THE ALPS TOGETHER, BARBAROSSA DOGGING THE CAR, BUT NEVER APPROACHING IT."
SPREAD OUT! GIVE HIM NO CHANCE OF RETREAT!
CLEVER-NESS WILL NOT HELP HIM NOW.
NOW WE EARN OUR MONEY.
"THIS WAS THE MOST DANGEROUS PART OF THE JOURNEY. THEY WERE LIMITED TO A NARROW MOUNTAIN ROAD.
"AND EVERYTHING FAVORED BARBAROSSA.

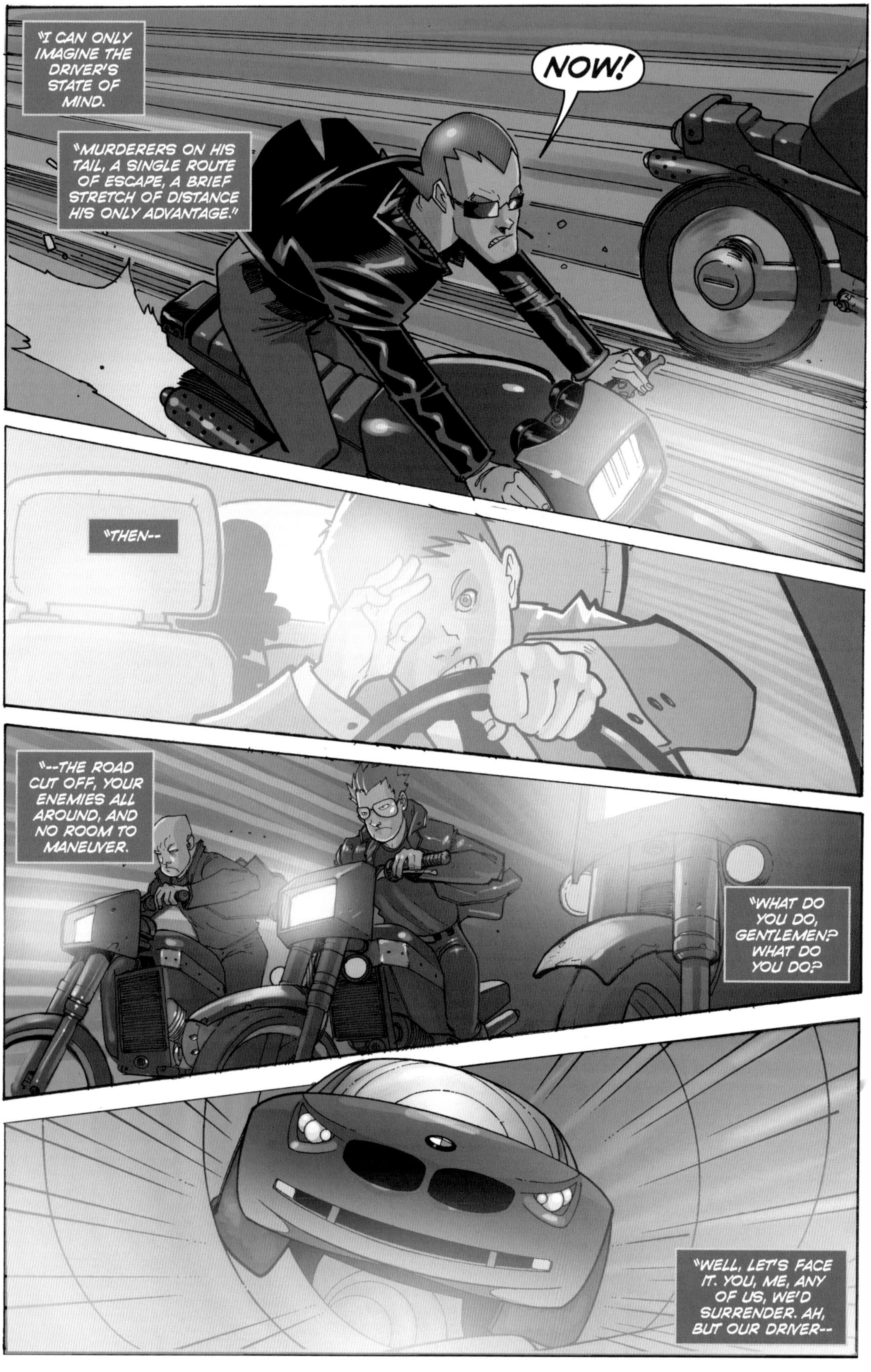
"I CAN ONLY IMAGINE THE DRIVER'S STATE OF MIND.
NOW!
"MURDERERS ON HIS TAIL, A SINGLE ROUTE OF ESCAPE, A BRIEF STRETCH OF DISTANCE HIS ONLY ADVANTAGE."
"THEN--
"--THE ROAD CUT OFF, YOUR ENEMIES ALL AROUND, AND NO ROOM TO MANEUVER.
"WHAT DO YOU DO, GENTLEMEN? WHAT DO YOU DO?
"WELL, LET'S FACE IT. YOU, ME, ANY OF US, WE'D SURRENDER. AH, BUT OUR DRIVER--

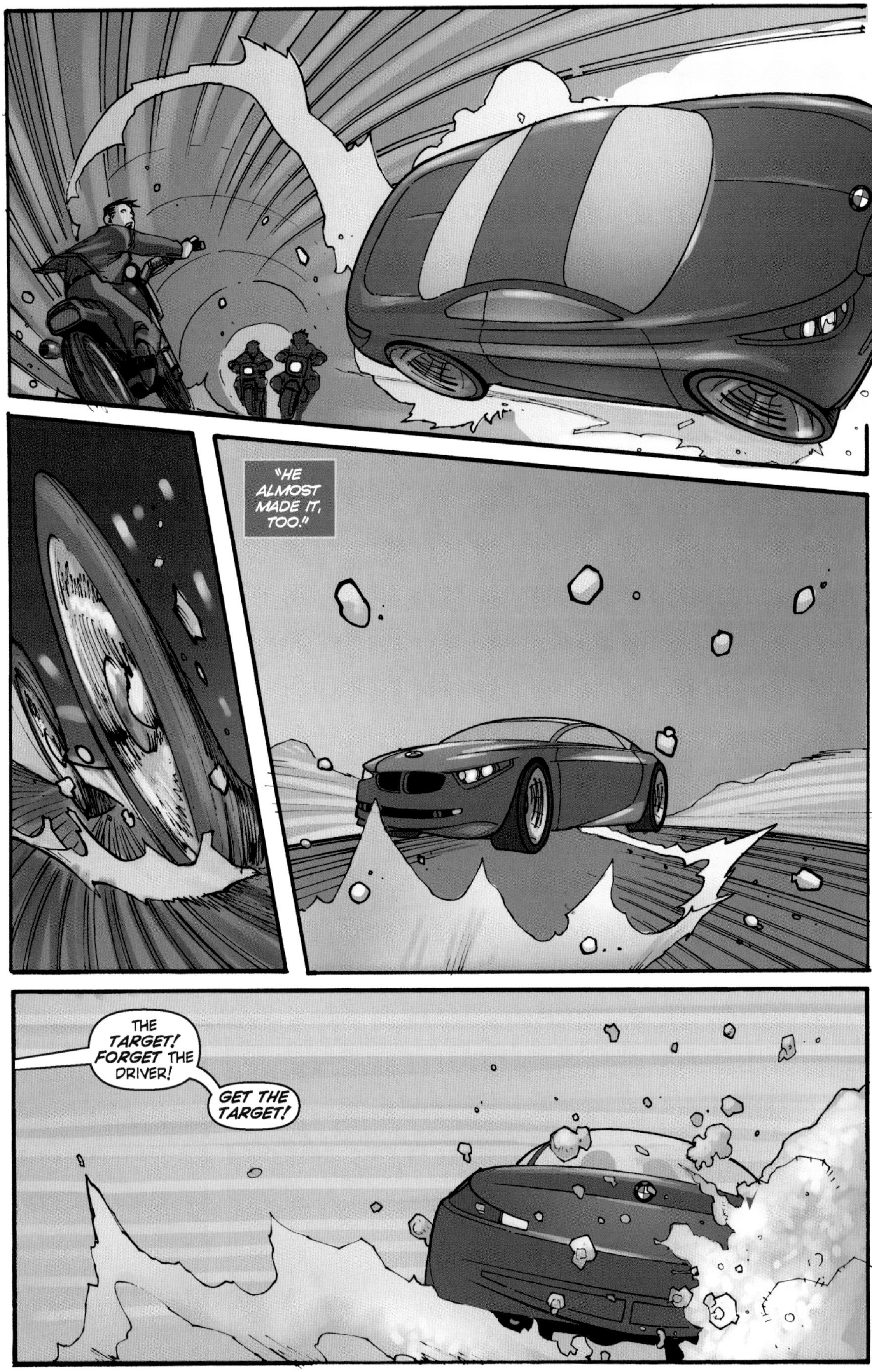
"HE ALMOST MADE IT, TOO."
THE TARGET! FORGET THE DRIVER!
GET THE TARGET!

IT'S A DOLL! HE'S NOT HERE!

"WAVISH! WHAT ON EARTH? BUT *YOU* WERE IN THE BACKSEAT!"

ALL IN TIME, PHILIP. THIS ISN'T ABOUT *ME* AT THE MOMENT.

WHERE IS WAVISH?

THINK YOU'RE *SMART?* YOU'RE *USELESS!* *TRANSPARENT!*

SORRY, MATE, YOU'RE ON ABOUT *WHAT,* AGAIN?

HE CAN BE ONLY *ONE* PLACE.

PARDON-- BEFORE YOU SHOOT UP MY TRUNK-- I'D RATHER NOT LOSE MY RENTAL DEPOSIT--

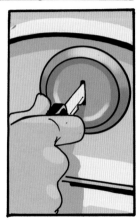

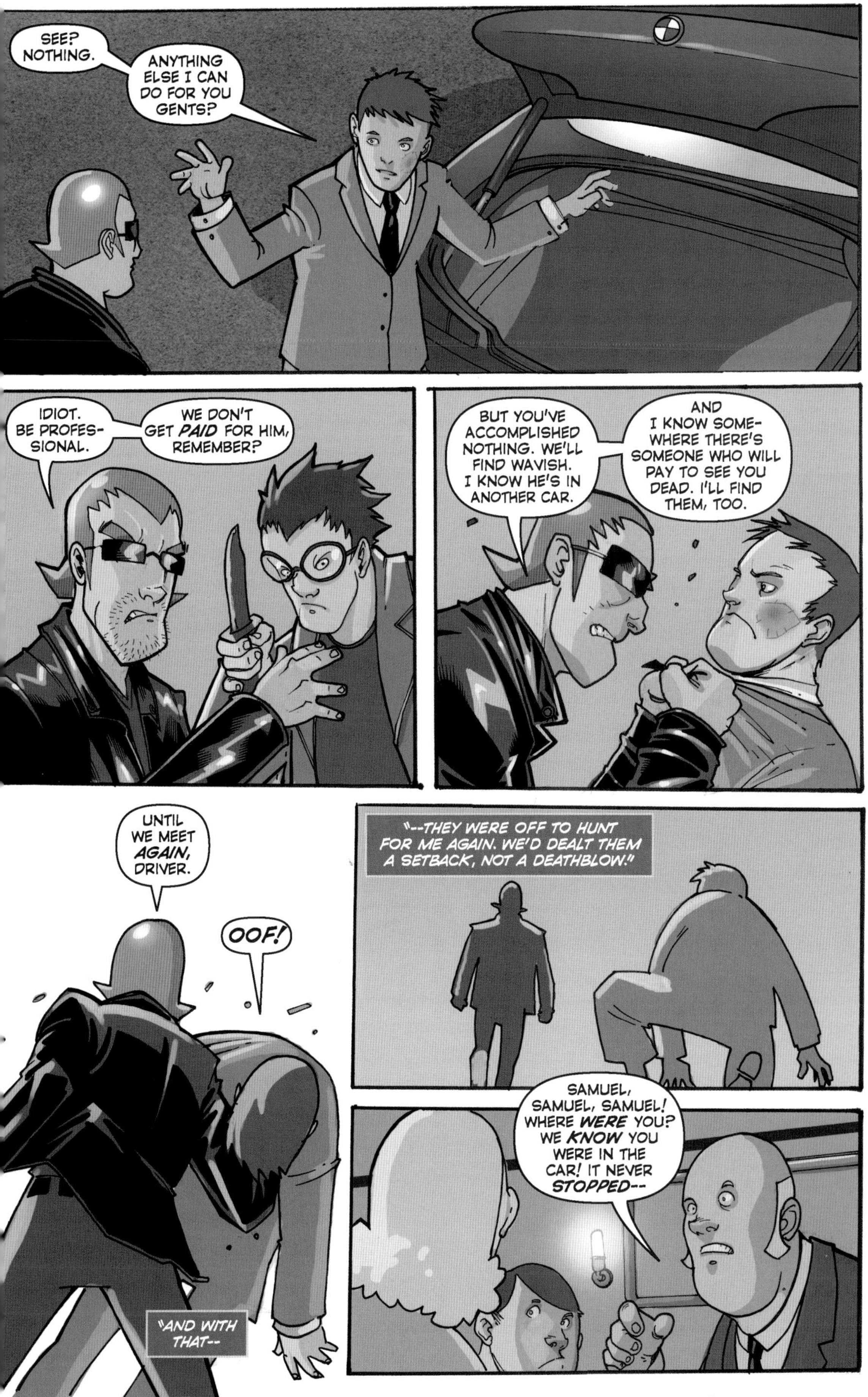
SEE? NOTHING.
ANYTHING ELSE I CAN DO FOR YOU GENTS?
IDIOT. BE PROFES-SIONAL.
WE DON'T GET *PAID* FOR HIM, REMEMBER?
BUT YOU'VE ACCOMPLISHED NOTHING. WE'LL FIND WAVISH. I KNOW HE'S IN ANOTHER CAR.
AND I KNOW SOME-WHERE THERE'S SOMEONE WHO WILL PAY TO SEE YOU DEAD. I'LL FIND THEM, TOO.
UNTIL WE MEET *AGAIN,* DRIVER.
OOF!
"AND WITH THAT--
"--THEY WERE OFF TO HUNT FOR ME AGAIN. WE'D DEALT THEM A SETBACK, NOT A DEATHBLOW."
SAMUEL, SAMUEL, SAMUEL! WHERE *WERE* YOU? WE *KNOW* YOU WERE IN THE CAR! IT NEVER *STOPPED--*

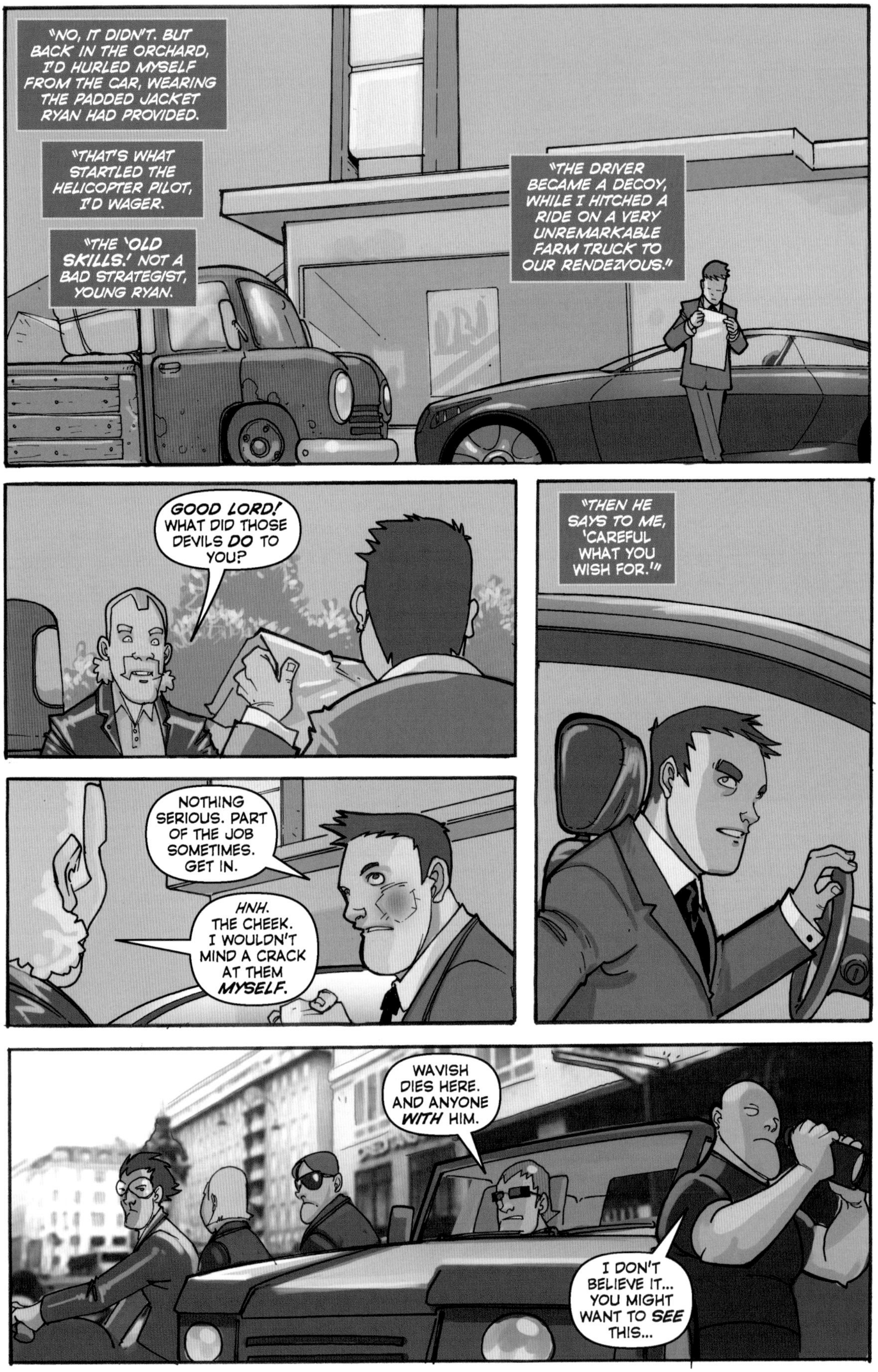
"NO, IT DIDN'T. BUT BACK IN THE ORCHARD, I'D HURLED MYSELF FROM THE CAR, WEARING THE PADDED JACKET RYAN HAD PROVIDED.
"THAT'S WHAT STARTLED THE HELICOPTER PILOT, I'D WAGER.
"THE 'OLD SKILLS.' NOT A BAD STRATEGIST, YOUNG RYAN.
"THE DRIVER BECAME A DECOY, WHILE I HITCHED A RIDE ON A VERY UNREMARKABLE FARM TRUCK TO OUR RENDEZVOUS."
GOOD LORD! WHAT DID THOSE DEVILS DO TO YOU?
NOTHING SERIOUS. PART OF THE JOB SOMETIMES. GET IN.
HNH. THE CHEEK. I WOULDN'T MIND A CRACK AT THEM MYSELF.
"THEN HE SAYS TO ME, 'CAREFUL WHAT YOU WISH FOR.'"
WAVISH DIES HERE. AND ANYONE WITH HIM.
I DON'T BELIEVE IT... YOU MIGHT WANT TO SEE THIS...

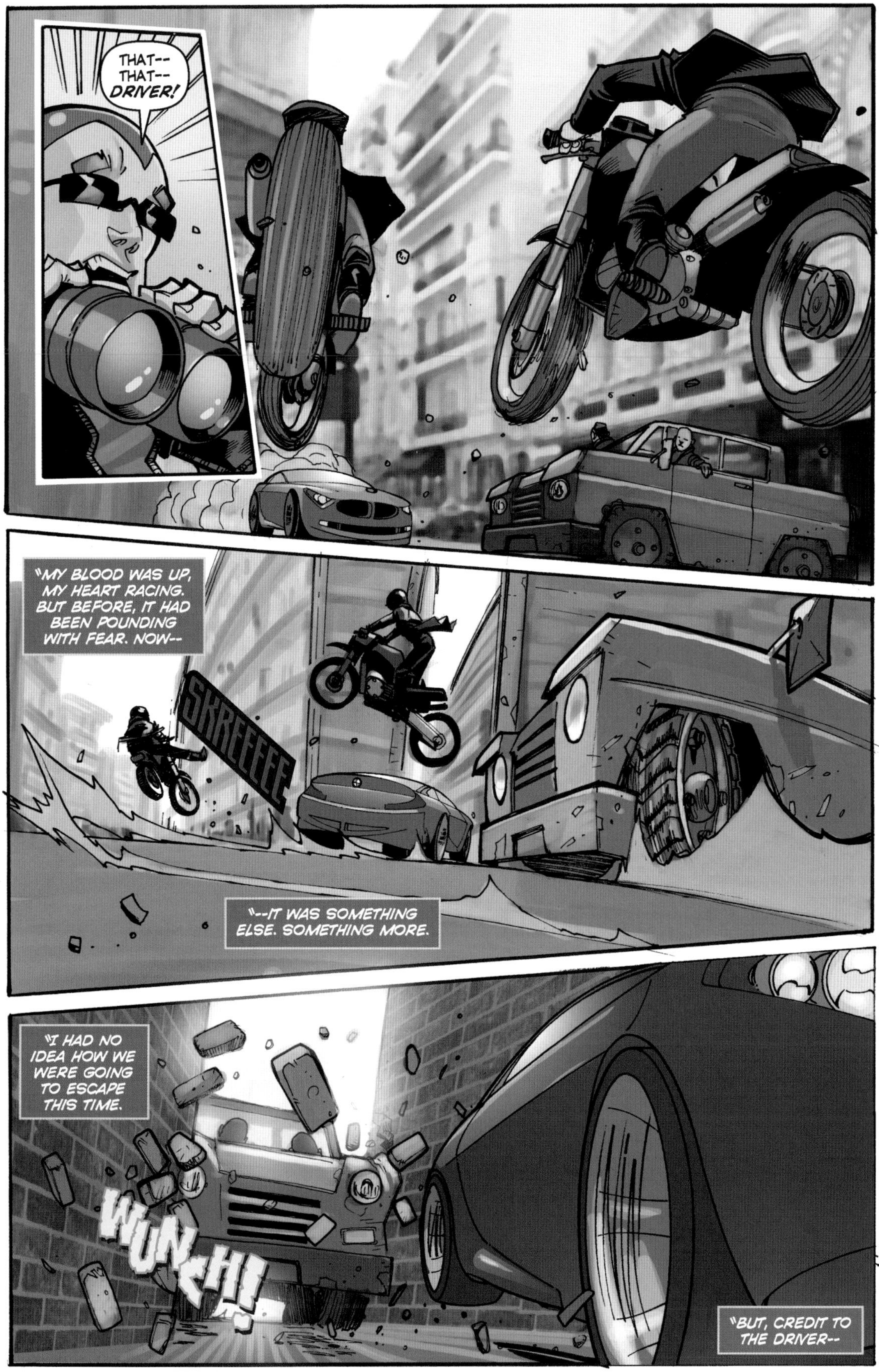
THAT-- THAT-- DRIVER!
"MY BLOOD WAS UP, MY HEART RACING. BUT BEFORE, IT HAD BEEN POUNDING WITH FEAR. NOW--
SKREEEEE
"--IT WAS SOMETHING ELSE. SOMETHING MORE.
"I HAD NO IDEA HOW WE WERE GOING TO ESCAPE THIS TIME.
WUNCH!
"BUT, CREDIT TO THE DRIVER--

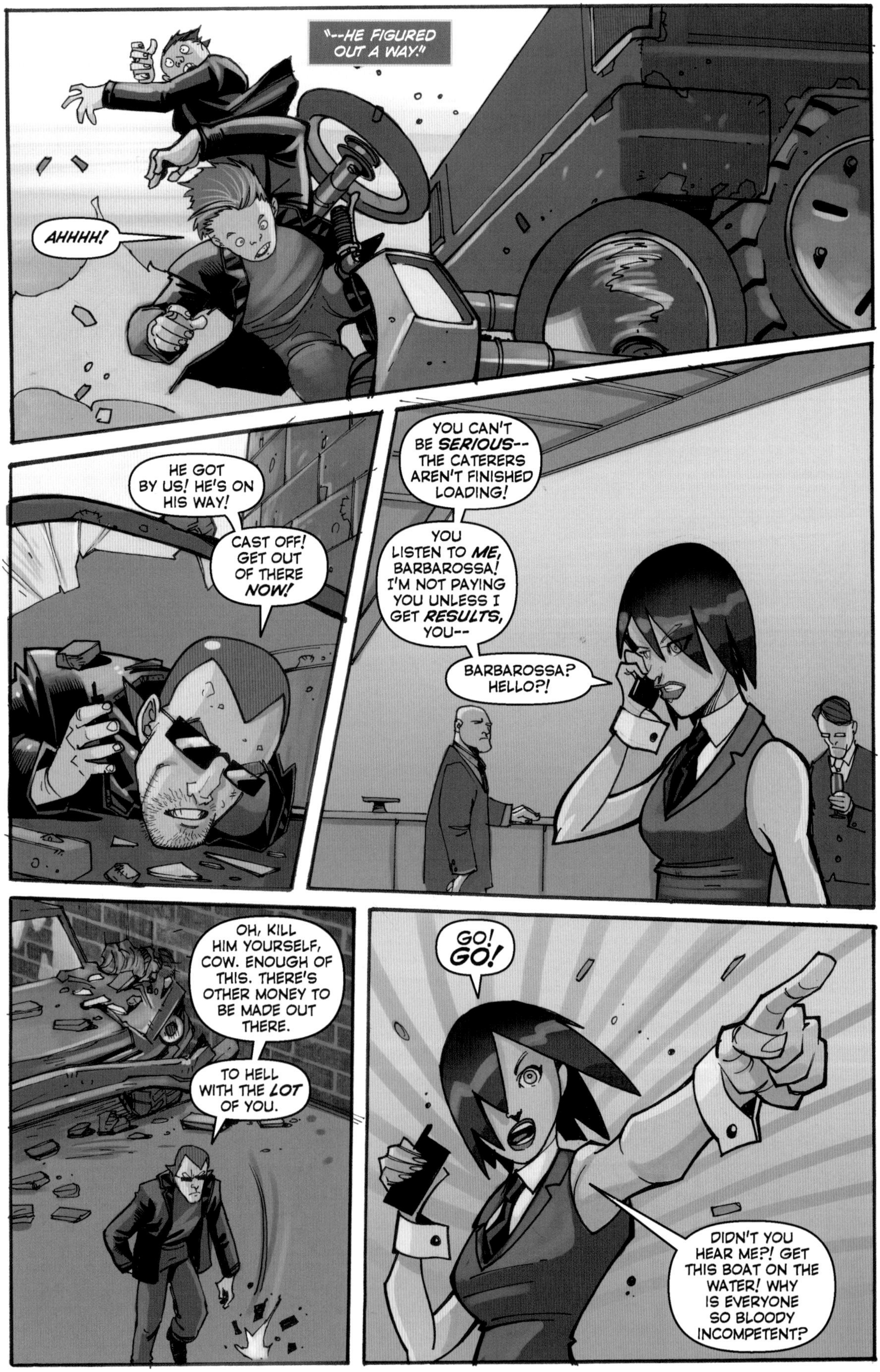
"--HE FIGURED OUT A WAY."
AHHHH!
HE GOT BY US! HE'S ON HIS WAY!
CAST OFF! GET OUT OF THERE NOW!
YOU CAN'T BE SERIOUS-- THE CATERERS AREN'T FINISHED LOADING!
YOU LISTEN TO ME, BARBAROSSA! I'M NOT PAYING YOU UNLESS I GET RESULTS, YOU--
BARBAROSSA? HELLO?!
OH, KILL HIM YOURSELF, COW. ENOUGH OF THIS. THERE'S OTHER MONEY TO BE MADE OUT THERE.
TO HELL WITH THE LOT OF YOU.
GO! GO!
DIDN'T YOU HEAR ME?! GET THIS BOAT ON THE WATER! WHY IS EVERYONE SO BLOODY INCOMPETENT?

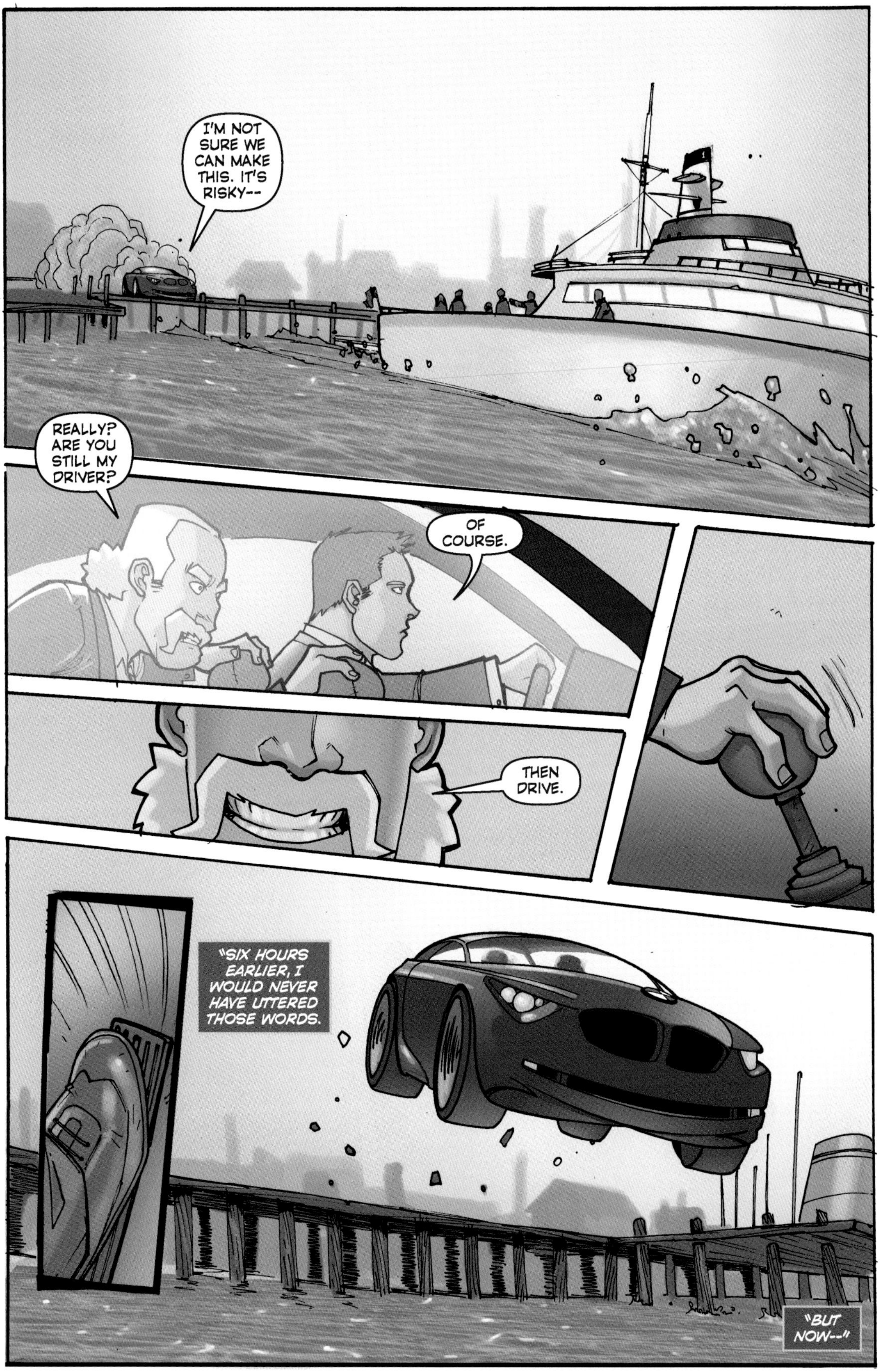
I'M NOT SURE WE CAN MAKE THIS. IT'S RISKY--
REALLY? ARE YOU STILL MY DRIVER?
OF COURSE.
THEN DRIVE.
"SIX HOURS EARLIER, I WOULD NEVER HAVE UTTERED THOSE WORDS.
"BUT NOW--"

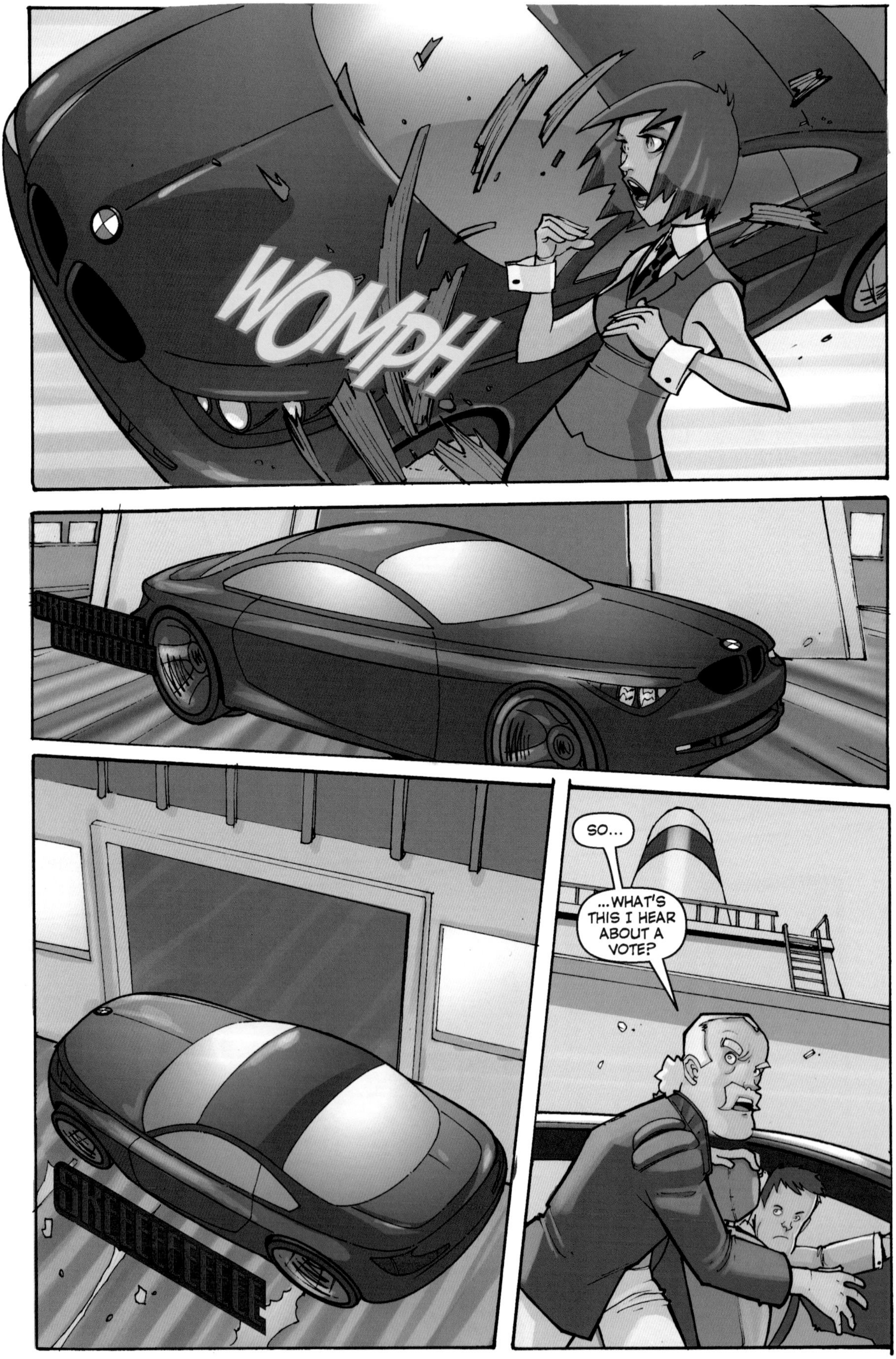
WOMPH
SKREEEEEEEEEEEEEEEEEE
SKREEEEEEEEEEEEE
SO...
...WHAT'S THIS I HEAR ABOUT A VOTE?

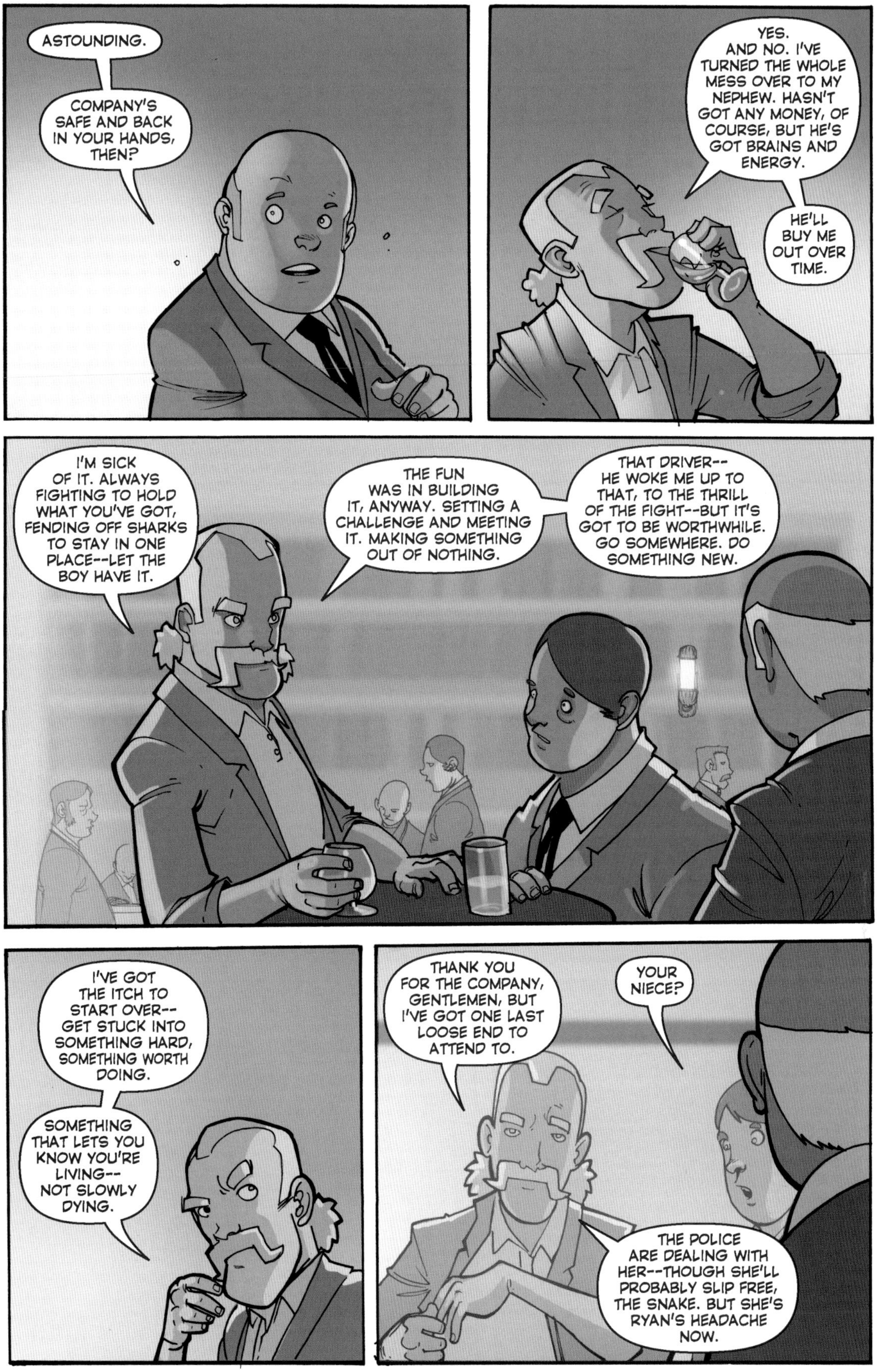
ASTOUNDING.
COMPANY'S SAFE AND BACK IN YOUR HANDS, THEN?
YES. AND NO. I'VE TURNED THE WHOLE MESS OVER TO MY NEPHEW. HASN'T GOT ANY MONEY, OF COURSE, BUT HE'S GOT BRAINS AND ENERGY.
HE'LL BUY ME OUT OVER TIME.
I'M SICK OF IT. ALWAYS FIGHTING TO HOLD WHAT YOU'VE GOT, FENDING OFF SHARKS TO STAY IN ONE PLACE--LET THE BOY HAVE IT.
THE FUN WAS IN BUILDING IT, ANYWAY. SETTING A CHALLENGE AND MEETING IT. MAKING SOMETHING OUT OF NOTHING.
THAT DRIVER-- HE WOKE ME UP TO THAT, TO THE THRILL OF THE FIGHT--BUT IT'S GOT TO BE WORTHWHILE. GO SOMEWHERE. DO SOMETHING NEW.
I'VE GOT THE ITCH TO START OVER--GET STUCK INTO SOMETHING HARD, SOMETHING WORTH DOING.
SOMETHING THAT LETS YOU KNOW YOU'RE LIVING-- NOT SLOWLY DYING.
THANK YOU FOR THE COMPANY, GENTLEMEN, BUT I'VE GOT ONE LAST LOOSE END TO ATTEND TO.
YOUR NIECE?
THE POLICE ARE DEALING WITH HER--THOUGH SHE'LL PROBABLY SLIP FREE, THE SNAKE. BUT SHE'S RYAN'S HEADACHE NOW.

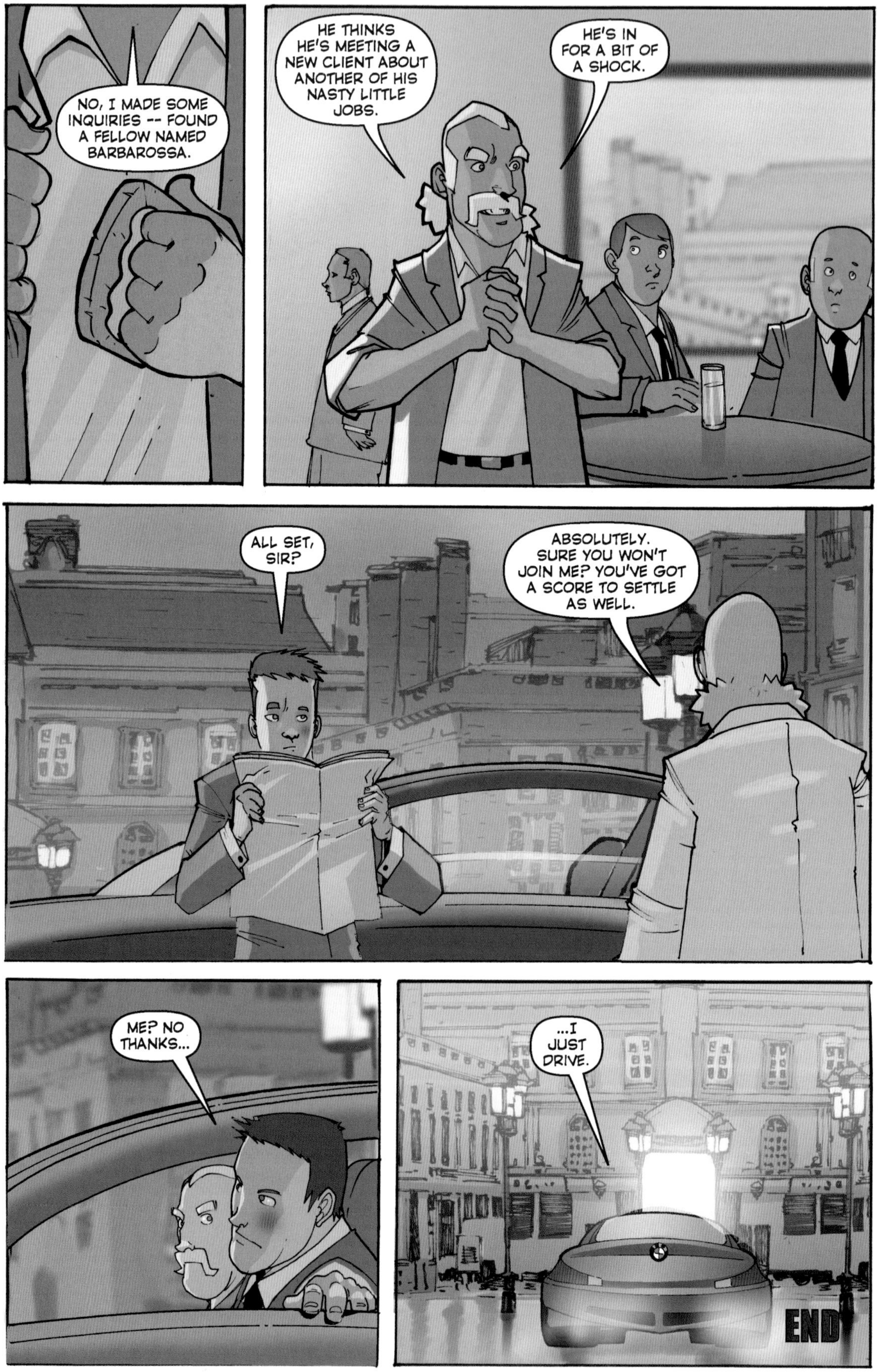
NO, I MADE SOME INQUIRIES -- FOUND A FELLOW NAMED BARBAROSSA.
HE THINKS HE'S MEETING A NEW CLIENT ABOUT ANOTHER OF HIS NASTY LITTLE JOBS.
HE'S IN FOR A BIT OF A SHOCK.
ALL SET, SIR?
ABSOLUTELY. SURE YOU WON'T JOIN ME? YOU'VE GOT A SCORE TO SETTLE AS WELL.
ME? NO THANKS...
...I JUST DRIVE.
END

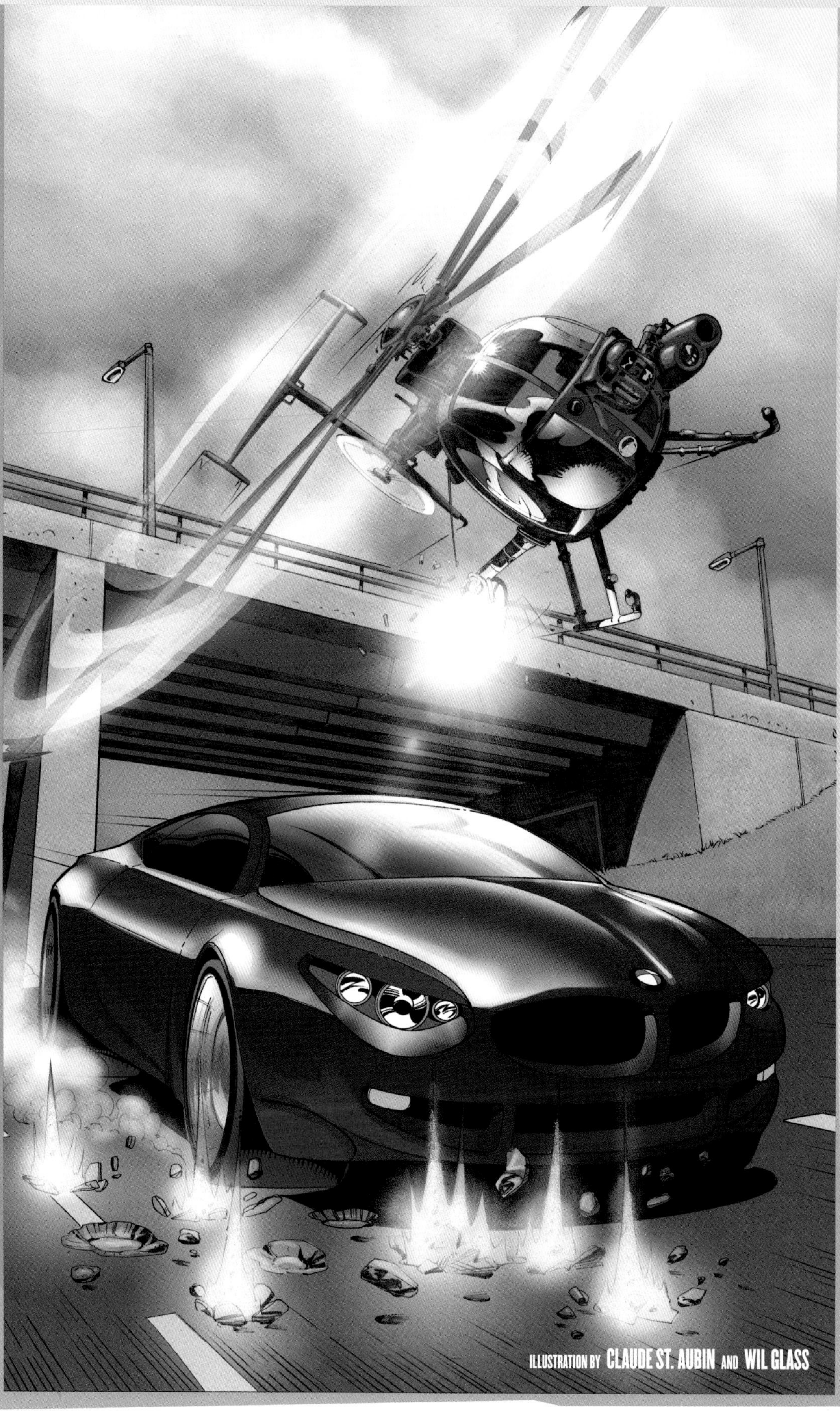
ILLUSTRATION BY CLAUDE ST. AUBIN AND WIL GLASS

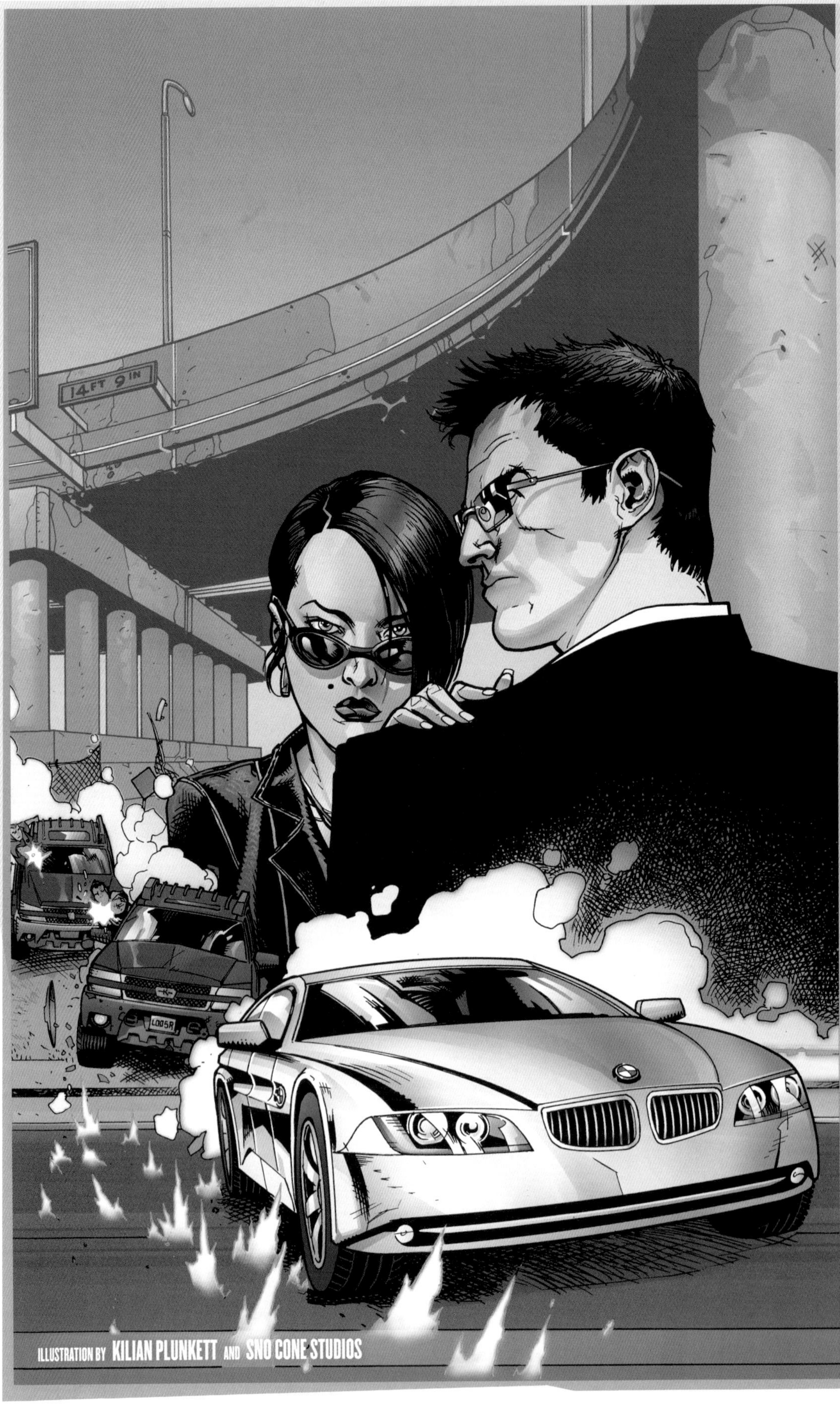
14 FT 9 IN

ILLUSTRATION BY KILIAN PLUNKETT AND SNO CONE STUDIOS

ALSO FROM DARK HORSE BOOKS

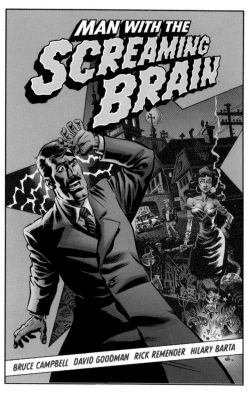

GRENDEL: RED, WHITE, AND BLACK

By Matt Wagner and others

These short stories are vignettes of the devious misdeeds of Hunter Rose, the first incarnation of Grendel. The tales are illustrated in stark black, white, and blood red by some of the top talents in comics, including Zander Cannon, Andy Kuhn, Ashley Wood, Tom Fowler, Mike Huddleston, Cliff Chiang, John K. Snyder, and more.

$19.95

ISBN: 1-59307-201-5
Softcover, 200 pages, black & white & red

MAN WITH THE SCREAMING BRAIN

By Bruce Campbell, David Goodman, and Rick Remender

Based on the film written and directed by and starring Bruce Campbell. The story of a wealthy American busi-nessman determined to exploit the crippled economy of a former Soviet state torn between communist roots and capitalist greed, who soon finds himself in the grip of a mad scientist with a twisted brain-transplant scheme worthy of Dr. Frankenstein.

$13.95

ISBN: 1-59307-397-6
Softcover, 104 pages, full color

AVAILABLE AT YOUR LOCAL COMICS SHOP OR BOOKSTORE

To find a comics shop in your area, call 1-888-266-4226
For more information or to order direct visit darkhorse.com or call 1-800-862-0052
Mon.–Fri. 9 A.M. to 5 P.M. Pacific Time *Prices and availability subject to change without notice

 **DARK HORSE BOOKS**™
darkhorse.com

Grendel: Red, White, & Black © 2003 by Matt Wagner. Grendel™ is a trademark of Matt Wagner. Text and illustrations of *Man with the Screaming Brain*™ © 2005 Bruce Campbell and David Goodman.

ALSO FROM DARK HORSE BOOKS

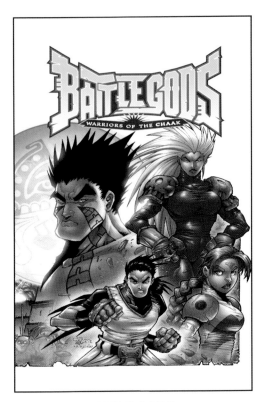

BATTLE GODS: WARRIORS OF THE CHAAK

By Francisco Ruiz Valasco

Featuring 240 pages of mighty warriors, exotic locales, professional jealousies, personal vendettas, Mexican wrestling, street fights, illegal motorcycle races, and Aztec zombies all wrapped around a thousand-year-old Mayan legend that portends the end of the world!

$19.95
ISBN: 1-56971-562-9
Softcover, 240 pages, full color

LONE WOLF 2100 VOLUME 1: SHADOWS ON SAPLINGS

*By Mike Kennedy
and Francisco Ruiz Valasco*

A young girl may hold the key to saving the world or destroying it. A corporation wants her secret—no matter what it may be. Her only companion is an android who is accused of killing her father. A ground-up re-imagining of the original *Lone Wolf and Cub* manga.

$12.95
ISBN: 1-56971-893-8
Softcover, 104 pages, full color

AVAILABLE AT YOUR LOCAL COMICS SHOP OR BOOKSTORE

To find a comics shop in your area, call 1-888-266-4226
For more information or to order direct visit darkhorse.com or call 1-800-862-0052
Mon.–Fri. 9 A.M. to 5 P.M. Pacific Time   *Prices and availability subject to change without notice

 **DARK HORSE BOOKS**™
darkhorse.com

Text and illustrations of *Battle Gods: Warriors of the Chaak*™ © 2002 Francisco Ruiz Velasco. *Lone Wolf 2100*™ copyright © 2006 Dark Horse Comics, Inc., Koike Shoin, and Liveworks.